The Fields Beneath

. . . In succession
Houses rise and fall, crumble, are extended,
Are removed, destroyed, restored, or in their place
Is an open field, or a factory, or a by-pass.
Old stone to new building, old timber to new fires,
Old fires to ashes, and ashes to the earth
Which is already flesh, fur and faeces,
Bone of man and beast, cornstalk and leaf.

T. S. Eliot, FOUR QUARTETS

'Happy are those who see beauty in modest spots where others see nothing. Everything is beautiful, the whole secret lies in knowing how to interpret it.'

Camille Pissarro (1893)

The Fields Beneath

The history of one London village

GILLIAN TINDALL

London

First published by Maurice Temple Smith in 1977
This paperback edition published in the United Kingdom
by Eland Publishing Limited
61 Exmouth Market, London EC1R 4QL in 2010

ISBN 978 1 906011 48 2

Cover image: *Laying Monster Tubes from the
New River*, 1855 by James Baker Pyne (1800–70)
© Guildhall Art Gallery, City of London/
The Bridgeman Art Library
Typeset in Great Britain by Antony Gray
Printed in Spain by GraphyCems, Navarra

This new edition of the book is dedicated to Mrs Bridget Tighe, born in County Sligo, Ireland in 1919, long time inhabitant of Kentish Town.

For all her unobtrusive help in my house over twenty-eight years, while I wrote this and many other books, I offer grateful thanks to her and to fate.

Contents

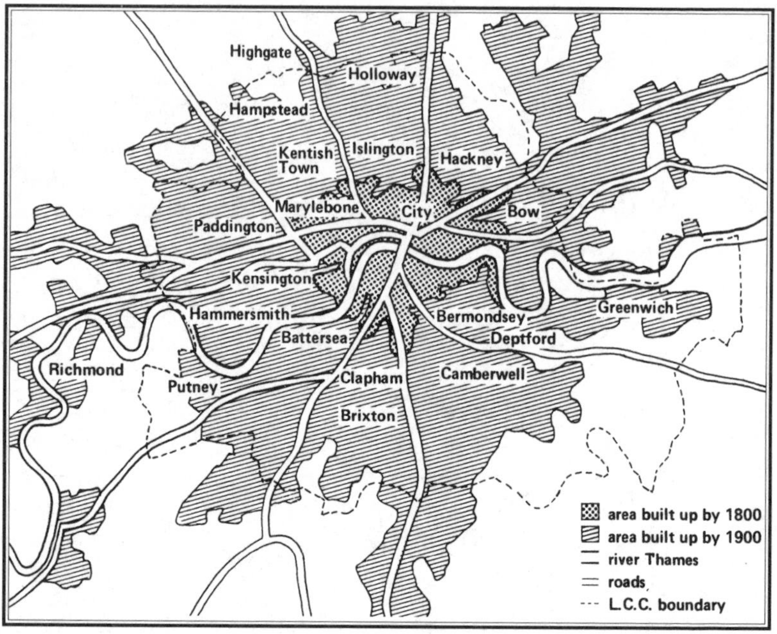
Highgate
Holloway
Hampstead
Kentish Town
Islington
Hackney
Marylebone
City
Bow
Paddington
Kensington
Hammersmith
Battersea
Bermondsey
Deptford
Greenwich
Richmond
Putney
Clapham
Camberwell
Brixton
area built up by 1800
area built up by 1900
river Thames
roads
L.C.C. boundary

A: The growth of London

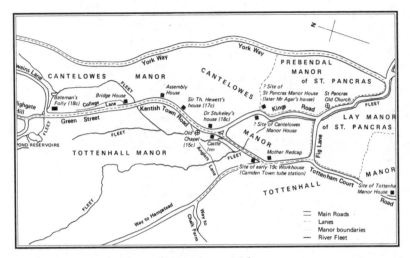

B: Pre-nineteenth century St Pancras parish

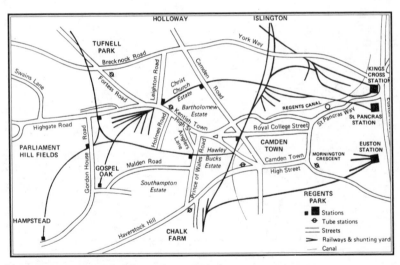

C: The same area by the early twentieth century

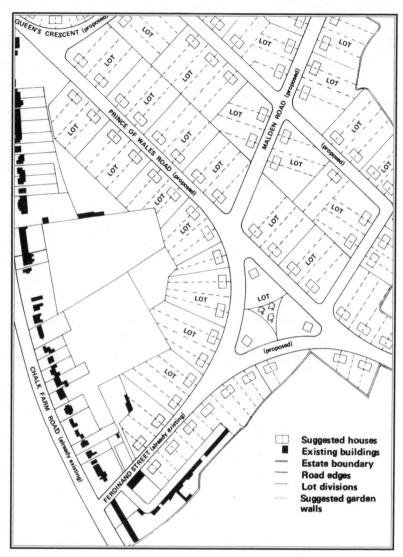

D: Part of the plans for the Southampton Estate, west Kentish Town (1840)
   *Each lot for sale was typically about 200 ft square and was envisaged as
containing four houses arranged two by two, semi-detached.*

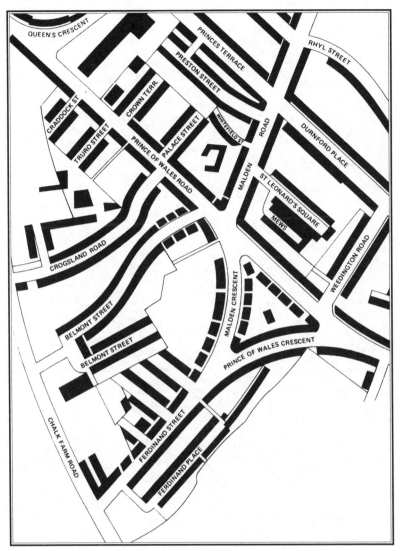

E: The Reality: the same part of the Southampton Estate by 1880

A frontage of 200 ft now often holds a dozen houses, terraced, each with a narrow strip of back garden. Extra streets, especially cul de sacs, have been slotted into the holdings.

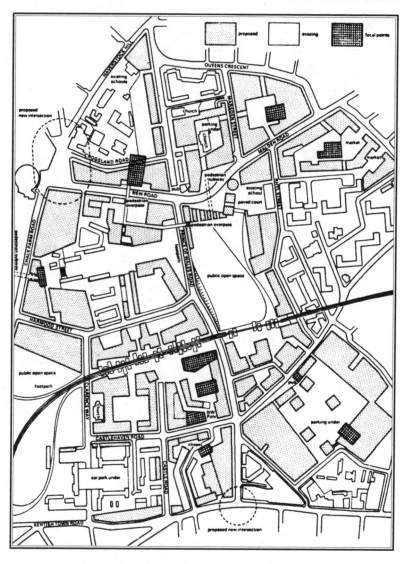

F: Further fantasy: plans for re-developing the same area, drawn up by the local authority in the early 1960s but happily never implemented.

Postscript 2011

It is almost thirty-five years now since the first edition of *The Fields Beneath* appeared. Other editions followed, but I was not able to update the work with anything more than a brief note. Not that 'update' is quite the word, for to keep a book of this kind accurate in each current detail – noting changes in shops, the enhancement or loss of buildings – would require constant, impractical revising and, at another level, would not be desirable anyway. Books of history do not go obviously out of date in the way that some other forms of writing tend to, but nevertheless a book is always a product of its own time, embodying the assumptions, hopes, fears and preoccupations of that time. This Postscript does not attempt to revise my earlier views, but it seems a good moment to take a general look at the way my chosen example of a village engulfed by a great city has continued to evolve over the past generation.

The overall theme of the book is, in any case, change. In the course of sixteen hundred years or so, Kentish Town was transformed from a small settlement beside a track some miles out of London into the busy inner-city district it is today. But this change, however momentous, was sporadic. For centuries nothing much happened, and at one point in the later middle ages the settlement even seems to have declined in size. A minor building boom in the sixteenth and seventeenth centuries produced the rural retreat within easy reach of town that was Kentish Town's character throughout the eighteenth and early nineteenth century, though the wind of change began to blow more strongly after the end of the Napoleonic wars. The truly cataclysmic change came in the 1840s, '50s and '60s, when the pastures and market gardens that had been the backland to the High Road were covered inexorably, field after field, with terraces of houses. This was followed by the coming of a mainline railway, which bisected the district and destroyed, for the next hundred years, most of the pretensions it had had to prettiness and gentility. In the space of less than thirty years a sooty townscape was created, as if by a black-hearted fairy. These were essentially the streets that still make up NW5 today.

Because to us past eras are over, fixed and known, we tend to under-estimate how traumatic such developments were to people living through them. In the mid-1970s I wrote: 'To believe that change, and in particular the *speed* of change, is something peculiar to the twentieth century, is an error, at least where the physical environment is concerned. Except in a few specific places . . . the changes seen by many people living today are as nothing compared with the paroxysms of alteration and despoilation weathered by their great-grandparents.' This, in 2011, should read 'great-great-grandparents', but it remains just as true.

It so happened that, when I was researching and writing *The Fields Beneath*, the lesser paroxysm of post-war redevelopment had only recently abated. I was thus able to describe this saga of misplaced idealism and Stalinist authoritarianism disguised as democracy while it was still very recent – see the book's last chapter. But what is significant is that I have no comparable upheaval to report for the period between the late 1970s and today. Just as, by the 1870s, Kentish Town had acquired much the form and social composition that it was to have for the next eighty-odd years, so, after the intervening storm of the late-1950s and '60s, the place settled down again into very much the one that we still inhabit, more than thirty years on, and shows every sign of continuing for the time being in the same way.

In the 1970s some people feared that 'by the year 2000' (a then distant, mythic date) areas such as Kentish Town would have deteriorated into urban "jungles' on the American model, dangerous to cross after dark and full of racial tensions, while others were optimistically convinced that the ever-rising price of property would ensure that Kentish Town in 2000 would be as affluent and exclusive as Chelsea. For more than one reason, I am pleased to report that neither of these predictions has turned out valid. The changes I have to signal are all relatively minor ones, in the scheme of things and in Kentish Town's long and chequered history.

The trends visible in 1977 have simply become more evident. The district has remained remarkably mixed, socially, with inhabitants ranging from the obviously poor to the discreetly wealthy, and only the lower-middle class under-represented. You have to be relatively well-off, today, to buy a Victorian house in one of the area's many pleasant, leafy side streets, and very few of these houses are still in multi-occupation: the old ladies who let lodgings have gone. However, the large amount of housing that remains in local authority hands continues to ensure that the district is hardly in danger of becoming exclusive. But one has to say, too, that the difference between one part of Kentish Town and another, often not far off geographically, has become more marked; and the foreboding that Kentish Town might become parcelled out, into expensively gentrified streets on the one hand and single-class ghetto estates of Council flats on the other, has to some extent come true. The planning-blight that descended upon west Kentish Town in the 1950s and '60s had a permanent effect, and though the partial destruction and rebuilding in the name of 'improvement' in the years that followed was much less extreme than originally intended, it has confirmed west Kentish Town's character as the less desirable side of town. Excepting, of course, places such Kelly Street and the Crimea enclave: these, once narrowly saved from demolition, are now carefully conserved, worlds away in character though not in distance from the ill-designed housing blocks and litter of Malden Road.

East Kentish Town has, by good luck, avoided such obvious ghettois-ation. Here a whole grid-pattern of streets was initially bought by the local authority for demolition, but a belated change of heart meant the terrace houses were then rehabilitated as flats and maisonettes for Council tenants (see pages 231–2). These proved very popular, with the inevitable result that since the right-to-buy legislation of 1980, many of the properties have passed out of the Council's stock of homes and into private ownership. They have often been sold on subsequently (something that the advocates of Council house sales apparently failed to envisage) and so the social mix is changing again, with the arrival in these streets of prosperous middle class youngsters starting out in life, or of older single people with some equity. Meanwhile, the Council has considerably fewer properties to offer to than it had thirty-five years ago. Also, the change in the allocation rules, from a system of points to the priority of need, has had the effect of excluding many solid citizens who would once have been offered Council accommodation. In Kentish

Town, as all over London, this has meant that Council tenants, except for the entrenched elderly, tend to form an underclass without the profile of respectable ordinariness that they had in the recent past.

The most significant single change over the last generation has been Council's embrace (at any rate in theory) of the idea that old buildings form a valuable heritage, and hence the designation of more and more sections as Conservation Areas where neither house-owners nor developers are free to alter windows, doors, roof-lines or back-additions at will, let alone demolish. The first CA, conservatively confined to a small collection of Georgian houses at the High Street end of Leighton Road plus the oldest part of the picturesque Leverton Street, was mapped out in 1985. That Area itself is now being widened to include the grid of small streets to the north and east, and some houses have been Listed. In the intervening years Torriano Cottages, most of the Christchurch and St Bartholomew estates, the Jeffreys Street-Rochester Square Area, Kelly Street, Harmood Street and the Crimea Area have been added to the canon, as well as the entire Dartmouth Park estate up Highgate Road.

The complete and admirable turn-about this represents, after the destructiveness of the preceding era, cannot be under-estimated, and I wish I could write that all anxieties about Kentish Town's physical future could now be laid to rest. But it was in 1989, well after the principle of conservation was established, that the ancient Bridge House in Highgate Road was demolished over one weekend, because someone in the Planning Department had not checked their records (or this book). And at the time of writing, a protracted wrangle is still in process about the integrity of Little Green Street, a small cobbled way containing the area's only surviving run of eighteenth century one-time shops. Inadvertently (or so it is said) Camden Council gave outline planning permission to a property developer planning to build a block of flats some way away down a pedestrian way (College Lane), not understanding that the developer was intending to turn Little Green Street into permanent vehicular access for all the future flat-owners and their projected underground garages. The impassioned row that has followed, in local and national press and elsewhere, may well be imagined by those who know what heat such issues these days arouse.

Sometimes, today, passions for the past can seem almost too enthusiastic. It is no longer the case, as it was in the 1970s, that the general public thinks that picturesque places like Hampstead have 'history' but that more ordinary and battered places like Kentish Town do not. Much more informed and detailed material has been published on various districts of Camden (see revised Sources) and interest remains great, though sometimes, as ever, a little fanciful. I became familiar with fantasies about remembered 'farms' when I was researching *The Fields Beneath*, but no one then tried to tell me, as they have recently, that Leverton Street was 'originally built for a colony of expatriate Portuguese fishermen'. (Under what circumstances a Portuguese fisherman would come and settle in Kentish Town was not explored). The basis for this tale is, I think, that these one-time railways workers' cottages, which long ago were painted in standard shades of peeling margarine, are now a rainbow of different colours, from palest green through subtle blues and greys, unashamed pink and virile terracotta – the influence, no doubt, of the holidays abroad taken by the new generation of owner-occupiers. But one may be extremely thankful that the same emotion of pride and love for the immediate environment that dreamed up the Portuguese fishermen also, in 2002, saved the Pineapple public house half way up the street from imminent disappearance. Neighbours enlisted every local celebrity to the cause and got the pub's intact Victorian interior spot-listed by English Heritage. The place continues to thrive.

Many other pubs have closed in Kentish Town and Camden Town in the last decade. The writer who complained in *The Builder* in 1854 that there far too many of these edifices were being built might be gratified to know how few of these traditional meeting places remain, but of course this does not point to any decline in alcoholic intake, but simply to changing habits. Famous pubs such as the Castle, or the Old Farmhouse which were rebuilt in the mid-nineteenth century but retained their ancient names, are now many of them unrecognisable as restaurants, wine-bars or 'music venues'. Others, especially in the side streets, have been converted into private flats. This was what a developer had hoped to do with the Pineapple, since such handsome buildings are often of more value now as real estate than in their designated usage. Others again have simply been swept away. The Assembly House survives, and now flourishes in responsible hands with much of its interior cut-glass intact, but it went through a bad patch in the 1990s, when the ornate window-glass that had lasted for almost a hundred years was either smashed or sold off by a series of dishonest tenant landlords. At the same period the commemorative marble table, which had been in the pub since the early eighteenth century (see pages 99–100), disappeared for good.

Relaxation in the licensing laws in recent years has brought late-night animation and frequently noise, fights, drunkenness and drug-trading to the heart of Camden Town. The huge and garish expansion of Camden Lock Market (now, unfortunately, 'world famous') has also had its effect. The determination of Kentish Town residents (backed, it should be said, by the local authority) has to date stopped Kentish Town from being degraded in the same way. An agreement seems to have been forged, among those who know the respective areas, that Camden Town is one place and Kentish Town is another, as historically they always have been, and any pushy bar-developer or his lawyer who think they will get the same licence in both places is in for a disappointment. Recently, the respective locations have been lettered into opposing sides of the wall of the railway viaduct across the road, which has long stood like a portcullis-gate where Camden Town might be said to end and Kentish Town to begin.

A visitor from the recent past would, I think, find much of Kentish Town rather cleaner than before, with less peeling paint, more elegant railings back in place, and fewer patched windows and rubbish-haunted front gardens, but the change is a matter of degree rather than a striking difference. The High Street is still choked with traffic morning and evening, but it flourishes, perhaps more than it did thirty years ago, with numerous walk-in supermarkets, green-grocery stalls, a long-established butcher-fishmonger, a smart halal alternative, an independent book-shop, a proper jewellers, a specialist needlework shop, a stationers, a baker's, a hardware store resembling Alladin's cave in its copious and varied stock, a large health-food store and several restaurants. (The one-time Daniel's shop, later the site of Sainsburys, is currently a Somerfield store, with Sainsbury's located further north, so any references to the position of the long ago Old Chapel should be adjusted to this).

By great good fortune rather than by any prescient plan, when a large section of the derelict one-time railway land was redeveloped it was for occupation by various light industries, a postal sorting office, a recycling centre and a car pound. None of these has impinged on the High Street's continuing success as a traditional shopping centre, whereas a large supermarket with parking would have inflicted considerable damage. Unlike many other old urban centres Kentish Town has had a lucky escape. It is merely rather a pity that the lack of any coherent plan for the railway land has meant that an old right-of-way across it in the direction of Hampstead has never been restored, as, with informed planning, it might have been. The wide road built to service the various works now occupying ex-railway land leads, absurdly, to a choice of dead ends, in a wilderness of blocked-off railway arches, without even a much-needed footpath through these into west Kentish Town.

Rather more planning has gone into the 'Secret Railway' which, in the 1970s, was delapidated and threatened with closure (see pages 219–20). Its old-fashioned wooden station has gone, and passengers have to reach it through the tube station entrance, but it is now no secret, being part of the busy Thameslink line. The separate line through West Kentish Town Station has also been upgraded, and appears on tube maps. Meanwhile historic St Pancras, the site of its one-time manor house, Agar Town, numerous burial grounds and much else besides, has found a new and high profile role as the terminus of Eurostar.

Highgate Cemetery, which was previously shut for burials and prey to vandalism, has received, some might say, all too much attention in the last thirty years. Care has been lavished on many of its fine monuments, but at present a brisk trade in graves combines uneasily with the place's modern role as a major tourist attraction, complete with entry fee and turnstiles.

As for John Betjeman's 'curious Anglo-Norman parish church of Kentish Town', that was built in 1790 to replace the chapel of ease and rebuilt in 1843, it now houses a Christ Apostolic Church. It is attended by a congregation almost entirely black, many of whom travel in from distant suburbs. The Church of England faithful have moved off to St Benet's, on the one-time estate of Dame Eleanor Palmer; while St Luke's in Oseney Crescent is Listed but currently mothballed, awaiting a resurrection. The Methodist congregation, who originally enjoyed the large church in Lady Margaret Road that they ceded in the 1970s to the Roman Catholics, occupied the ex-Catholic chapel in Fortess Road for about thirty years but gradually evaporated. That chapel has recently been demolished, though the ex-Presbytry next door still wears tell-tale crosses on its stonework.

The much-contested Talacre Open Site continues to flourish, as does the Kentish Town Farm. The Governesses Benevolent Institution in west Kentish Town that later became a series of schools is now, like the public houses, converted into flats, but on its wrought iron gates the initials GBI still entwine. Baroness Burdett-Coutts' stable block that survived so long in St Albans Road has been replaced by an over-sized residential block. The ungainly sweet-shop in front of Village House is now a house-agents' premises of equally ill-assorted design. The theme of land and property value evidently haunts this Postscript: it has been a significant part of the story of the last thirty-five years. The residential children's nursery in Leighton Road, which was earlier a casual ward, relieving station and soup kitchen, and earlier still an old house where the Crane family lived and tossed colourful insults over the wall at Mr Pike and his family, has been rebuilt as a Housing Association estate of uninspired but harmless houses in traditional London stock brick.

In the house that was once the Pikes' a typewriter has become in itself an object of nostalgic memory, but the person who was typing on it when *The Fields Beneath* first appeared is still using a keyboard today in the same upper room.

I

Introduction

Written in 1977

One day in the early 1970s I was roaming through a particularly disjointed and run-down area of Kentish Town, London NW5, and passed a row of houses which were then occupied by squatters engaged in a cold war with Camden Council. They were – and are – unremarkable houses; a mid-Victorian terrace of the type that has been demolished all over London in the past two decades, with none of the Georgian cottage appeal that might commend them to preservationist forces. In stock brick, three storeys, with a dank basement area below and a parapet wall on top, they faced a busy road; the most quintessentially ordinary houses, you would say, though of a uniquely English kind, built by speculative builders for Philistines, unloved now for decades, doomed soon, perhaps, to extinction.

Then I saw that over the lintel of one of them someone had carefully carved an inscription: the letters, cut through the sooty surface into the fresh yellow brick below, stood out clearly –

The Fields Lie Sleeping Underneath.

It is deeply satisfying to come unexpectedly face to face with your own private vision in this way. For years, walking round London, I had been aware of the actual land, lying concealed but not entirely changed or destroyed, beneath the surface of the nineteenth- and twentieth-century city. It has been said that 'God made the country and man made the town', but this is not true: the town is simply disguised countryside. Main roads, some older than history itself, still bend to avoid long-dried marshes, or veer off at an angle where the wall of a manor house once stood. Hills and valleys still remain; rivers, even though entombed in sewer pipes, still cause trouble in the foundations of neighbouring

buildings and become a local focus for winter mists. Garden walls follow
the line of hedgerows; the very street-patterns have been determined by
the holdings of individual farmers and landlords, parcels of land some
of which can be traced back to the Norman Conquest. The situation of
specific buildings – pubs, churches, institutions – often dates from long
distant decisions and actions on the part of men whose names have
vanished from any record. The more you know about the past of one
district, the easier it becomes to perceive the past of any district through
the confusing veil of the present.

From this, it is only a short step of the imagination to envisage the
one-time fields being themselves still there, with their grass and buttercups and even the footprints of cows, merely hidden beneath modern
concrete and asphalt – as if you had simply to lift up a paving stone in
order to reveal it. And while this is not literally true, what *is* true is that
once you get outside the inner areas of old cities (whose ground has
usually been so heavily disturbed by building and rebuilding through
the centuries that the present houses rest on packed rubble) you do not
have to go far down to find real earth, the kind cows walked on and
crops sprang from, lying there fallow beneath the weight of stone.

In this sense the past can be said to be still *there*, not just existing in the
minds of those who seek it, but actually, physically still present. The
town is a palimpsest: the statement it makes in each era is engraved over
the only partially-effaced traces of previous statements. Freud used
the image of the ancient city as a metaphor for the Unconscious: he
envisaged a city 'in which nothing that has once come into existence will
have passed away and all the earlier phases of development continue to
exist alongside the latest ones.' He was talking about the Unconscious of
one individual, but perhaps the city is a more obvious metaphor for
Jung's Collective Unconscious of the race: we may know nothing about
our nineteenth- or seventeenth- or fourteenth-century predecessors on
the patch of territory we call ours, but their ideas and actions have
shaped our habitat and hence our attitudes as well. In Blake's poetic
vision 'everything exists' for ever: experience is total and cumulative,
nothing, not one hair, one particle of dust, can pass away. And in point
of fact he was right. Matter is hard to destroy totally, even though it may
be transformed by time and violence out of all recognition. In the

pulverised rubble lying below modern buildings is the sediment of mediaeval and pre-mediaeval brick and stone. Modern techniques of soil analysis can tell one what crops and wild-flowers grew in fields now buried several feet beneath modern streets. Many of our London gardens owe their rich topsoil to manure from long forgotten horses and cattle or vegetable refuse from meals unimaginably remote in time. Moreover there are a great many buildings still standing whose bricks are the compressed product of other fields, usually not far distant, whose clay was dug out in the early nineteenth century and fired in local kilns. The process is not just cumulative but to some extent cyclic also –

> Old stone to new building, old timber to new fires,
> Old fires to ashes, and ashes to the earth
> Which is already flesh, fur and faeces,
> Bone of man and beast, cornstalk and leaf . . .

Seeing the past is not a matter of waving a magic wand. (Though traditionally local historians have behaved as if it were, contrasting past and present as if the two were totally separate realities, beginning paragraphs 'It is hard now to imagine . . . ') It is much more a matter of wielding a spade or pick, of tracing routes – and hence roots – on old maps, of reading the browned ink and even fainter pencil scrawl of preserved documents, whose own edges are often crumbling away into a powder, themselves joining the fur, flesh and faeces to which they testify.

People have suggested or hinted to me that surely the only places whose local history is worth going into in depth are 'interesting' areas – 'historical' ones, like Hampstead or Greenwich, or York or Bath. When I ask them if they don't suppose that other places also have a history, they say 'Oh yes, but you know what I mean.' As a matter of fact I do know exactly what they mean; they mean that, unless an area actually has a number of 'old' buildings standing, which in London usually means eighteenth-century buildings *not* disguised behind modern shop-fronts but nicely white-painted and readily recognisable, they do not care to envisage its past. This is a perfectly acceptable point of view, but it is not one I share.

In the local history of towns and districts where so much is already

patent and indeed on display, the dynamic tension between what you
see and what you know to have existed once and still to exist in some
fragmented or symbolic form, is largely missing. Moreover townscapes
which have managed to retain such a homogeneous aspect over a large
stretch of time are, by definition, areas which have not suffered the
complex social upheavals and physical dislocations that make their
history worth studying. Tales about Beau Brummel in Bath ('where one
can so easily still imagine him') or Keats in Hampstead – where one can
still imagine *him* – are fascinating to local inhabitants, but they do not
actually lead one anywhere; one cannot draw any general social or
historical conclusions from them. Places that have been socially and
architecturally pickled are too atypical to be examples of anything but
themselves. Paradoxically, these places in which local 'concern for the
past' is often so marked among successive generations of moneyed and
leisured inhabitants, actually tell one less about the past as a whole or
about the processes of historical evolution than do more ordinary,
battered places.

In addition, not only is the past history of an accredited 'historical'
area obvious for all to see, but often what is still hidden has been so fully
documented already by a series of scholars, plagiarists, band-waggoners
and chatterboxes, that little discovery remains to be done and what
there is can only consist of the unattractive task of setting others right
regarding some cherished piece of local fable. Books on areas like
Hampstead (to choose the example so near at hand to my own territory
that their outlying fields touch) are legion. Some, both old and modern,
are excellent. Many are virtually worthless, typical examples of the 'Idle
Stroll Around the Old Stones' school of local antiquarianism, which
endured for so long in the nineteenth century and the first half of
the twentieth, but now at last is being displaced by something more
stringent. In those nineteenth-century compendia about London and its
surroundings, often copiously illustrated with cheap engravings which
antiquarian dealers now chop out and mount, the same localities – and
the same stories about them – occur over and over again, while vast
tracts of London are barely touched upon. Typical is the attitude of
Howitt, friend of Mrs Gaskell and author of *The Northern Heights of
London* (1869), who did the usual rounds of Hampstead and Highgate

with a glance in the direction of Kilburn Priory (site of), but dismissed Camden and Kentish Towns with the remark 'these places do not lie within the limits of this work.' One might give Mr Howitt the benefit of the doubt and assume he was speaking geographically, but it is hard to escape the conclusion that the 'scope' implied was social as well: at his period, the once-favoured villages of Camden and Kentish Town were steadily declining into urban working class districts and, as such, were apparently becoming invisible to gentlemen with antiquarian interests. In fact, Mr Howitt lived on Highgate West Hill, well within the fringes of what was, or had recently been, considered part of Kentish Town. Nor were his eyes fixed resolutely upwards: he writes with moving pity at one point of the plight of horses straining under repeated lashes to drag heavy loads up this steepest of hills, and of his own attempts to get something done to alleviate their distress. But evidently it didn't occur to him that the streets through which these horses had just passed might be a worthwhile subject for investigation.

So Kentish Town, like most of the other districts which now form London's 'inner ring', is for the historian comparatively untouched and therefore particularly tempting. It is, to use an archaeological metaphor, like a dig on a new site where earlier comers have not been burrowing about disturbing things and perverting evidence. In addition, there happens to be a wealth of archive material concerning the district, hardly any of which has been exploited: most of it was collected over the course of two lifetimes by members of the Heal family – owners of the big furniture shop in Tottenham Court Road – and is now in the archives of Camden Public Library. The other reason for the choice of Kentish Town is more fundamental: by a combination of circum-stances, it exhibits many of the classic and most interesting features of the long-term metamorphosis of mediaeval village into twentieth-century renewal-area.

There have, for centuries, been pressures on Kentish Town, formative and conflicting ones; its present equivocal situation, geographically mid-way between city and suburb and partaking of some of the characteristics of both, reflects a struggle that has been going on certainly for two hundred years and perhaps for much longer – that between the needs of the district *as* a district in which people live, work and sleep, and the needs of the rest of London and the country to use it as a corridor. In the beginning, certainly before the Normans, perhaps even before the Romans came, there was a road, passing somewhere near St Pancras old church and continuing northwards. From it dates the existence and history of Kentish Town, as of very many other places, and from it stem most of its problems.

Kentish Town is not special – except of course to me, but I cannot expect any but other local inhabitants to share my particular attachment to it. I have taken it as a subject, not because it is special but because it is archetypal. The general outlines of its story are those, with modifications, of a million other ancient villages gradually absorbed into metropolises; not just round London but in many parts of England, and not just in England either. Paris, too, has its Kentish Towns. So has Moscow – though there they would be harder to disinter. If, therefore, I dwell on particular local events, personalities or structures, it is because I am using them to demonstrate a pattern, geographical, historical and social. I am using Kentish Town to give a local habitation and a name to the expression of something far more general, and in the hope that some readers may perhaps be sufficiently interested and inspired to look at other, comparable, areas with fresh eyes afterwards.

I am also conscious of being typical of my own era, just as Mr Howitt was of his, just as the Rev. Dr Stukeley, eighteenth-century resident, Druid, and enthusiastic Roman camp-finder, was of his. That I should wish to live in and even write about a district as traditionally 'un-promising' as Kentish Town, is, I have no doubt at all, symptomatic of certain social shifts that have taken place within my adult lifetime. In the last fifteen years or so large areas of this inner-city ring have become visible again in a way they were not when Mr Howitt was writing. Paradoxically, it is now these areas, which appear so unattractive to the outsider travelling – traffic himself – through the traffic-wracked main street, which actually attract the most passionate loyalty and commitment from inhabitants of several different social levels. It is perhaps here, rather than in the self-conscious, ex-rural 'villages' of the Bucks, Herts, and Sussex commuterlands, that something resembling an old-fashioned identification with the soil of the place can most readily be found, even though that soil is represented by tarmac, asphalt and the sort of old

York stone slabs which 'no local authority could afford to buy and lay in these days' (in the words of the urban historian H. J. Dyos).

Possibly the very existence of commuterlands, spreading wider and wider, and more and more dependent on the car, devaluing the rural image by associations with the phoney, has helped to revive the idea of attachment to a physically compact urban landscape, and to the 'urban values' reassessed by sociologists such as Peter Willmott and Jane Jacobs. Certainly the wholesale destruction of large parts of London and many other towns since the Second World War in the name of 'planning' has led to a massive loss of confidence in shining visions of a Brave New Future and to a revaluing of such districts as still retain some of their traditional aspect. The loss of a sense of place that follows upon big urban redevelopment schemes is not just due to the physical disturbance and remodelling of the territory: even when the new tower blocks, motorway junction or whatever have become familiar to the eye, they still convey little idea of being *here*, on some ordinary but individual patch of land. This is partly because they have no local distinguishing features and 'could be anywhere', but more because the whole scale is wrong – non-domestic, monolithic, discouraging. Urban motorways work very well when you are in a motorcar, and tower blocks work well too when seen from a car speeding along: soothing white oblongs that rise and sink before your eyes, dream cities, not quite real. But none of it works well for the pedestrian on the ground. By contrast, areas like Kentish Town are, despite huge traffic problems passing slowly through them, essentially pedestrian areas to the people who live in them. If you want to get to your place of work, or to a school or a shop or a street market or to visit a friend on the far side of Kentish Town, you don't get the car out or wait for a bus: you walk, in just the same way, and quite likely along the identical route, that other people, hundreds of years ago, walked on similar errands. Their paths, their muddy cart-tracks, their hedgerows, lie beneath your feet.

'The Fields Lie Sleeping Underneath' still, at the time of writing, proclaims itself from the lintel of the house in Prince of Wales Road. But the squatters have been evicted (or, as they insist, have managed to induce the Council to re-house them) and the house is in the hands of builders. Originally it was supposed to be knocked down as part of a

grandiose scheme for the area, conceived at a period which now seems
laughably remote. That was why the squatters found it empty in the first
place – a theme in Kentish Town's most recent history to which I shall
be returning at a later stage in this book. The bit of land on which it and
the rest of the terrace stands was originally 'scheduled as an open space'
in the jargon of the planning report, and had that been carried through
the field underneath would indeed have been revealed again as the
inscription seems to predict, though perhaps without its cows and buttercups. But in fact local resentment about the destruction of inoffensive,
liveable houses became so intense in the early 1970s that the plan was
abandoned, at any rate for the moment. Currently, the house is being
rehabilitated (the jargon of *this* decade). The roof has been taken off and
put on again, at the upper storey a large expanse of new, yellow London
stock bricks shows the house's original pristine colour by contrast with
the greyish tinge the rest of it has now assumed. The variegated windows
are being restored to the correct, twelve-paned uniformity. When
Camden Council does decide to do up an old house for its own tenants,
it restores it to its original appearance with a care and knowledge few
private owner-occupiers emulate – which, ironically, leads the casual
passer-by to the false assumption that the house has been acquired by
middle-class owner-occupiers. Since this book will inevitably contain a
number of harsh words about those who are now the public custodians
of a very large slice of Kentish Town, I should like to put their care on
record also.

Perhaps some council servants, reluctantly abandoning the authoritarian, late-1940s planning precepts on which many of them were reared,
have come round in recent years to the realisation that William Morris's
famous dictum still has validity today. It is often quoted, but I make no
apology for quoting it again here; it needs perennial restatement: ' . . .
These old buildings do not belong to us only . . . they belonged to our
forefathers and they will belong to our descendants unless we play them
false. They are not in any sense our property, to do as we like with them.
We are only trustees for those who come after us.'

Roads and Rivers

In the beginning there was the road. But before the road, there was the river.

Present-day London has a number of buried rivers: there is the Wandle, which has given its name to Wandsworth, the Tyburn which for centuries gave its name to the crossroads we now call Marble Arch, the nearby Westbourne which further downstream flows in a pipe over Sloane Square tube station, and several others. But the best known of all is the waterway called for most of its length the Fleet. Kentish Town lies neatly in the valley of the Fleet, and it is this circumstance which has shaped it and made it a corridor – a natural route in and out of London since time before history. It is also from the Fleet, according to divers explanations, that Kentish Town derives its name (Ken-ditch = the bed of a waterway. 'Ken' in this sense is common in place names).

Yet this once-important watercourse, which for centuries provided not only the *raison d'être* of the village but also its transport, its principal source of water for men, beasts and crops, the power to turn its mills, and its only drainage, has become invisible. Most people who live in the area, or in Hampstead to the north, where other tributaries of the same river rise, have vaguely heard of the Fleet, but few have much notion of where it once ran – or rather, runs. Local building firms, not to mention large national ones, seem similarly ill-informed: it is not uncommon for the foundations of a new council block in west Kentish Town, or a new in-filling development of 'town houses' on the Brookfield Estate, to become inundated with water, to the consternation of all concerned. Yet a glance at the maps of 150 years ago would have shown architects all they needed to know. Perhaps because of this vaguely apprehended building hazard in Kentish Town, other people seem to have a general impression that the Fleet may be *anywhere*: any time a cellar in the area shows signs of rising damp, tales circulate of people lifting up floorboards in their basement kitchens and finding 'the bed of the Fleet' underneath. One imagines a clear but shallow stream, with bright, round pebbles and fronds of weeds, a few minnows and perhaps a corroded anchor or two from a long-ago ship.

Such an anchor was in fact found in the eighteenth century, when the section of the stream then running open at the back of the Castle Tavern tea-garden was dredged. No date, even conjectural, was assigned to it, and writers commenting on it not long after seem to have imagined it as belonging to something akin to a Spanish galleon, or a mythic vessel of some remote but resplendent golden age not locatable in actual chronology. One should perhaps qualify statements about 'whole navies' having once come up river as far as Kentish Town with the observation that, in distant times, 'ships' (like 'rivers') came in modest sizes. It seems however likely that the Romans sailed their boats up the Fleet: in the foundations of St Pancras Old Church (early mediaeval, but known to be on the site of an older building or a series of them) lie courses of Roman brick and fragments of their tiles. So perhaps the church, like St Paul's Cathedral itself, in whose gift it was for so long, lies on the site of a pre-Christian temple. It was confidently asserted in the eighteenth century that the bones of an elephant, brought to Britain by the Romans 'to frighten the barbarians', had been dug up not far from the church; but twentieth-century scholarship, with rather more accurate perception of the aeons of time that lie behind us, is more inclined to regard these as the bones of some prehistoric mammoth, overtaken by death while seeking a drink at the crackling, frozen verge of the Ice Age Fleet. Even further back in time there are indications that the whole area was covered by the sea: an unsuccessful boring for water in the nineteenth century got down to beds of carbonised shells.

Returning to a more measurable time-scale, the facts are these: one or more main tributaries of the Fleet rise near the Vale of Health on Hampstead Heath and flow in one stream via Hampstead Ponds and South End Green along Fleet Road to Gospel Oak. This stream then proceeds due south through west Kentish Town, crossing Prince of Wales Road just below Angler's Lane (the derivation is obvious) and then continues in a slightly more eastwards direction till it crosses the lower part of Kentish Town Road below the Castle Inn, at almost the same place where the Regent's Canal has run since 1820. But just before making this cross to the eastern side of the road it is joined by its other main tributary, a stream which rises in the grounds of Ken Wood, and flows down through Highgate Ponds (which are old reservoirs) on the edge of Parliament Hill. This stream veers east under Highgate Road at about the level of St Alban's Road where it is joined by the rivulet of the Brookfield brook: the end houses of St Alban's Road stand in what was once a sizeable pond, utilised in the late eighteenth century for a gentleman's ornamental water garden. It continues due south, then veers west again back under Highgate Road at the particularly bleak point where two large factories now stand right on the road. Behind them, somewhere in the waste of railway lands and abandoned scraps of pre-urban Kentish Town fields, it picks up another little stream coming from the north and then continues on its way through west Kentish Town to join with the Hampstead branch.

Once joined, somewhere near the railway bridge which spans the main road like a portcullis at the southern end of present-day Kentish Town, the enlarged stream proceeds determinedly onwards following the curve of St Pancras Way – or, to be more accurate, the line of St Pancras Way still follows the curving route of the pack-horse track that once followed the bank of the stream. It passes close beside St Pancras Old Church, which was built either on a natural hillock above the marshy watercourse or on land specially embanked there to lift the building clear of the spring floods. It then continues on, down under the complex of railway bridges north of the main line stations, down past King's Cross where Bagnigge Wells once were, through Clerkenwell and on – its name now transiently the Olde-bourne – down Farringdon Street, past the site of the one-time prison that bore its name, past Fleet Street, and finally out into the Thames itself and hence at long last to Gravesend and the sea. Today, from the Highgate and Hampstead ponds onwards, it is encased in cast iron pipes the whole way to the Thames.

There is evidence that, from the thirteenth century on, there was chronic concern about over-use and misuse of the river. In 1290, the eighteenth year of the reign of Edward I, we find the White Friars, near Ludgate Hill, complaining that putrid exhalations from it stifled the smell of their incense at Mass, and this was a complaint which was to be repeated up and down stream, with variations, till the Fleet's final imprisonment. In 1307, according to Stowe, there were complaints that whereas 'in times past the course of water, running at and beside London under Olde-bourne Bridge and Fleet Bridge in to the Thames, has been of such bredth and depth that ten or twelve ships laden with goods, could sail there together,' it was now 'sore decay'd'. The blame was laid on the tanners, who polluted the waters, and on those who raised wharves beside it, but the principal problem seems to have been that the water was diverted to turn the paddles of mills built near the stream. The struggle for supremacy between those who wanted to use waterways for industrial purposes and those who wanted to use them to transport heavy goods about, is a constant theme in mediaeval and post-mediaeval life. Successive laws were passed and efforts made in the following centuries to clean the river, dredge it, remove the mills and so forth, but it was never brought back to its old breadth and depth, and came to be regarded less as a river than as a brook. The last plan for cleaning and canalising it was by Christopher Wren. But, like most of Wren's grandest plans, including his scheme for rebuilding London after the Fire with a new street pattern like a classical Italian city, this idea for turning the squalid outflow of the Fleet at the Thames into a Venetian-style asset did not come to anything. London has a long tradition of rejecting visionary planning schemes, though this has not prevented twentieth-century planners from seeing visions and dreaming dreams just as revolutionary as those of a Wren or a Haussmann.

Waterways lead a life of their own, and there may have been other factors in the Fleet's decline apart from the wasteful, despoiling ways of those who lived upon its banks. One identifiable cause for its progressive degradation was the late sixteenth-century formation of the pond-reservoirs north of Kentish Town, with conduit pipes made of elm trunks leading the water off to supply London. This lowered water levels further downstream – though not enough to prevent the occasional disastrous flood in the Battle Bridge (King's Cross) district, overturning brick walls and drowning cattle. Where the stream ran through Kentish Town it still seems to have been reasonably sweet and clean up to the end of the eighteenth century or even later, which was just as well when you consider that it was still the main source of water for many people living in its vicinity: only middle-class houses, in the eighteenth century, had water laid on, and then usually only in the kitchen or yard. But lower down, towards Clerkenwell and Holborn, where it was now known as the Town Ditch, it had by then become a byword for filth:

> . . . Fleet ditch, with disemboguing streams
> Rolls the large tribute of dead dogs to Thames,
> The king of dykes! than whom no sluice of mud
> With deeper sable blots the silver flood. (Pope)

Gradually, as the eighteenth century progressed, more and more of this fetid open drain was arched over and confined to a brick culvert. Its lower reaches became a general sewer into which scores of latrines, built out over the backs of houses, discharged directly. And, as London gradually increased in size, so the brick gulley extended higher and higher up the watercourse since, above a certain population density, human beings seem inevitably to pollute and foul their streams. The Fleet was still open just north of St Pancras church in the early nineteenth century, perhaps because this was then a very sparsely populated area, but a large segment disappeared underground when the Regent's Canal was constructed. (It crosses *under* the canal, but for a little way through Camden Town the canal takes the exact route of the old river, as if replacing it.) It was still capable, in the 1820s, of causing floods in the Kentish Town area, principally at the point where it crossed under the lower part of what is now Kentish Town High Road and what was known for centuries before as 'Water Lane'. Indeed the watery habits of the Fleet made themselves known again at that point some twenty-five years later, when the North London Junction Railway was being constructed by unwary engineers and several arches of the viaduct collapsed with a rush of water at the foundations. Further up, its fluctuating levels did less harm. In 1825 the pond where the stream crossed under Highgate Road (near the entrance to College Lane) was said to be thirteen feet wide at flood, and so it was there that the water-carts regularly came. A house where the carters refreshed themselves, Bridge House, stood there and in fact still stands (but see page 16), disguised behind the pebbledashed modern facade of a metal dealer's offices.

But the population explosion experienced by Kentish Town as the nineteenth century went on – the transformation scene which will be a dominant theme in this book – had a terrible effect on the Fleet, which suffered the fate of rivers up and down the country in that newly-industrialised era. Typical of many general laments for the lost stream, that archetypal playground of lost childhood, lost innocence, is that of James Hole, a housing reformer of the same generation as the great sanitary propagandist, Edwin Chadwick. He wrote in 1866: 'The inhabitant whose memory can carry him back thirty years recalls pictures of rural beauty, suburban mansions and farmsteads, green fields, waving trees and clear streams where fish could live – where now can be seen only streets, factories and workshops, and a river or brook black as the ink which now runs from our pen describing it.'

Kentish Town was by then rapidly filling up with inhabitants, increasingly working-class, and between them their cess-pits, street drains and workshops did for the Fleet. As each new area of land disappeared under paving and foundations, another section of the brook was arched over. In 1872 the Metropolitan Board of Works finally encased its whole course, from Highgate Ponds, in a new sewer, some of it as much as fifteen feet below the level of the modern street. Two years earlier, Samuel Palmer, the principal and almost the only historian of St Pancras, had written:

There still remains a few yards in our parish where the brook runs in its native state. At the back of the Grove, in the Kentish Town Road, is a rill of water, one of the little arms of the Fleet, which is yet clear and untainted. Another arm is at the bottom of the field at the back of the Bull and Last inn, over which is a little wooden bridge leading to the cemetery. [Highgate Cemetery]. It is pleasant of a summer evening to walk the meadow, or lean over the little bridge, and allow fancy to range back when that running rill flowed on to join the River of Wells, pure and clear, which emptied itself into what was then the clear and stainless Thames . . .

Palmer's vision of the primitive world was that of the Pre-Raphaelite painters, every leaf and petal standing out in childlike colour, of Ruskin or of William Morris's escapist *Earthly Paradise*, which never existed historically, or at any rate not in the pristine form envisaged:

> Forget the spreading of the hideous town
> Think rather of the packhorse on the down,
> And dream of London, small and white, and clean,
> The clear Thames bordered by its gardens green.

> (Morris)

From then on *all* references to the Fleet are couched in this elegaic tone, obsessionally contrasting past with present in favour of the former. The river, having disappeared below ground, had ceased to be a perceived fact but had become a myth, a mysterious presence, an embodiment of all that civilisation has lost.

Yet it is fair to add that so rapid and complete was the transformation of Kentish Town, as of many analogous areas, between roughly 1840 and 1870, that there must indeed have been many inhabitants of the district in the last quarter of the nineteenth century and the first part of the twentieth, whose own childhood memories had assumed the quality of an improbable dream. This is an old man writing to a local newspaper in 1909:

> The Angler's Lane of today connects Prince of Wales Road with Kentish Town road, and is, of course, a lane of brick and mortar. When I knew it as a boy it was one of the loveliest spots imaginable – so deserted in the early hours of the morning that, when the anglers were not there, some of the youngsters from the cottages around, and some who were not youngsters, used to bathe in the river.
>
> I passed through Angler's Lane some time ago, an aged man in a bathchair, and I found it hard to realise that my wheels were rolling their way over the Fleet river!

The history of the Fleet river has been described as 'a decline from a river to a brook, from a brook to a ditch, and from a ditch to a drain'. The drain is the classic symbol for man the destroyer, but in fact, today it is only a 'drain' in an innocuous sense, not the more usual fetid one. It has become a storm relief drain, taking the overflow from particularly heavy downpours. This is essential in cities, for whereas rain sinks readily down through grasslands or ploughlands or indeed unpaved roads, and is soon absorbed, rain in areas largely covered by stone, asphalt and tarmac cannot sink away and must be channelled. Harmless, necessary Fleet.

Because the river was there, defining the contours of the land, the road came. But where the earliest road lay is not absolutely certain. Norden, the Elizabethan topographer, identified Watling Street, the ancient road to Chester, as the way that is now Tottenham Court Road, Hampstead Road as far as Camden Town, then Chalk Farm Road, Haverstock Hill and so on to Hampstead and the north. At all events Watling Street seems to have been a pre-Roman track, which was improved and perhaps partially paved by the Romans and then, during the Dark Ages, was allowed to fall into decay till resurrected by Abbot Leofstan of St Alban's shortly before the Norman Conquest.

It has been suggested that an alternative route for Watling Street is the one described by Norden as also very ancient: the way from Holborn on the edge of the City, up Gray's Inn Road to King's Cross (site of an undetermined ancient battle, as its old name, Battle Bridge, suggests) and thence up what is now called St Pancras Way but was for centuries called Longwich Lane and then the King's Road. At the level of the present day Crowndale Road (Fig Lane, where a fig tree survived till the late nineteenth century) the road would have forked, one branch curving west to pick up the route of what is now the Hampstead Road and the other continuing north through Kentish Town to Highgate.

I slightly prefer the second of these alternatives, for several reasons. Firstly, it follows the course of the river and hence the valley, the most logical place for an early road to be. Secondly, it starts from a point much nearer the City than Tottenham Court Road: it is a little hard to see why, in very distant times, the main road to the midlands should have been located so far to the west of the small settlement that was London. Thirdly, the route up Gray's Inn Road passes at least two very ancient sites, Battle Bridge and St Pancras church itself. There have been Roman finds near Gray's Inn Road: two cremation urns. By contrast, the other route up Tottenham Court and Hampstead Road is not known to pass by any ancient settlement (Camden Town is modern – 1791, to be exact); the only significant building recorded there is the one from which the present day Tottenham Court Road takes its name, the manor house of Totenhale near the present Euston Road underpass, sometimes mis-leadingly called St John's Palace, the earliest parts of which seem to have been mediaeval.

In addition, two other roads concern us. One is the eastern fork from Gray's Inn Road leading up York Way (anciently Maiden Lane), across Copenhagen Fields to Holloway, Hornsey and Muswell Hill. The Maiden Lane section was the eastern boundary of the ancient parish of St Pancras and of the manor of Cantelowes (of which much more later); it is still the eastern boundary of the modern metropolitan borough of Camden, and is also the farthest possible eastern limit of Kentish Town. The dual and contradictory nature of a road – a means of connection to those who travel it, a social demarcation line and barrier to those who live around it – is no new thing.

The other road, a latecomer dating only from 1386, is the by-pass road for the above, built through Holloway and up Highgate Hill by the Bishop of London, who charged tolls for its use (hence High-gate).

There is yet another road which ultimately became important in shaping the whole northern inner-suburb area. It determined the position of the three big stations, Euston, St Pancras and King's Cross, and thus had a profound effect on the later development of Kentish Town. But it was constructed so many centuries after even the Bishop of London's road that it hardly seems relevant to this chapter. This was the New Road, deliberately built as a by-pass through uninhabited fields in the mid-eighteenth century, and one of the few far-sighted road schemes for London which did become reality. Today, it is called the Marylebone Road, Euston Road and Pentonville Road. It was in 1800, and still is today, the demarcation line where central London gives way to more outlying parts. We shall return to it.

When the area north of London was surveyed at the time of the Norman Conquest, it consisted mainly of forest, infested by outlaws, robbers and beasts of prey. Trees and scrub are the natural vegetation of a large part of England. The first mention of St Pancras church as such occurs at the period of the Conquest, but there seems to have been some form of

clearing and settlement in the vicinity of the church – or *a* church –
hundreds of years before this, probably since about AD 400. At any rate
St Pancras was made a prebendal manor by King Ethelbert and granted
by him to the Dean and Chapter of St Paul's Cathedral in 603.

Slowly over the centuries we now call 'dark', a few changes took place.
By the time of the Domesday Survey (1086) four manors are recorded,
though one is not called a manor, plus some other land, covering roughly
the area that was to become the Borough of St Pancras (merged into
Camden in 1965 when the LCC became the GLC). The named manors
were St Pancras itself, Totehele (Totenhale) and Rugmere. Each manor
had a plough or two (Totenhale had three and 'another half can be
made'), each had its handful of villeins, some pastureland, and 'wood
for hedges and for pigs'.

Almost exactly a hundred years after the Domesday Survey, the
propagandist FitzStephen wrote in his 'Survey of the Metropolis' that the
St Pancras district had 'cornfields, pastures and delightful meadows,
intermixed with pleasant streams, on which stands many a mill whose
clack is grateful to the ear.' The number of mills (typical service industries)
suggests that the area had already embarked on the beginnings of its
long-time special role as country-by-the-town. FitzStephen added that
the cornfields were not of a hungry, sandy mould but 'as the fruitful
fields of Asia, yielding plentiful increase and filling the barns with corn'.
He continued: 'Beyond them, a forest extends, full of the lairs and coverts
of beasts and game, stags, bucks, boars and wild bulls.' Clearly, the
frontiers of the great Forest of Middlesex, for so it was, had by now been
pushed back, outlaws and all no doubt, to more manageable proportions:
it formed the main hunting grounds for the citizens of London.

The hamlet centred on St Pancras grew. According to a Visitation of
the Churches made in 1251, there were by then thirty ordinary houses in
the parish, four manor houses, and two moated, stone-built ones – the
vicarage and the rectory.

London was also growing, however slowly, and its needs were growing
– for food and fodder and fuel. In 1218, the second year of the reign of
Henry III, an edict went out that the forest lands should be cleared. As
trees were cut down they went to build new timber houses in the city, or
to replenish the hearths of those already built, and gradually more and

more of the land came under the plough and had its rough contours smoothed into those rounded slopes which, in western Europe, we regard as natural landscape but which are really nothing of the kind. At first considerable portions of the forest were preserved, being now reserved hunting grounds for royalty: no doubt it was the presence of their hunting lodges in the area which have given rise to persistent tales of 'King John's Palace' and the like. But time, and the ever-present needs of the nearby town, gradually eroded these preserves. Today the only remaining scraps of the once enormous Forest of Middlesex are Highgate Woods, and Ken Wood within Hampstead Heath, just on the edge of Kentish Town.

Those familiar with the area may possibly, by now, be asking themselves when I am going to stop discussing the general history of St Pancras and home-in on Kentish Town proper. After all, St Pancras church and the early settlement round it is one thing, but Kentish Town, a mile or so up-river, is surely quite another?

As a matter of fact it isn't. Or rather, it is now, but as far as one can tell, it wasn't in the Dark Ages, nor yet at the Norman Conquest nor yet in 1400. Until about the middle of the fifteenth century the names 'Kentish Town' and 'St Pancras' appear to have been synonymous, and either name could be used for the hamlet. Frequently on documents relating to property the place is styled 'St Pancras alias Kentish Town'. In fact in Kentish Town we have an interesting example of a village that was apparently established in one place for a considerable period – perhaps a thousand years – and then drifted off to another locale.

In an often-quoted passage, the late-sixteenth-century Norden wrote:

Pancras-church standeth all alone, as utterly forsaken, old and wether-beaten, which, for the antiquitie thereof, it is thought not to yeeld to Paules in London. About this church have been many buildings now decayed, leaving poor Pancras without companie or comfort, yet it is now and then visited with Kentishtowne and Highgate, which are members thereof; but they seldome come there, for they have chapels of ease within themselves; but when there is a corpse to be interred, they are forced to leave the same within this forsaken church or church-yard, where (no doubt) it resteth as secure against the day of resurrection as if it lay in stately Paules.

So, by the Elizabethan period, Kentish Town, with its new chapel of ease 'within itself' was being regarded as a separate entity. The chapel had been built some hundred years earlier, in 1449, on land given by a local landlord, Robert Warner, after some parishioners had made representations to him on the subject: evidently there was local feeling by then that the old church was now too remote from most of the currently inhabited buildings. The plot of land chosen was in the heart of the present-day Kentish Town, in the high road, the site to be occupied in the early twentieth century by part of Daniels's department store and, today, by Sainsbury's supermarket. The raising of this chapel was both an indication of the shift of habitation which had already taken place and a confirmation of it: once the chapel was there the tendency would be to group any new houses near it and to abandon still further the old site down the King's Road. When another hundred odd years had passed since Norden's description of 'poor Pancras, without companie or comfort', a William Woodehouse, JP, amateur antiquarian and local freeholder (*c.* 1700), wrote in the manuscript book he inscribed for his own pleasure and interest:

Ah, Pancras, deserted, timeworn, decayed, Pancras, why Pancras, thy village answers to the cognomen Kentish Towne, thy population are there congregated, thy whole tide of fame and life are there, and in its neighbour Hamlet of Highgate, while around the old time-honoured Church is naught but fields, ditches, its ruined and moated vicarage-house, and its old elms, the only sign of true life there, the clear and running Fleete, that noted river of Wells, which still skips and meanders on its way as it did a thousand years gone by. [But see 'A Note on Sources', pages 239–40.]

Why did the village move? The best explanation lies, in fact, in the 'only sign of true life there' – the persistent Fleet. This was hinted at by Robert Warner himself, declaring that his new chapel would be a boon for those who could not get to the church itself 'when foul ways is and great waters'. We know that flooding was a perpetual hazard of the low-lying land around it: already, when the church was substantially rebuilt in 1331 and a new vicarage and rectory built near it, reference was made to the 'overflowings of the River Fleet', which had presumably become worse as the stream got silted up lower down its course. An Inquisition taken of Totenhale manor, lying west of the Fleet, in 1350, paints a picture of dilapidation – a half-ruined house, unkempt woods, one hundred acres of fairly decent land worth 4*d*. an acre 'and 100 acres worth 2*d*. an acre and no more because the land is marshy'. Also 'ten acres of Marsh Meadow worth 5 shillings by the year and no more, because they were overflowed and could not be mowed, except in a dry time.' The general neglect could have other causes besides the flood menace – two years earlier, the Black Death had first visited England – but a map of the same manor seventy-two years later in 1422 shows, as well as a water-mill just above St Pancras church, extensive marshy reed beds lining the stream on its western side. So it was quite logical for the inhabitants of Kentish Town, especially those that could afford decent houses, to take themselves by degrees to the higher, drier land about a mile up the Fleet, where by now another road (Tottenham Court – Hampstead Road) joined the King's highway. Just north of this junction, where the Castle Inn was and is today, the new Kentish Town established itself, and there it has remained – except that a slight drift further northwards becomes apparent in the nineteenth century, and was confirmed by the siting of railway and Underground stations.

In archaeological terms, then, the area round St Pancras church is a deserted mediaeval village. This has to be understood if early document-ation on Kentish Town is to make sense; and when it is not, much confusion results. Admittedly the fact does not spring to the eye, mainly because the phrase itself conjures up something quite different: a bare field on which, from a low-flying aircraft or the slope of an adjacent hill, faint lumps, circles and shadows can be picked out. But this, in fact, is what you would probably have seen in the area round the old church in the seventeenth and eighteenth centuries, had you been able to achieve the right vantage point. (A balloon, perhaps?)

Dr Stukeley, the mid-eighteenth-century divine, and Kentish Town house-owner, was convinced that the area was the site of an extensive Roman camp. But Roman remains, representing classical civilisation, were more fashionable in his era than they are today, and the many centuries that separated the hypothetical Roman construction workers from the eighteenth-century antiquarians were lightly passed over. Today, were archaeologists able to trek with Dr Stukeley over the lumpy fields of St Pancras, they would no doubt be able to diagnose there a rise and fall of pre-Conquest and mediaeval buildings which the Doctor does not even seem to have suspected.

But those lumpy fields are, unfortunately, no longer there, even in concealed form, for modern archaeologists to excavate. A fundamental problem of research into the past in an overcrowded area like the south of England is that field archaeology, which is used to reveal ancient road and field patterns, strip farming patterns, house-sites and the like, can only be done over a fairly wide area at once. The chances, in any built-up area, of an archaeologist having at his disposal any more than a small fragment of a field or village site, are slight. But urban excavation, which takes a small area such as the site of one demolished building and combs it intensively, is only appropriate to centre-city sites that have been built upon for centuries and are therefore, with any luck, a rich layer-cake of successive building deposits. Forced, as an archaeologist would be in St Pancras, to use urban techniques on what was until the nineteenth century a field site, he would not discover much. Moreover the foundations, post-holes and fragments of paving which it is tempting to imagine somewhere down below the surface of the modern streets, would not even be there any longer to find. In an area that has been open country since, such remains are never more than a few feet down because there has been nothing much to pile on top of them. Virtually all the old house remains of the original Kentish Town would therefore have been scooped out and cast aside, together with the compressed evidence of former crops, when the basements of the nineteenth-century terrace houses that came to cover the area were constructed. Our deserted mediaeval village was finally dispersed into dust, and the dust scattered far and wide, when the Russell family laid out what was first optimistically known as 'Bedford New Town' and is now more commonly called, after its tube station, 'the Mornington Crescent area', or 'that bit between Camden Town and Euston'.

This brings me to a fundamental problem for a writer who picks a particular area: not only its aspect but its very demarcation lines change as fields disappear under streets. When a place – Kentish Town or any other – is a small settlement, whether compact or straggling, and is surrounded by open country, even a quite distant field, being ancillary to the village, may be regarded as part of it. But once that field has been put to more intensive use and sown with houses instead of wheat, perception of it changes. The new 'place' will be given a new name, and will develop as an entity quite separate from the original hamlet. When Lord Camden was empowered, by special Act of Parliament in 1788, to grant building leases on his lands near St Pancras church, the bill was called 'The Kentish Town Act'. Yet the new town he built there was, of course, Camden Town.

Thus the parish of St Pancras *alias* Kentish Town, which in the middle ages stretched from the top of Tottenham Court Road in the south up to Highgate in the north, is today many districts: Euston, King's Cross, Mornington Crescent, Camden Town, part of Chalk Farm, Gospel Oak; Parliament Hill, the Dartmouth Park area and the Holly Lodge Estate – as well as the modern, reduced Kentish Town proper. What I mean by 'Kentish Town' must therefore, of necessity, be variable also; references are determined by what the inhabitants of any particular era thought of as Kentish Town – a large tract of land in the middle ages, a more concentrated centre with some outlying districts in the sixteenth, seventeenth and eighteenth centuries, an increasingly sharply defined area in the nineteenth and twentieth.

Not only as it was built over did Kentish Town reduce in area; the reduction, in terms of the inhabitants' own perceptions, continued as social decline set in, after the coming of the railways in the 1860s. An inhabitant writing to the historical column of a local paper *c.* 1900 pointed out: ' "Kentish Town" has ceased to be "genteel" and it has therefore become smaller and smaller.' The various neologisms – or euphemisms – for the out-lying parts of Kentish Town, in the hundred years after about 1860, become familiar to anyone who consults local archives and local memories: Parliament Hill, Highgate Rise, Dartmouth Park, Brookfield, North St Pancras, Holloway, Camden New Town – all these were employed to avoid the use of those despoiled and shaming words 'Kentish Town'.

Students of present-day inverse snobbery, however, may care to note that, since about the mid-1960s, the trend has been reversed. There has been a slight but distinct influx of the professional middle class into Kentish Town proper and also into the outlying quarters of Parliament Hill, Camden Square etc. The result is many of these newer inhabitants of the once euphemistically-named outlying districts now claim, stretching a point, to live in Kentish Town. Evidently Kentish Town, as well as becoming properly visible again for the first time in a century, is also growing larger. The day has not quite come when Millfield Lane, a charming example of pickled rurality leading from Highgate West Hill past Parliament Hill Ponds to the secluded and woody Fitzroy Estate, calls itself Kentish Town again, but it cannot, I feel, be far off.

However, those who live indisputably within present-day Kentish Town show a considerable unanimity on the subject of its boundaries. 'Real' Kentish Town is contained, north and south, by two railway bridges, visual barriers like the gates of a mediaeval city. The northern one crosses Highgate Road at the level of Gordon House Road, shortly before the apparent open country of Parliament Hill on the west is deceptively reached – though there is a good case for Kentish Town continuing, on the eastern side of the main road, as far as Swain's Lane. The southern one crosses Kentish Town Road and Camden Street; the viaduct whose arches collapsed spectacularly during building in 1849 because the Fleet had been insufficiently considered. Below that, and over the sizeable barrier of the Regent's Park Canal, one is abruptly in Camden Town.

East and west the frontiers are less defined; but most people agree that west Kentish Town bleeds off fairly quickly into Chalk Farm about two-thirds the way along Prince of Wales Road, going toward Haverstock Hill. On the eastern side one might take Camden Road (a piece of early nineteenth-century town planning) as the obvious frontier, and this is about right – except that, from the accident of its name, Camden Road and its environs seem to enjoy a spurious participation in Camden Town. There are those who would see even the district over to the east of Camden Road, the Camden Square district, 'Camden New Town' of the mid-nineteenth century, as a part of Kentish Town, right to the old frontier of York Way (Maiden Lane), with Agar Grove as its southernmost outpost –

but then this is sliding into the area that *was* Kentish Town once, but had become, by 1600, Norden's 'utterly forsaken' place.

Further up the Camden Road, from its junction with York Way, there is no dispute. The ancient route of York Way becomes, at that point, Brecknock Road, and nobody at all in Kentish Town has the slightest doubt that what lies on the far side of Brecknock Road is alien territory, unknown, unvisited. It is Islington, a different borough with different schools, shopping centres and communication-systems. The very names of its roads are unfamiliar, even to those who live only a few minutes walk away. It is known that Dr Crippen murdered his wife among those roads, but that is all.

In this way, by subtle and variegated signs that go unperceived by the stranger, the inhabitants of any urban area define and colonise their particular bit of territory. Only to the uninformed eye, or the jaundiced eye of a commuter passing through districts that are not his own and never stopping there, is a townscape a 'formless morass'. London may be, as Chesterton said, a collection of submerged villages, but to the inhabitants they are not even fully submerged. People's attachment to 'their' street may be just as tenacious and appreciative as the attachment of a smallholder to his particular fields, of a hunting tribesman to a known area of scrub and woodland. The instinctive allegiance which primitive man gives to a natural habitat (large trees, hills, streams, etc.), urban man transfers to man-made landmarks, but the essential nature of that allegiance remains the same.

Yet town planners have persistently ignored this component in human life and, in ignoring it, have done obscure violence to it. In their rationalistic cosmopolitanism, they have failed to grasp that just because you transfer the descendants of ploughmen to paved streets, or turn villages into urban areas, you do not in fact alter human beings; they will still make their villages where they can. The only difference is that their tenancy will be more precarious, more at the mercy of ill-informed bureaucratic decisions, or vainglorious architectural experiments. And if imposed controls produce a landscape which diverges *too* far from the traditional, a desert without domestic scale or subtlety or variety, then the instinct of attachment to the place wilts and fails. We are very ready, today, to concede people's need for 'meaningful human relationships', yet we fail almost entirely to realise that other relationships, with places, objects, views – other supports for the human psyche – may be just as profoundly important, and that, if these are denied, the resulting impoverishment of the person may have deep and lasting consequences.

3

Manors and Gentlemen's Seats

Local history develops its own local conventions. It has become customary for anyone writing about the St Pancras – Kentish Town area to quote the Domesday list of its manors and then to go on to discuss the subsequent ownership of each in some form that makes apparent sense. Compilers of potted histories in local borough publications have made much use of evasive phrases such as 'the manor then passed to' or 'came into the possession of' such-and-such a family, and statements plucked from contemporary documents give apparent authenticity and authority to the whole. I say 'apparent' because, however true individual statements may be, the overall effect they are used to produce – that of a clear and logical sequence of landlords through the centuries in each of four clearly defined manors – is to some extent fictitious. The fact is that the four manors mentioned in Domesday, one of which in any case is not called a manor, probably bear only a tenuous relationship to the later mediaeval manorial holdings in the district.

Nor, for that matter, is the mediaeval pattern itself entirely clear. It has been confidently reiterated that in the old Borough of St Pancras (roughly the once-extensive parish of St Pancras church) we are dealing with four manors as follows: the large manor of Tottenhall (Tottenham Court), the smaller 'lay' manor of St Pancras, the even smaller prebendal manor, and the larger manor of Cantelowes which is usually identified with Kentish Town. In addition, there was the somewhat spectral manor of Rugmere, thought to have occupied part of Regent's Park. But in fact the evidence that there ever were two absolutely distinct manors of St Pancras is rather slight; only one St Pancras manor house is ever referred to. In the ecclesiastical survey of 1251 the *parish* of St Pancras is reported as containing three manor houses. It seems not unreasonable to identify these as Tottenhall (near the site of the present Tolmer Square, behind Euston Road); St Pancras, which I personally believe to have stood on the east side of the King's Road (St Pancras Way) near the present Agar Grove; and Cantelowes, which I believe to have stood in the same area but a little to the north and on the opposite side of the road.

Lists of the lords of the various manors, with dates, sound similarly incontrovertible, but are not actually much use in determining who was effectively in charge of what land. All three manors (or four, if we count St Pancras as two) belonged ultimately to St Paul's Cathedral: they were granted by the Dean and Chapter to other people as 'prebends' – the term can also be applied to the holder himself as well as to the grant made to him. But this simply meant that the revenue from those manor lands would go to the possessor and to his immediate heirs: to be a prebend, or to hold a prebend, did not necessarily mean, therefore, that one lived in the place and farmed it oneself – usually not, in fact. The manorial system had started, probably long before the Conquest, as a method of social organisation. Originally it depended on serfage, a form of slavery; the lord of the manor protected the serfs in return for their labour on his land and their allegiance to him in battle. But, as the middle ages progressed, more and more serfs gained the limited freedom of peasants; under the 'copyhold' system, which was not finally abolished till 1922, they became tenants of the manor lands, paying a nominal rent. Thus, in time, the old intimate bond between master and man slackened, and by the fourteenth century very many villagers were in effect small tenant farmers under an absentee landlord. To be a lord of the manor was no longer necessarily to sit in a manor house presiding over the doings of a subservient body of churls: instead, manors had become commodities to be bought and sold, like industrial concerns today. Indeed the comparison between an early feudal manor held 'in hand' by the lord himself, and the same manor several centuries later, is like that between the mediaeval workshop, with a master presiding personally over a handful of journeymen and apprentices, and a present-day public company in which anyone can hold shares and which may be only one part of a much larger combine anyway.

Thus the same ground landlord might own more than one manor in the same area (as did St Paul's); or two manors adjacent to one another might, further down the scale of control, be in the effective possession of the same family. This would naturally lead to a blurring of distinction between them. Or, alternatively, old manors might be split up into two or more smaller holdings (as seems to have happened originally with Kenwood at Highgate, and Kentish Town, or indeed with the two manors of St Pancras). Nor were men who had simply rented manors, or married into them, averse to assuming the role, if not the actual title, of 'the lord'. Moreover a district might include a substantial freehold house belonging to a notable, who might well be the nearest thing around to an actual lord.

Nor, indeed, is the traditional school history book image of a manor house, as a substantial residence set squarely in the centre of the manorial lands, necessarily realistic. In many areas, manorial holdings were split up, because of buying and selling and marriages and bequests, into several segments. Nor was the manor house where one existed (which was by no means always the case) necessarily 'fit for a lord'. In manors where the land was seldom, if ever, in hand, the manor house might be no more than a farm with outbuildings, lived in by the steward or let off to another tenant. The manor courts, attended by copyholders, which performed many of the functions of the later vestry councils, were held as often as not in inns.

Later, after the upheavals of the Civil War and the Commonwealth, there was a tendency for land-holdings in London to become concentrated in the hands of a few great families. Cantelowes manor, consisting of about 210 acres on the east side of the town, was seized after the execution of Charles I and sold off to two London merchants; ten years later, after the Restoration, it was returned to the family who had held it just before the Commonwealth. From thence, by a route that is not clear, it passed about 1670 into the possession of the Jeffreys family, of Judge Jeffreys fame – the Judge is reputed to have owned a house in Kentish Town. In the following century a Jeffreys granddaughter married Charles Pratt, who was created Baron Camden in 1765 and Viscount Bayham and Earl of Camden in 1786. It was this first Earl of Camden who managed to get an Act through Parliament to enable him to lay the southern part of his estate out in building leases: hence Camden Town, and the streets in it which take their names from

Camden family connections. There is a Jeffreys Street in Kentish Town, one of the oldest and most architecturally attractive of the area, and Brecknock (as in Road and Arms) was a Camden family seat.

In contrast, the St Pancras manor or manors became divided, as time went by, into several parcels. In the sixteenth century the Skinners Company Estate and what was to become the Foundling Hospital Estate became separated off in the south, in present day Bloomsbury, as did the Aldenham (Platt's) Estate near the church on the west of the Fleet. After the Restoration, the Somers family acquired most of the rest of that area – whence Somers Town. The smaller section to the east of the Fleet, apparently known as the prebendal manor (as distinct from the lay manor) passed through several different tenancies in the late eighteenth century before being acquired by the Agar family, the notorious shantytown landlords who are commemorated in Agar Grove.

Tottenhall Manor, having been leased by St Paul's to the Crown in the sixteenth century, was also seized on the establishment of the Commonwealth and sold to one Ralph Harrison. At the Restoration the manor reverted to the Crown, and from thence came into the possession of Isabella, Countess of Arlington, who left it to her son, Charles Fitzroy, one of Charles II's many progeny. It was still in the Fitzroy family in the late eighteenth century, when the current Charles Fitzroy became Lord Southampton. He had only a leasehold interest in the property, but, through the good offices of his uncle, the Duke of Grafton, then Prime Minister, he managed to have an Act put through Parliament converting his leasehold to a freehold to himself and his heirs for ever. The annual compensation paid to the then-prebendary and to the Church was trifling by comparison with the enormous value which the estate, as building land, acquired over the next two generations. A writer in the *Morning Chronicle* in 1837 (cited by Howitt) reckoned that, for an outlay of only £17,784 to date, the Southampton family had by then received at least a million and a half from this estate, and more was to follow. Such was the nature of the speculation in land to which the old manorial holdings finally lent themselves. West Kentish Town was part of the result, including the house which today proclaims its fields beneath.

Once manors and lords were a thing of the past in St Pancras, a folk memory of them lingered on, sentimentalised by Victorian notions of rustic Good Old Days. Until about the middle of the nineteenth century a timbered building of Elizabethan or Jacobean origin still stood half way up Kentish Town High Road on the right hand or eastern side; in fact this was the house built *c.* 1600 for Sir Thomas Hewett, whose father had been a Lord Mayor of London. The estate later passed to his son George Hewett, who inherited at the age of eleven and lived to become Viscount Hewett of Gowran, Co. Kilkenny. He left it to Robert South, a canon of Christ Church, Oxford, who in turn left it to his college when he died. This was the Christ Church Estate, which was laid out during the nineteenth century with roads named after Oxford associations – Caversham Road, Islip Street, Peckwater Street etc. Until it was built on, the land was leased from Christ Church by the Morgan family, prosperous local farmers of whom we shall hear again, and the old timbered house became known as 'Morgan's Farm'. Thus the history of this house is clear: it was not a manor house. Yet, by the end of its days, it had acquired a local fame as 'The Old Kentish Town Manor House'; pictures of it were so labelled by the Heals, father and son, in their local history collection, and the belief has continued to lead a life of its own.

A persistent confusion has also occurred between this house and a fifteenth-century house which disappeared much earlier and which in any case almost certainly stood in a different part of the district, nearer to St Pancras church. It was owned by an illustrious inhabitant of Kentish Town, who was not lord of any manor. His name was William Bruges (or Bregges or Bridges) and he is remembered as having been the first Garter King of Arms, a diplomatic post placing him way above the level of a local squire. Appointed Garter by the newly crowned Henry V in 1415, Bruges probably attended the installation of the German Emperor Sigismund (the title was a Holy Roman Empire one) in the Order of the Garter in the early summer of 1416: at any rate it appears that later in the summer, while the Emperor was still in England, he entertained him at his house in Kentish Town.

The grandeur of this official function was considerable; Kentish Town has never seen the like again. Among those invited were representatives of the City livery companies, the mayor, assorted knights and heralds, the Bishop of Ely on a palfry clothed in white and gold and with suitable attendance, two dukes, several lords, the Prince of Hungary and the Emperor Sigismund himself, each with their retinue, besides sundry other gentlemen, esquires and officers at arms. It is recorded that they set out in mounted cavalcade, 'with exceeding great pomp', covered in 'Jewels, Gold Chains, rich embroideries etc. [which] dazzled the eyes of the innumerable multitude of people who flocked from the City of London.' A mile outside Kentish Town, in a field described as 'arable' (presumably this meeting took place after harvest time?) Bruges and his retinue were waiting to greet their noble guests, Bruges himself on his knees, cap in hand. After extravagant courtesies on both sides, the procession made its way to the house, where minstrels were playing. Then everyone sat down to an almost unbelievably extensive meal, among whose ingredients were casually included such choice items as '7 sheep', '200 pigeons', '100 green geese', '30 great carp', '1 gallon welks', '1,000 eggs', '200 lbs butter' and 'cock-combs innumerable'. The cost amounted to the then enormous sum of £192. 17s. 8½d.

It was all for one sitting: the record does not say that the party stayed at Kentish Town; nor could any mere country house of the period have been large enough to accommodate them. One is inclined to imagine an orgy of gluttony going on for hour after hour, but the answer is probably that they didn't actually eat it all and weren't meant to. Feasts of such dimensions were in the nature of a public-relations exercise, a crude display of conspicuous consumption intended to impress rather than to sustain. They remained so for many centuries afterwards, in fact into the Victorian era. Doubtless, therefore, the less grand inhabitants of Kentish Town lived royally for weeks on the ample remains. It is worth noting that the feast consisted almost entirely of meat in various forms plus eggs and fish – protein and yet more protein, at a time when the staple diet of the labouring classes was rye bread and wheaten bread eked out with diary products and probably only an occasional meat dish, when a pig or an ageing plough-ox was killed. Despite the social dislocation of the Black Death (first visitation, 1348) and a consequent rise in the wages of skilled men like masons and thatchers, the social inequalities of the fifteenth century were still massive. I do not know how large the hamlet of Kentish Town was then. In the whole of St Pancras parish, 125 years earlier, there had been only forty households. A few new houses were apparently built when the church was re-modelled in 1330, but it was probably not a great deal larger by Bruges's day, since populations increased slowly in those harsh times.

Thus, as early as 1416 the nature of life in Kentish Town was already modified by the presence in the hamlet of wealthy outsiders, whose main life and work and even dwelling did not actually lie there. In this respect, villages within easy walking or riding distance of a large town are subtly affected in their social organisation centuries before their external appearance is greatly changed. Kentish Town retained its air of a typical English village certainly into the eighteenth and almost into the nineteenth century. Yet long before that time it had ceased to be an autonomous rural community, and for centuries before it was built over its agriculture was affected by the needs of London.

Bruges referred in his will to the chapel belonging to his house and to his great barn there. The property had a frontage of some 130 yards on the London–Harringay highway, and in 1446 Bruges was authorised to take a twenty-foot strip off the road in order to make a ditch to protect the place. This would not however have been a moat in quite the early mediaeval sense of the term for, as the engines of war became more sophisticated, the old style fortified manor house ceased to offer any real defence; its moat, tower etc. became more a matter of tradition and grandeur than of strict utility. Indeed the fifteenth century saw the first building of the English country house, whose presence was to dominate English landscape and society for centuries; the earliest appearance of the rural idyll, which we shall meet again and again in the course of this account. Bruges was therefore a typical and fashionable example of his era, and his moat was most likely intended for keeping fish in for household consumption. Not, however, that he lived to enjoy it. He must have been getting on in life in 1446, thirty years after the famous dinner party, and he died in 1449. The house itself was not disposed of in his will, but he bequeathed a number of its chapel fittings to a church in his native Lincolnshire, so it looks as if he intended it to be sold. At all events it appears to have been bought in 1452 by a Sir Thomas Ive, a court official.

The Ive family figure quite prominently in local records for this period, and later, in the seventeenth century, we find them still in the area. In the fifteenth century they seem to have been a troublesome and a litigious family. Because of the habit of calling sons and grandsons after fathers, it is always difficult to know which generation one is dealing with – the sparse manor court records that record rows about land-holdings were kept as minutes for people who knew personally whom they referred to and had the unlettered habit of keeping all information in their heads anyway. But I assume that the Thomas Ive referred to in the 1490s was the grandson of the original one who would by then have been rather old for such activities – 'Thomas Ive has broken and entered the pinfold of the Lord [i.e. lord of the manor] and driven away his cattle there. 12*d* taken for trespass and pasture.' The following year we find him, undaunted, litigating about felled trees and obstructed water-courses. There were also debts complained against him.

I think it was, however, the first Thomas Ive, the court official and the grandfather of the hedgebreaker, who maintained a running battle with Robert Warner or Wariner a generation earlier. This Warner, another local landowner of some substance and a member of the Grocers' Company, was the one who, in 1440, presented to the parish the plot of land in the new centre of the village on which the chapel of ease was built (see Chapter 2). To the parishioners who came to ask him to sell that plot, he said that he had bought it only recently and that if he were to sell it again people would say he was in need of the money, so 'for the worship of God and the welfare of the parishioners' he preferred to give it to them. He marked out the ground himself with stakes, leaving room at the front for processions, gave £5 towards the building, though other parishioners also contributed, and apparently superintended the building himself. It is clear that Warner, whatever his legal title in the village, was playing the authoritarian and possessive role of Squire Bountiful, familiar in later centuries. Perhaps Thomas Ive did not like this and saw Warner's handsome gesture as a threat to his own position – he who had just bought Bruges's fine mansion for 360 marks. At any rate a struggle for precedence took place between the two families, with Ive and his lady and their servants marching in and sitting in Warner's own pew in the chancel. Upon this, Robert Warner declared 'it would be the worse for them all', and took the key away from the vicar on several occasions, saying that no service should be held in the chapel while Ive was present. Thomas Ive eventually brought an action against Warner in Chancery (says Godfrey in the *London Survey*, Vol. XIX but he does not say how the matter was finally resolved).

The next century brought far-reaching changes in England, with the dispossession of the monasteries, the Reformation, and finally the increasing prosperity of the Elizabethan period. Church livings, always financial assets, became delicate political commodities. In 1551, under Edward VI, the boy-king son of Henry VIII, we find Dr Ridley, then Bishop of London (later to be martyred under Mary) attempting to obtain the living of St Pancras for one or another of his protégés:

> Now there is fallen a prebend in Paul's with the Vicarage of a poor parish in Middlesex called the prebend of Cantrells and Vicarage of St Pancras, by death of one Layton [who had been in any case dispossessed by Henry VIII]. This prebend is an honest man's living of thirty-four pound and better and the Vicarage very small in the King's books. I would with all my heart give them unto Master Grindall and so I should have him continually with me, and in my diocese to preach.*

Someone else, a master William Thomas, one of the clerks to the council, was apparently after the same living. In the end Ridley gave it not to Grindall but to another protégé named in his original letter – one Bradford. But those were difficult times. Neither Grindall nor Bradford appear in the *London Survey* list of vicars; by 1569, when Ridley had died under Mary and Elizabeth had been queen for eleven years, the ruling authorities were for some reason taking steps to stop Grindall preaching at 'St Pancras otherwise Kentyshetowne' and sending him fierce notes about it.

There is a persistent tale that St Pancras Old Church was the last parish church in England where the Catholic Mass was said, and that this was allowed to happen because there was an aged priest there who was a favourite with Queen Elizabeth. I do not know if this is true; what *is* true is that in 1584 a clerk, one Thomas Sherlock alias Thomas Toothdrawer – which sheds an interesting light on the money-making shifts resorted to by dispossessed priests – was arraigned for saying a

* This letter is quoted by Woodehouse, in his *Journals*.

private Roman Catholic Mass at Kentish Town, together with Katharine Bellamy, widow of Richard Bellamy. This probably took place not at the church but in Katharine's own house: she had two, one at Kentish Town which had been purchased from Lord Paget, and another at Uxenden. It is clear that the Bellamys were a family of some means and distinction, whose obstinate adherence to the old faith was bound to attract official disapproval: Norden listed Richard Bellamy as a person of note in the London area. Two years later, in 1586, poor Katharine was implicated in a plot, during which a priest called Babbington was hidden in her Uxenden house. She was imprisoned in the Tower, the favourite prison for upper-class criminals, and died there. Then in 1593 her son Robert was imprisoned in Newgate for saying Mass, where he was possibly tortured and where he too died. He was fifty-two then, so seven years earlier he would have been forty-five, which argues that his mother when she went to the Tower was at least sixty-plus, and probably nearer seventy. Her property passed to her younger son Thomas.

There were other substantial families living in Kentish Town in the late sixteenth century. Ridley's reference to the 'poor parish' presumably refers to the vicar's living rather than to the inhabitants in general. Some of their doings were chronicled by a man named Machon who lived in the district then. Of him and his diary, Heal has this to say:

> . . . This manuscript diary is one of the volumes which suffered severely by the fire of the Cottonean Library and is much burnt away from the upper parts of the pages. The writer was a citizen of London but of no great scholarship, some have taken him for a herald, others for a painter in the employ of Heralds. He first lived in the parish of Trinity . . . in the 56th year of his age he retired to Kentish Town; his diary begins in 1551 and continues to 1563. It is thought he died of the plague raging at that time.

The life Machon depicts is a happy one: as so often with contemporary documents, there is no hint of recent strife or social upheaval. In June 1560, two years after Elizabeth ascended the throne, he reports a big wedding party at William Bellise (or Bellay's) house, 'the manor house of Pancrasse'. Bellise was an Alderman of the City of London and a vintner: in spite of the similarity of his name in some versions to that of the Bellamy family, it seems that they were a different family. The marriage was not apparently of a member of the Bellise family in any case, but the triple wedding of the three daughters of Atkinson, a scrivener of Kentish Town (if Machon was indeed employed by the College of Heralds, a scrivener would have been his exact social equal. There were still Atkinsons in the district a hundred years later). The three girls were married in St Pancras church wearing 'III goodlye capes garnysshed with laces gylt and goodlye flowrs and rosemare', and headgear with pearls and precious stones. There was a masque and mummers at the St Pancras manor house afterwards.

Then, in September of the same year, there died one Master Richard Howlett 'Esquire of this parish', and he was buried in St Pancras churchyard complete with his armour. The land around the chapel of ease, which Warner had designated a hundred years earlier for church processions, was not apparently consecrated for burial though it is known that some burials did take place there, since it is recorded that, when the building was pulled down in the late eighteenth century, gravestones were salvaged and used for paving. Howlett's funeral, however, took place properly at the church where he lay, no doubt, as Norden said, as secure against the day of resurrection as if he lay in stately Paul's. It was the occasion for a big dinner at 'the Howse' (presumably, again, St Pancras manor house). It was a meatless dinner, as befitted the solemnity of the occasion, which meant that it consisted of 'all kindes of fyse bothe fresse and saltes' (Did Machon actually fail in pronunciation to distinguish between 'sh' and 'se', I wonder?) and was 'the godlyest dener that has beene in Pancrasse'. Evidently he did not know about the Bruges repast some 140 years earlier. But, as at the Bruges dinner, 'ther was unfinished' – to regale, no doubt, the inhabitants of humbler houses round about.

Bequests to the poor figure prominently in the wills of the period. To local parishes, this was an important source of charitable funds: to the bequesters it was a painless way of purchasing a small stake in the Everlasting Mercy, a form of insurance premium against spending too long in purgatory. Heaven and hell being real places to most of our ancestors, the steps they took to safeguard their own future in these regions were real and practical likewise. Before the Reformation, a

charitable bequest was in the nature of a formal bargain: money or
goods in kind were left to the poor on condition that they would repeat
Masses for the soul of the departed at regular intervals, and a sum was
usually set aside specifically to defray the cost of these Masses 'for ever'.
How long is 'for ever'? In practice, it seems to mean merely while there
is anyone left alive who remembers the person – or until the next
big socio-religious upheaval. Probably few of the Masses ordered 'in
perpetuity' in the first half of the sixteenth century were still being said
a generation (and a Reformation) later, but the effects of the more
secular charitable bequests made after the hold of the Church was
broken have proved surprisingly long-lasting.

Typical is the generous will made by John Morant who died in 1547,
setting up various charities for the poor of St Pancras including a bequest
of the proceeds from twenty-eight acres of land 'next under Haymans in
the hamlet of Kentish Town'. This land lay on the eastern side of the
Kentish Town high road and formed part of what eventually became
Hewett's estate and then the Christ Church Estate (see illustrations).The
shape of the holding, clearly defined in the sketch map appended to the
bequest, is still readily discernible three and a half centuries later on a
detailed map of 1796: field boundaries are often very tenacious, outlasting
buildings and even footpaths, since fields, once defined, tend to be
bought, sold or bequeathed as lots, and this remains true when they
are sold for building. The shape of the fields in Morant's bequest was
eventually to determine the layout of the roads in the Christ Church
Estate, with Oseney Crescent fitting into a triangular patch
at the end. And while the other streets – Gaisford, Caversham, Islip,
Peckwater – form a regular grid pattern with their cross streets, the size
of the gardens is less regular, diminishing as the field boundary tapered
at one end. This is readily discernible on maps of 1870 onwards: it is less
clear on the modern map because Peckwater Street was demolished
after the Second World War, but still the northern boundary wall of the
estate that covers that area will be found out of parallel with the next
street, just as the line of the hedge was marginally at an angle to the main
road centuries earlier.

At some point in the unheavals of the sixteenth century the Church
apparently lost this land. But a large parcel adjoining it on the south,

which was given by a Sir John de Grey in 1315 to St Bartholomew's Priory and Hospital, in return for the usual Masses for his soul, was still in the possession of Bart's in the mid-nineteenth century, when streets were laid out on it bearing Bartholomew's name.

An even clearer persistence through time is found in the case of Heron's Gift, consisting of £8 left in 1580 for repaving the roads of the hamlet. By 1861, when the various 'paving boards', an untidy legacy from the eighteenth century, were finally swallowed by the Metropolitan Board of Works, this legacy had, with investment, swollen to £41. 19*s*. 8*d*. – though, taking inflation into account, this does not seem an overall gain. I owe this piece of information about Heron's Gift to Palmer (*History of St Pancras*, 1870). But what Palmer does not seem to have guessed at is a possible connection between Heron's gift in 1580 and the curious presence in the borough of some old slate paving, on which he comments: 'One of the peculiarities of Kentish Town still preserved . . . It certainly bears a very clean and pleasing appearance, and very soon becomes dry, but in wet and frosty weather is dangerous in the extreme. The slabs of almost polished slate make it as difficult to walk upon as the polished oak floors of our ancient family mansions . . . '

In 1582 Sir John Stonehouse 'of Kentish Town, Knight', whose wife had died before him, left capital represented by forty shillings to be given yearly in bread to the poor of St Pancras, to twelve poor men a frieze gown, shirt and pair of shoes and to twelve poor women of the same parish a frieze gown, shift and pair of shoes. He stated that this should be done on October 1st each year – in time for the winter chill and wet. But Woodehouse, noting this in his journal 120 years later, commented 'No such charity now known'. Money, being flexible in use, lasts longer than more precise bequests: much more durable was Platt's Gift, also given (in 1637) in memory of a deceased wife. It consisted of some of the revenue from lands given to St John's College, Cambridge in what is now the north part of Kentish Town but was then a separate hamlet within St Pancras known as Green Street – £20 yearly for the poor of Kentish Town. That twenty pounds is still on offer today; notices are posted about it in the local public library. But it is not always easy to find ten modern old age pensioners who will stand up in a public meeting and ask for it.

Equally and more profitably durable was Palmer's Gift. Eleanor Palmer was the daughter of a cofferer of Henry VII and wife to John Palmer of Kentish Town, whom she out-lived. She seems to have been of a slightly higher social class than her husband, and the extensive copyhold lands they held in both Cantelowes and Totenhale came from her side of the family. One of their daughters married a son of Lord Paget – he who sold his house at Kentish Town to the ill-fated Lady Bellamy. When she died in 1558, Eleanor bequeathed to the poor of Kentish Town a third part of the profits of three acres of land situated near the Fortys Field (now Fortess Terrace, Fortess Road – which has nothing to do with 'fortress'). Writing about this property in 1870, Samuel Palmer (no relation, I think) remarked that 'In 1696 it produced £2. 10s; in 1810, £14, and now it produces £50 per annum.' It had by then been built upon and its revenue was helping to fund some almshouses: 'On the renewal of the lease,' he added, 'it will bring in a very much larger sum.' This remark, indeed, might stand as a classic understated comment on the history of once-farm land turned into brick and mortar. Today, the revenue is the property of The Fortys Field Housing Association, a charitable trust, and part of it is occupied by a primary school, built in the late 1960s to replace an older one and called Eleanor Palmer. I hope she would be surprised and pleased if she knew.

The most remarkable will preserved from this period and district is that made by Richard Bowdler in 1603 as he lay dying in St Pancras parish, to which he had retired. He was a member of the Society of Merchant Adventurers 'for Muscovie and the East Indies', a Freeman of the Drapers, and erstwhile citizen of London. He seems to have been an extremely wealthy man with property in various parishes, but he asked specifically in his will to be buried at St Pancras. He left numerous charitable bequests naming quite large sums: £60 for a dinner for the parish inhabitants and his friends, other monies for releasing 'poor prisoners' (perhaps debtors?) in various itemised prisons. He sounds a man of compassion and imagination, but the endless bequests, both to the poor and to his own family, become repetitive: one wonders if it was all quite realistic. He claimed to be 'very sick in body but of good and perfect memory', but perhaps this was not the case. His name does not seem to crop up in other local records, which one feels it should have if

he was really such a substantial citizen. Unless, of course, the connection
with St Pancras was merely his retirement there when already old.

This, indeed, is a tale that many wills tell by implication. The hamlets
of 'St Pancras in the Fields' – Kentish Town, Green Street and Highgate
(whose inhabitants often preferred to go to church more conveniently
in Hornsey) – were suitable places within easy reach of London to retire
to. Well-to-do people like Lady Bellamy, Eleanor Palmer and Sir John
Stonehouse bought or leased houses there in old age in the same way
that their modern counterparts might retire to Gloucestershire, Sussex
or Spain. Often, as with their modern counterparts, their country houses
in St Pancras were not the only ones they possessed. They were rustic
retreats, a sign of the new prosperity among the merchant and civil
servant classes. Speaking of Middlesex in general, Norden wrote:

> This shire is plentifullie stored and as it seemeth beautified with many
> faire, and comely buildinges, especiallie of the Merchants of London,
> who have planted their houses of recreation not in the meanest places,
> which also they have cunningly contrived, curiously beautified, with
> divers devises, neatly decked with rare invencions, invironed with
> Orchards of sundrie delicate fruites, gardens with delectable walks,
> arbers, allees and great varietie of pleasing dainties . . .

Exactly where these houses were, it is now usually impossible to say.
Someone, no doubt, lived in Bruges's mansion: Woodehouse, a later
occupant of the house, says that Queen Elizabeth granted it to Sir Roger
Chomondley or Chomley, who founded and endowed Highgate School,
but the Chomondleys, like the Cornwallises with whom they intermarried, are more likely to have lived in Highgate, always the smartest
end of the parish. More often than not, at this period, the occupant of a
house was not its owner. Another member of the family, Sir Hugh
Chomondley, who died in 1601, owned a house in the Green Street area,
but, again it is not known whether he occupied it himself. Woodehouse
lists six substantial local landowners for the Elizabethan period, in
addition to the manors.

Kentish Town was also, by reason of its nearness to town, a favoured
hunting district. Game laws, intended to preserve game as far north as
Hampstead and Highgate, had been in force since Henry VIII's day.

Machon's diary records that a hunt by the Lord Mayor, that started in Holborn Fields, ended with a fox being killed by St Pancras church. There was a hunting lodge in Fig Lane (Crowndale Road) near the church, and the Castle Tavern is thought to have been another. Local tradition had it that this had been, like Tottenhall Manor, 'a palace of King John', but, as a nineteenth-century antiquary remarked, popular tradition habitually assigns old buildings either to the Devil or to King John (his representative on earth?) and there seems to be no reason for placing the origins of this building so far back in time. When the house was demolished in 1849, to be replaced by the present Castle public house, the *Illustrated London News* reproduced pictures of it, inside and out, which suggest a typical Elizabethan or early Jacobean house.

There was another house of much the same style a little to the north of it, and there must have been others again of which no traces survived into the era of watercolourists and engravers. One, built on part of the Deaconsfield, which had once been owned by Bruges and later by the Ive family, stood between Swain's Lane and the Bull and Last – in the Green Street area. It was probably built by John Draper, citizen and brewer of London, whose family did very well for themselves in Elizabethan times. Later an eighteenth-century house occupied the same plot – Bateman's Folly.

What was happening in Kentish Town in the Elizabethan era was happening all over England. With new prosperity, villages were being rebuilt, and the new homes were not the old scrap-wood and mud erections which a couple of generations of wind and rain would reduce to ruin again, but were built with good, new oak timbers. The new middle class, many of them for the first time *rentiers* living on the proceeds of property, built on a comfortable domestic scale very different from Bruges's great hall and thick stone walls. In other parts of the country many of the houses built at this time are standing today, and a number of those built in Kentish Town *could* be standing today if they had not been pulled down in the mid-nineteenth century by businessmen who did not realise they were destroying a potential treasure trove (to put the matter at its lowest). Forty years after the old house had been destroyed, the Castle Inn was done over with such olde-worlde additions as a historical picture in coloured tiles. But you would have thought that someone earlier in the century would have seen which way the wind was blowing, for even as Tudor and Stuart buildings were being demolished up and down the country in favour of Victorian stock brick, Gothic architecture was coming back into fashion. Timbered Clerkenwell was demolished at the very time that the Pre-Raphaelite Brotherhood were converting the middle ages into high fashion. The destruction was carried out in the name of commercial necessity, but it didn't, in the end, even make commercial good sense.

Among those lost by 1860 was Sir Thomas Hewett's house. I have already said that it has been wrongly labelled as – variously or together – Cantelowes Manor House and Bruges's house. It may, of course, have occupied the site of an older mansion, but in itself it was unmistakably a house of the period of which I am writing – a substantial gabled place in a mixture of rendered brick or stone and half-timbering of *c.* 1600. It seems to have captured the local imagination like no other building. J. F. King, the early nineteenth-century artist of Kentish Town, of whom we shall be hearing again, provides still further myths concerning it:

> Its early history is not correctly known; some record it as being built in the reign of Henry VIII, others that it was a hunting seat of Nell Gwynn and Charles II; also that it became a Lodge belonging to the Earl of Essex where he kept his Harriers. Be that as it may, it seems to have been in times gone by a very Aristocratic residence until it fell into the possession of a wealthy farmer.

Frederick Miller (*St Pancras Past and Present*, 1874) supplies a different story:

> A legend exists amongst the old inhabitants, that more than a hundred years ago the then-proprietor of the Old Farm House engaged a reaper at harvest time, who soon afterwards conceived the diabolical idea of murdering and robbing his new master. He succeeded in his object, but retribution speedily overtook him. He was tried, found guilty, and sentenced to be hanged near the spot where his crime was committed. The Old Farm House was, therefore, associated for some time with the crime and the execution of the criminal. For many years of late the premises had a deserted appearance.

'More than a hundred years ago' would take us back to about 1760. There is, however, no newspaper cutting of the period relating to this crime in Heal's collection, as one might expect if the story were true. Later the house, by now in a ruinous state, was described by Albert Smith, a popular nineteenth-century novelist, in *The Adventures of Mr Ledbury*, as a hide-out for coiners. He evidently enjoyed himself dwelling at length on the details of its state:

> . . . The brickwork of the walls is crumbling and disjointed, in some parts riven throughout its entire structure; the windows are mere frames of blackened and decaying wood, allowing free entrance to the interior, in mockery of the corroded padlocks still fixed to some of the doors; and the inside of the dreary building is equally dismal. The ceilings have fallen down upon the floors, and the boards themselves have rotted from the joists and lie about the apartment, sometimes standing out, like the coffin planks of a teeming burial ground, from the dirt and rubbish that half cover them . . .

As I have said, a popular taste for Gothic romance was well-established by the nineteenth century.

Rather earlier, probably, than Mr Smith's word picture (which may or may not be accurate) is the testimony of A. Crosby, an amateur water-colourist of considerable talent who was familiar with the St Pancras area and painted a whole series of pictures depicting various points along the Fleet (soon to be much transformed). He also did pictures of the Castle Tavern, the Old Farm House and several other buildings. He had a particular interest in the Old Farm House, and in the late 1830s made a great many small sketches of panelling, stairs and so on, and took exhaustive measurements, with descriptions of materials used in the building. He also drew a carved mantelpiece, apparently Tudor work, from 'Nell Gwyn's room'. These papers now repose in a small wallet among a collection of his pictures in the Guildhall Library. Along with them is even a piece of 'the parlour wallpaper', which looks like a late eighteenth-century 'Chinese' pattern: just the thing for an aspirant gentleman farmer. It was probably laid on the walls when the Morgan family, who farmed extensively in the district, took the place over. Crosby wrote in his notes: 'Kentish Town Old House. Mr William

Morgan carried on the farming business there about 58 yrs. He left in October 1831. Held of Christ Church College Oxford. Manor of Cantlows. Ancient Moat on North and East side of House. A Walnut and Mulberry Tree in Orchard.' He adds on another sheet: 'The house materials are to be sold for £60.'

So much for the house of Sir Thomas Hewett, son of a Lord Mayor of London, whose own son was raised to the peerage, and whose house may or may not have sheltered the private affairs of Charles II and Nell Gwynn. The last remains of it were not swept away till 1860, when the new streets were laid out.

4

Ordinary People

Nearly all the landscape of England and many of the houses have been created or tended by people whose very names are forgotten. The 'history' of an area inevitably tends to be a recital of the doings of a few literate property-owning people who left records in a comprehensible form. Those left by the ordinary, unlettered people, though ubiquitous, are far harder to read. Lanes are records, and so are farmsteads and the names of fields. Hedgerows are particularly good records, and, using Max Hooper's rule-of-thumb that for every separate type of tree in one hedge you can count a hundred years of existence, it can be established that many still-existing hedges are seven or eight hundred years old or even older. Nor was the presence of all these species fortuitous. Hedges, now considered part of our 'natural' landscape, are of course planted, and men tend to plant at each era what is useful to them, so that the hedge is not just a barrier but a source of essential material. The Normans, materially ambitious and far-sighted, planted oaks near London, many of which were harvested as splendid trees about five hundred years later (and not, sadly, replaced) and went to make the ships for Elizabeth's navy and the new, fine houses for her successful traders. Probably Hewett's house in Kentish Town, like many others, was built with timbers from Norman trees, so that by the time it was demolished the wood in it had been in existence in one form or another for close on nine hundred years. Come to that, the best beams were not burnt even then, since Crosby tells us that the materials were sold for £60. Very possibly somewhere not far away even now some of that oak is surviving, buried in the stuccoed structure of a Victorian villa.

A century later, according to FitzStephen, St Pancras was famous for yew trees – presumably also deliberately planted or fostered, since yew was much used for making bows. Since it is poisonous to sheep, it could only be grown in an area where much enclosure took place at an early date and where the places where manorial flocks roamed free were therefore limited. (This accounts for the traditional presence of yew in a churchyard – the only piece of properly enclosed land available in many districts in strip farming days.) Land in St Pancras, lying close to London, was under all sorts of pressures and a good deal of enclosure took place centuries before The Enclosures: a map of the Totenhall manor in 1422 shows a well-established field pattern, and by the eighteenth century there was little common land left. At the same time as the yew, no doubt, ash saplings were also planted – for arrows. Blackthorn was planted for sticks and the handles of farming implements – there are some very old thorn trees among the vestigial hedge lines on Parliament Hill. Later, when wooden palings became common, chestnut was often planted for this purpose. Later again, when furniture became more plentiful and more lightly fashioned, elm was much used, and the hedgerow elms of the typical eighteenth-century enclosure landscape became ubiquitous.

These, then, were the records of generation upon generation of ordinary people, whose unrecorded, unremitting labour laid the hedges and trimmed them, just as they must also have helped to build the timber and mud houses once scattered along the high road. Their record remains in many places, and remained in Kentish Town till just over a hundred years ago. Little of it can now be found. And yet more survives, because of the extended nature of building in London, than in such typical 'concentrated' cities as Paris or New York. Compressed, the one behind fortifications against the Prussians and the other on an island, these two cities have between them created the twentieth-century stereo-type all-urban habitat, which has been imitated around the globe. But at the same period – the mid- to late-nineteenth century – London, though expanding at an immense rate, was continuing to do so in the old haphazard fashion of towns from time immemorial: a tavern here, a gentleman's residence there, a row of other houses there, but all quite spread out and close to the ground.

Judged by Continental standards, land use in London has traditionally been very wasteful, and still frequently is. Even today, more than 50 per cent of all the land in inner London is actually open to the sky: some of it is road space, some park or housing-estate public space, but a great deal is individual garden. From the sky, even quite densely-built areas which, at ground level and in the street present a greyly urban aspect, are a patchwork in which green predominates. The typical London street is a *trompe d'oeil*. The fronts of the houses, often nothing *but* false fronts, all stucco and pretension slapped inappropriately onto humbler brickwork, are meant to persuade you that these are grand town houses in the latinate manner, but when you walk through the house and out at the back the illusion is dispelled; irregular back-additions, cottage-like chimney stacks, sheds, betray the houses' origins in an essentially rural tradition. Some have only paved yards, but very many have actual garden plots, with grass, roses, lilacs, flowering fruit-trees and even vegetables whose existence you would never guess at from the barren street.

It is here, at the inaccessible back of the houses, where so much of the inhabitants' life goes on, that the pattern of the older field systems, and sometimes the hedgerows themselves, are clearly discernible. I have already mentioned the way the 1860s streets of the Christ Church Estate in Kentish Town were fitted into the existing field shapes; this is a particularly clear example, but a more fragmented preservation of hedge-rows is commonplace, and often some of the actual components of the hedge survive physically. Typically, the rows of gardens behind the houses in one street end in a wall backing onto the gardens of the houses in the next, thereby creating a green enclave out of the public eye. The shared garden boundary separates the development along one street from that along another – which may indeed have been developed by a different speculator or at a different period. This boundary, then, is the historically significant one, often being much older than the line of the street itself, and it is here that surviving hedgerow trees may be found. If you take up a position (usually difficult, unless you are the tenant of one of the houses) looking *along* the bottom wall of a line of gardens, you may find that you are looking at a row of elms or willows, some of the trees in one set of gardens, some in another, according to the thickness of the original barrier and lie of the modern wall or fence. Elsewhere the signs of an old hedge may be more fragmentary, but a scattering of poplars or horse-chestnuts along the range of gardens may indicate its spectral presence. Very many London houses owe the substantial tree at the end of their gardens not to any great arboraphilia on the part of nineteenth-century speculators (who tended to prefer manageable privet and laurel) but to the land's more distant incarnation as pasture, which required leafy barriers both to keep the stock in and to afford them shade and wind shelter. For the fields near London were pasture land, or land for hay, for centuries before they were ploughed up to make bricks.

The description of the St Pancras district in the Domesday Survey suggests that much of it was then ploughed; FitzStephen, a hundred years later, spoke of it being 'as the fruitful fields of Asia . . . filling the barns with corn'. Clearly its main function then was to act as a granary for London: the corn was milled in the many mills of the Fleet whose sound FitzStephen found 'grateful to the ear' – indeed the section of the Fleet running down to Battle Bridge was known then and for several centuries as Turnmill Brook. It will be remembered also that Bruges, when he rode out to meet the Emperor Sigismund near his house in Kentish Town, knelt down to greet him in an 'arable' field. Up to the Elizabethan period crops were sown; Norden remarked that on this side of London:

> . . . the soyle is excellent, fat, fertile and full of profite . . . Yet doth not this fruitefull soyle yeeld comfort to the wayfairing man in the winter time, by reason of the claiesh nature of soyle; which after it hath tasted the Autume flowers, waxeth both dyrtie and deepe. But unto the countrie swaine it is as a sweet and pleasant garden, in regard of his hope of future profit . . . The industrious and paineful husbandman will refuse a pallace, to toyle in there golden puddles.

Yet other commentators of the time suggest the swains were already discovering that, in the vicinity of a big city, simple hay-crops (grass) can be the most profitable crop of all, and moreover one that can be harvested several times a year. An anonymous writer of the same period referred to something being 'as plentiful as haycocks in St Pancras', as if these were already an established fact.

In an age when all haulage and travel by land takes place by horse-power, hay, the fodder of horses, is the fuel of commerce: it is as essential a commodity as petrol is in our own times – and this is in addition to its use as food for sheep and cattle, the equally essential meat and milk-providers for the city's inhabitants. Not surprisingly, therefore, with the growth and growing commercial sophistication of London during the Stuart period, more and more of the land adjacent was turned over to grass. The 'clayish nature' mentioned by Norden was in any case not ideal for agriculture. A hundred or so years later, William Woodehouse was confidently writing: 'There is now considered to be about 3000 acres of land in the Parish [of St Pancras], only a small quantity of which is arable and the soil generally gravel and clay; the pasture and meadow land is very good and produces moderate good rental.' He must have known, for he owned 45 acres there himself.

Looking ahead for a moment another hundred years, by 1810, when Thomas Milne drew up a detailed Land Utilisation Map of the London area, virtually all the land in the parish and in neighbouring Islington was grassland, except for a few nursery gardens and orchards. A French visitor of the same period (Louis Simond) was struck by this oddity in the environs of London, and also remarked on an obviously related fact that England was obliged to import a large quantity of its wheat and other foodstuffs from abroad – an absolute difference between England and France which remains today. A few years later, in 1822, Cobbett (of *Rural Rides*) remarked, with his usual asperity towards London, that the fields right out as far as Watford were nearly all turned over to hay to satisfy the needs of 'The Wen'. It was, he said, cut several times a year by gangs of travelling Irish labourers. Perhaps local swains had by then become rather thin on the ground – or, realising that the maintenance of grassland hardly provides a full-time occupation, had turned their attention to other service industries for the spreading town, becoming coachmen, gardeners and house servants.

But let us return to the end of the middle ages, when the ordinary parishioners of Kentish Town first became visible to us through the court rolls. These were the brief records kept by the manor court, which performed in each area some of the functions later taken on by the parish councils or vestries and also some of those of a local magistrate's court. Many rolls have been lost. Others, though often in existence, have never been transcribed or translated out of the Latin in which they were originally written. The Cantelowes court rolls were transcribed, in part, by one of the compilers of the LCC *Survey*, and these of course have the greatest interest for Kentish Town. The St Pancras manor rolls have apparently disappeared, probably destroyed – with symbolic fitness, perhaps, since most of the land that formed the manor or manors of St Pancras has similarly disappeared under the yards of the main line railway termini that front Euston Road, and every vestige of former landscape thus destroyed. The Tottenhall rolls, which are relevant to the western side of Kentish Town, were stated by the compilers of the LCC *Survey* to have been lost, but were recently found, lying quietly in the archives of County Hall. Doubtless many papers that, given time and scholarship, could be made to yield valuable information, lie similarly uncollated in libraries and archives up and down the country.

The Cantelowes court records tell us what was happening in Kentish Town, not in the long term but from one season to the next, and who was making it happen, both for good and ill. The oldest date from 1480, just as the middle ages were ending. Soon after that date, as mentioned in the last chapter, a Thomas Ive makes his appearance, accused of breaking and entering a pinfold of the lord and driving away cattle. These would have been his own cattle: the pinfold was the pound, in which straying beasts were put and released on payment of a fine. Ive was fined anyway – 12d. for 'trespass and pasture', which he seems to have paid on the spot. Such offences were common, and were not confined to what later generations would have called 'the lower orders'. The Ive family, as we know, were substantial property owners as well as the owners of Bruges's fine house. Offences simply listed as 'hedge-breaking' (e.g. 9 May 1482: 'John Wynter is a common hedge breaker') probably usually referred to attempts to remove or take back livestock. A later pound stood at the junction of Kentish Town and Hampstead Roads, exactly where Camden Town tube station now is, but I do not know if this pound was there in the fifteenth century, though there was a common there then (Holt Green).

Picturing a neighbourhood at any date before about the accession of Queen Victoria, one should remember the ubiquitous presence of animals: apart from the horses and cattle enclosed – or supposed to be enclosed – in fields, there would always have been single cows and goats browsing on the wide 'waste' by the side of the road, or pastured on the common land – in this case, principally the Kentish Town Green, which was land along the road going up towards Parliament Hill Fields; a little bit of it survives as a recognisable public green opposite Grove Terrace. One item in the rolls for this period refers to pigs 'being allowed' to dig on the common, but a generation later one reads 'Rd Tailour has annoyed the common with his pigs', so clearly their days as free-scavengers – descendants of the wild pigs of the Forest of Middlesex – were ending.

Depredations of one kind or another on the depleting store of common land in the district were a continual problem in an area adjacent to the town. When the fifteenth and sixteenth-century inhabitants of Kentish Town were not 'leaving dung on the waste', they were felling trees there (perhaps as beams for new houses) or else digging out cartloads of gravel from a gravelly oasis in the London clay on about the site of Highgate New Town. Fines hardly seemed to deter them. Nor did they always bother to turn up at meetings. The court held in November 1503 heard a particularly typical range of offences:

Joan Swyfte and the wife of John Drever are common tipplers.
Egidia Eustace is a brewer (widow).
The wife of John Watson snr. is a disturber and scold.
Reginald the servant of Hy Taylour is aged 12 and not sworn.
Thomas Walterlyn is obstructing the common way at Holt Green
    leading to the chapel of St Michael.

At this same meeting John Drever was made ale-taster, which should have suited his wife. The job of the ale-taster was to check that ale brewed for sale was as it should be and of specified strength: cases of brewing – and presumably selling – untested ale are so common, however, that it is hard to believe they were taken seriously, e.g. 'The wife of Giles Eustace, Joan Kempe, Florence Bartram are brewers. Meg Watson, Joan Wyse and Joan Pecher are common tipplers.' Joan Eustace, Joan Kempe and Meg Watson were still at it the following year, and Joan Eustace and Meg Watson the year after that, when Joan Eustace was also had up for gravel-digging on the much-pillaged Highgate Hill. The year after, though widowed by then, she was still continuing her brewing activities undaunted, and in subsequent years also.

Occasional fights are reported, but mostly these seem to have taken place between servants rather than among the more moneyed members of the community whose names constantly appear and reappear in small property transfers. For instance, in December 1508 there was reported an 'Assault between Jas. Aschu and John a Barowe, and Thos. Croche servant of Master Kyrton, with club and dagger. The first two fined 40*d*. each.' But a few years later Thos. Eustace, of the troublesome Eustace clan, assaulted his servant, and he too was fined 40*d*. The following year 'Wm Marshall keeps loose women of evil conversation and conduct; he is ordered to expell them from his house [presumably an ale-house]. Robert Couper offends the same.' Another entry, for a later year, is still more moralistic in tone: 'Wm Alsoppe by day and night keeps Margaret the wife of Robert Kynge in his house, committing adultery, to the evil example of the king's lieges.' The previous year he also took boughs of trees from the common, but it is not clear which offence was the most badly regarded.

The court was just a local gathering intended for settling disputes peaceably between neighbours. More serious matters were taken to the Court of Assize. Most of the crime reported from the sixteenth century seems to have centred on horse and cattle rustling. Richard Holmes, an Essex man, was hanged for this in 1549, when he had broken into a close at Kentish Town and stolen a grey gelding worth 26*s*. 8*d*. Seven years later another man, accused of stealing eight black steers, made use of the time-honoured dodge of 'pleading benefit of clergy' – that he was of priestly status and that his case should therefore be heard in the ecclesiastical court, where the death penalty was not applied. To substantiate his claim he read out a few verses of the Bible 'reading like a clerk' i.e. fluently. (The fact that this alone could establish a man's claim to be set apart from the common run of men gives one considerable insight into the degree of illiteracy, even among solid citizens who bought and sold property, carried on businesses and left wills. I doubt if any of the men and women who attended the manor courts at this time could read, except the steward who kept the notes, the vicar, and possibly the occasional 'gent' and his lady – though these showed a tendency to stay away and pay the absentees' fine instead. Even in the early eighteenth century, by which time literacy had become the rule among the trading classes, the ordinary working people could not so much as sign their names. Most of those who made depositions before William

Woodehouse in the early eighteenth century signed with a cross, or perhaps with a wavering initial letter only.)

By the mid-sixteenth century, when Kentish Town was securely established near the fork at the Castle Inn, the half-abandoned St Pancras church had become 'St Pancras in the Fields', and had inevitably become a spot for insalubrious activities. Norden wrote: 'Although this place be as it were forsaken of old, and true men seldom frequent the same but upon devyne occasions; yet it is visited by thieves, who assemble not there to pray, but to wait for praye, and manie fall into their hands clothed, that are glad when they escape naked. Walk there not too late.'

At the same period, a letter to Queen Elizabeth on the subject of crimes of violence in the suburbs noted 'The chief nurserys of all these evil people is fields of Pancrass and about the Churche, the Brick kylnes near Islyngton, and the Wells.' This is the earliest mention of either brick kilns or wells in the area, and they – and the crime – were to remain a feature of the district well into the nineteenth century. Evidently by Elizabeth's reign the area was already acquiring its character as urban-margin land – rustic in appearance but subtly deformed and socially affected by the town's proximity: the land given over to pasture for the town's milk and meat herd or the production of fodder for its coach-horses, the much-vaunted fresh air intermittently sullied by whiffs of industrial vapour, the inns developing fancy pleasure gardens and attracting riff-raff from the town, who trampled what crops remained, stole fruit and purses and made love in the fields.

There are gaps in the existing manor rolls. They come to an end in 1540, just at the time when, it is clear from them, a number of new, moneyed families were moving into the area. Old names – the Pechers, Eustaces and Warners – fade out. It may have been that the male line failed and their female descendants are disguised in later rolls under other names (the Pechers, for instance, were related to the Ives), but it may also have been that families simply moved out of the area as others came in. There has been a traditional tendency to underestimate the amount of social movement and change our ancestors experienced. It is clear that even very ordinary people in the pre-industrial world were not necessarily born, bred and buried in the same parish, though probably when they moved the distance could be measured in a few miles at most.

The rolls do not resume again till 1610, and cease in 1632 with the coming of the Civil War. During this twenty years the general picture they give is of a bigger and also more middle-class community than that of a hundred years earlier. The Ive family are still there; the Draper family have their property in Green Street. The Hewetts have arrived and another knightly family, by the name of Bonde; there are a fair sprinkling of Esquires among the manor's tenants. The Earl of Arundel was living on Highgate Hill in a house previously occupied by the Cornwallises, and was even (1626) installing lead water pipes in it.

Events of great national importance make themselves felt in the rolls only in a negative sense: by omissions and breaks in the record. The rolls resume their seasonal tale in 1658, a Civil War, a regicide and most of the Commonwealth having silently supervened since the last surviving entry. It is known from other sources that, under the Commonwealth, the Cantelowes demesne lands, some 210 acres, were acquired by one Utber, a London draper, but at the Restoration were handed back to the Dean of St Paul's. No whisper of this, however, appears in the rolls. At the court held on 10 May 1660, within a fortnight of Charles II's triumphal return to the throne, the chief interest was provided by Mr Fishbourne, who was entertaining cripples or vagabonds in his barn and was fined 20s., and by Kellam Collins, who had put a diseased horse on the lord's land. Evidently *which* or *what* lord was irrelevant to the business in hand. The sole reference to anything untoward having happened to ruffle the peace of the parish occurs the year before, when it was recorded that 'Hannah Dixon, spinster, who claims to hold a parcel of waste, a cottage and stable and a quarter rood of land at Holts Green has lost her copy of the Court Roll. Due to the Wars the Court has also lost its copy. It is granted to her.'

The upheavals of the Commonwealth and the Restoration were presumably the reason why, in 1664, a formal review of land ownership in the manor was made, to clarify holdings. Some of the fields had retained the names they had had nearly two hundred years earlier, but some had new names. Deaconsfield, which in the intervening time had figured as 'Dacond Field', 'Digglesfield' or 'Dykkyns field', is recorded as Dicas Field, and holds that name from then on. The Ives no longer figured as prominent landowners, though a member of the family makes several brief appearances later in the rolls as an inn-keeper in Highgate and owner of a small piece of land there. It rather looks as if, while other families had been climbing the social ladder, the Ives were on their way down. (They were to fall further. In 1867 a dispossessed RC priest, the Rev. Hardinge Ivers, died in a small house in Kentish Town from 'want of proper medical aid and nourishment'. He was said to have been a descendant of the Ive family.)

But individuals are always more ephemeral than habits, and in many ways daily life, judging by the rolls, had not changed very much. People were still failing to scour ditches and repair bridges and persisting in leaving dung on the waste land. The available waste for such activities must, however, have been rapidly diminishing, for by now there are numerous records of people enclosing parcels of it or building on it. It is a little hard to tell from the undramatic style of the entries whether the court was just noting what had come to pass or was registering disapproval of it. Some pieces of waste were expressly stated to be granted by the manor. Only sometimes is it clear, from the mention of a fine, that the copyholder had transgressed: for instance, in 1658 Thomas Howe was fined 3s. 4d. for setting willow trees on the common at Battle Bridge, which to a modern mind would seem to be a generous improvement to the amenity of that place. But presumably Howe's intention was to cut the trees down later to sell them, so he was in effect using the common as a plantation. The same year he was also had up for allowing gaming in his yard, a reminder that the Puritans were then still – just – in power.

Sir Thomas Hewett died shortly after the Restoration, leaving his fine house and his substantial property-holdings in the parish to his son George, then aged eleven – he who was later to acquire an Irish barony. In May 1666 an unprecedented number of deaths were recorded since the previous court in August the year before – which was, in itself, an unusually long lapse of time between sessions. Richard Wright had died, presumably at no very advanced age since he left sons of 16, 13 and 7. William Holmes, similarly, had died leaving a son who was still an infant. Thos Howe – of the willow trees and the skittles – had died. John Briscoe, a substantial citizen despite brewing peccadilloes, had died, and so had one Ed Stith. The number of copyholders was not great, and this is a disproportionately large number of deaths. The reason was probably not far to seek – to be precise, about three miles distant, in London itself, where the Great Plague had raged all the previous year. It is known that families retreating from the infection to country houses nearby carried plague with them, and also that, as the situation in London grew worse, poorer families fled on foot, sometimes to expire in the fields by St Pancras church.

Indeed a story is told concerning such plague victims and a prominent citizen of the parish and manorial copyholder, Elisha Coish. This man, a physician, is first listed as a faithful attender at meetings in the late 1650s, and later served a term as collector of rents for the manor. Of him, Lloyd, the nineteenth-century Highgate historian, had this to say:

> The High Dutch physician – newly come over from Holland, where he resided all the time of the Great Plague in Amsterdam, and cured multitudes of people that actually had the plague upon them . . . was indeed a charitable man to the diseased poor . . . There is a case told of his goodness to 13 poor people who were flying for their lives from London and Clerkenwell, and who intended to have gone north, away by Highgate, but were stopped at Holloway, as there the people would not let them pass, or not even suffer them to be in a barn for the night; so they crossed the field towards Hampstead, when Dr Coysh having heard of their distress, he had them brought to his barns, and there attended to and fed them for 2 days; he saw them got safe to Finchley Common, where they intended to wait until they were in hopes the cold weather would check the infection.

It would be pleasant to record this as an early instance of St Pancras parish's long tradition of accepting immigrants into their community and profiting by their presence – 130 years later a large influx of French *émigrés* altered the social mix of the southern end of the parish, and since then successive waves of Germans, Welsh, Irish, Greeks, Africans, West Indians and Asians have come and been absorbed. Certainly this story traditionally told about Coish (or Coysh or Coise) bears all the marks of a Good Jew story – a variant of the Good Samaritan prototype – in which an outsider of a despised race performs some deed of charity which puts the indigenous population to shame. To get the full flavour of it, you have to remember that England was intermittently at war with Holland during this period. Unfortunately, however, the idea that Coish was a foreigner at all appears to be a myth. The land he held near Swain's Lane was previously in the possession of the Blake family, who were relations of an Elizabethan Roger Coise, citizen and Grocer of London.

Living on the western side of the slopes leading to Highgate, Coish and his family were thus near to 'Traitor's Hill': indeed their property is referred to at one point in the rolls by reference to this landmark. This was a tree-covered knoll, now absorbed in Highgate Cemetery but clearly marked with its name on the map of 1796. There are therefore no grounds for the frequent false identification of Traitor's Hill with Parliament Hill further east – or indeed for the assertion that it got its name from being a meeting place for the conspirators of the Gunpowder Plot. Doubtless 'Traitor's Hill' – like indeed 'Parliament Hill', which may have been the site of a Saxon folk-moot – dates back long before the squabbles and disruptions of the seventeenth century. Nevertheless, before proceeding to the closing decades of the century, when many new names appear on the rolls, this is perhaps the moment to take a look back to the Civil War, that 'disturbance' which, once it was over, people were eager to forget.

During this event (referred to by Woodehouse as 'the great rebellion, now happily settled by our glorious King William') the Commons at one point heard a rumour that King Charles I and his army were marching upon London:

> In a great fright [they] did send unto the Mayor, and Citizens, to order out the trained Bands, and all men that could be spared, and even London Apprentices, to raise earthen bulwarks and fortifications around the outer parts and suburbs of London, and to man the said Walls to prevent the King entring his City. And at that time as I have heard many thousands of men, women and even children were seen to work in these fields, and many dreadful deeds and crimes were committed under the colourings of these patriotic mud and useless Walls ... The remains of their handy-worke are still to be seen through the whole length facing the Church, and after when these Walls were manned by the Trained Bands and Souldiers they made fires in this ancient Church and cooked their Victuals there, and tore up the seats and rails for firewood and left it in a most pitiful state. [Woodehouse's Book, *c.* 1700 – but see 'A Note on Sources', pages 239–40.]

This was one of the lowest points in the history of Norden's 'poor Pancras', already a lone surviving building in a deserted site whose village had moved away from it. It is not surprising that Woodehouse, writing half a century later, should add 'the Church is but dimly lighted and has but a very forlorn appearance ... divine service is now seldom performed in it.' The surprising thing is that, despite being semi-derelict for so long and despite the building of New St Pancras Church in the Euston Road in the early nineteenth century, the old church did survive and is there today, one of the oldest buildings in London, when so much else has gone.

Perhaps one of the 'dreadful deeds and crimes' Woodehouse had in mind was the event which is recorded in a contemporary (1643) pamphlet found bound up with his MS Book, and entitled with the brevity typical of the period: 'A Most Certain, Strange and true Discovery of a Witch, Being taken by some of the Parliamentary Forces as she was standing on a small planck board and sayling on it over the River of Pancrasse. Together with the strange and true manner of her death, with the propheticall words and speeches she used at the same time'.

This curious document provides an interesting example of the subsidiary violences which are committed in wartime on the pretext of patriotic and moral motives: it is no coincidence that persecution for witchcraft in England reached its peak in the mid-1640s. It also serves as a contrast with another account of 'witchcraft' by the same river from Woodehouse sixty years later (quoted in the next chapter). The change in the educated person's view of witchcraft between the time of the Commonwealth and the accession of Queen Anne is a striking witness to the general growth in sophistication and the social change that mark the Restoration era.

The pamphlet starts with a preamble against women, citing their feebleness of mind etc. and expressing surprise that the devil should choose such weak vessels to carry out his works. It continues:

A part of the Army [presumably the victorious Parliamentary forces, since the account was written shortly after] being at Pancrasse out of London and marching . . . one of them, . . . espied on the river being there adjacent a tall, lean, slender woman, as he supposed to his

amazement and great terror, treading of the water with her feet, with
as much ease and firmness as if one should walk or trample on the earth.

On taking a closer look the soldiers realized

> there was a planke or deale overshadowed with a little shallow water
> that she stood upon, and which did beare her up . . . still too and from
> she fleeted on the water, the boord standing firm, boult upright . . .
> turning and winding it which way she pleased.

When she landed, the commander of the soldiers ordered her to be
brought to him:

> In consulting with themselves what should be done with her, being it
> so apparently appeared she was a Witch, being lothe to let her goe and
> as lothe to carry her with them, so they resolved with themselves to
> make a shot at her . . . But with a deriding and loud laughter at them
> she caught their bullets in her hands and chew'd them.

When a carbine was held to her chest the bullet rebounded, and a sword
proved equally ineffectual.

> Yet one amongst the rest had heard that piercing or drawing blood
> from forth the veins that crosse the temples of the head, it would
> prevail against the strongest sorcery and quell the force of Witchcraft,
> which was allowed for trial. The woman, hearing this, knew then that
> the Devile had left her and her power was gone, wherefore she began
> aloud to cry and roar and teare her haire, and making piteous moans.

> With her last breath, she prophesied that the Earl of Essex 'shall be
> fortunate and win the field, and said no more . . . They immediately
> discharged a pistoll underneath her eare at which she straight sunk
> down and dyed, leaving her legacy a detested carcasse to the wormes.
> Here soule we ought not to judge of, though the evils of here wicked life
> and death can scape no censure.'

The account ends here. Was she, one wonders, a local girl and thus
known to all the parish? Even by the standards of a country at war with
itself, the soldiers' summary execution of her went against all law and
precedent. What story, one wonders, is really concealed behind the tall

tale and sanctimoniously approving words? Perhaps an attempted gang rape by the idling soldiers who, having been repulsed and having killed their victim in their annoyance, then felt they must concoct a suitable story to explain away her corpse?

At all events the little-habited area near the church was evidently maintaining its character as a place of ill-repute from which respectable citizens should be warned away. Twenty years later, shortly after the Restoration, it was the scene of a long-famous murder, that of the actor Clun. He had a house in Kentish Town village to which he was returning on horseback one summer night in 1664 after appearing in *The Alchemist* at the King's Theatre. As Pepys records it in his diary, the actor was set upon by footpads and, though he struggled a great deal, was bound and stabbed and bled to death in a ditch where his body was found the next morning. Pepys, with his usual inquisitiveness, went to view the scene of the crime several days later, and also learnt from London gossip that Clun had been sitting drinking with his mistress in town before going home, which was why he was riding back so late. One at least of those who set on him, an Irishman, was quickly taken, and later hung on a gibbet near the scene of the crime, by the roadside near St Pancras manor house. The presence of a rotting body in chains can hardly have improved the amenity of that already decayed neighbourhood. The gibbet remained there long after, as a warning to others tempted to similar crimes.

It will be noticed that what the unlucky Clun was doing was commuting. He worked in the centre of London but, despite having a mistress there, returned to Kentish Town apparently every night where he had a wife and children. This was a relatively new concept in 1664, and may point to some improvement in the condition of the roads since the beginning of the century, when mainly retired persons had taken houses in Kentish Town. Pepys himself found the place convenient enough for brief drives to take the air.

It was to be another three hundred years before the word 'commuter' became an accepted part of the English language. Yet the act itself was, in the course of the next century, to become a major feature of Kentish Town life.

5

'One hundred and twenty-two houses'

London was growing. It had been, in fact, for some time. The first strenuous attempts to limit its size were made by Elizabeth I in a famous proclamation of 1580, forbidding the erection of any new house within three miles of the City gates – she and her Parliament could, of course, do little about the existing houses, already snaking their way down the Strand, linking London with Westminster, covering the Moor Fields to the north, working their way towards Wapping in the east. In any case neither the proclamation nor the successive Acts of Parliament that followed it seem to have achieved much. It has been estimated that the population of London more than quadrupled during the queen's reign, but that by the end of it only one quarter lived actually within the City walls. The rest (about 170,000) lived in the outskirts.

Regulations were repeatedly ignored or circumnavigated. In 1603 we find Stowe writing, of a lane to the north of the City,

> . . . within these fortie yeares it had on both sides fayre hedgerowes of Elme trees, with Bridges and easie stiles to passe over into the pleasant fieldes, very commodious for citizens therein to walke, shoote, and otherwise to recreate and refresh their dulled spirites in the sweet and wholesome ayre, which is nowe within a few yeares made a continuall building throughout, of Garden houses and small cottages: and the fields on either side be turned into Garden plottes, teynter yardes, Bowling Alleys and such like, from Houndes ditch in the West so far as White Chappell, and further towards the East.

Stowe's particular complaint was that many of these 'garden houses' were built 'Not so much for use or profite, as for shewe and pleasure' – what one might call the country cottage or *résidence secondaire* syndrome that seems inevitably to affect a society's ecology in a time of prosperity. Further proclamations during the reign of James I, setting arbitrary limits on development close to London (limits ranging from two miles to seven) were made and continued to be ignored. It was becoming evident that cities have a hydra-headed life of their own. A poem written in 1614 by Thomas Freeman, called *London's Progresse*, declared that:

> Hogsden will to Highgate ere't be long
> London has got a long way from the streame,
> I think she means to go to Islington,
> To eat a dish of strawberries and creame.

It may be noted in passing that the abortive attempts at total restriction embodied the 'Green Belt' principle, which was only to become a semi-reality some 350 years of unimaginable growth later. There was nothing wrong with the principle. But no one seems to have faced then, or for centuries, the fact that you cannot have both an uncrowded city and an uncluttered surrounding countryside. Unlike most Continental cities, London ceased, after the middle ages, to feel the need to gird herself within defensive walls. In addition, the English tendency, at all social levels, to prefer a separate house for each family and to consider this the 'right' and healthy way to live, has been all along a perfect recipe for urban or rather *sub*urban sprawl. Thus the famous prophecy of Mother Shipton, a Yorkshire wise-woman of the time of Henry VII, was already, by the seventeenth century, acquiring a new and sinister meaning:

> Before the good folk of this kingdom be undone
> Shall Highgate Hill stand in the midst of London.

(In fact Highgate Hill, despite the vast development to the north of it, still does not really stand 'in the midst of London', for the open spaces of Hampstead Heath and Parliament Hill offer it some protection and an air of vestigial rurality. Descending Highgate West Hill, going into Kentish Town and therefore *towards* London, even today there is still a clear view to be had out over the green slopes of an apparently agricultural landscape – Parliament Hill – in between, much as there must have been in the eighteenth century. The building of a pub called the Mother Shipton in west Kentish Town around 1850 must have seemed, at the time, a cynical endorsement of the prophesy, but, as things turned out, the march of bricks just north of there was stayed – largely by the endeavour of private individuals.)

Charles I continued the attempts to restrict London's growth, though then, as always, it was not the new houses of the rich which were objected to but the higgledy-piggledy developments of the less well-to-do. Cromwell went on in the same vein, even introducing retrospective punitive fines for houses illegally built since 1620, but his laws about building proved as effective and workable as his laws against fornication. The regulations were renewed at the Restoration to even less effect, particularly as the Great Fire of London in 1666 brought the whole design of London into open question anyway. Many and grandiose were the schemes put forward for London's rebuilding on entirely new and rational lines, and all, like the County of London Plan of 1944, came to nothing in the end. One of them, by Sir William Petty, even embodied the idea of a 'Greater London', a modern megalopolis in a setting of rural amenity that would one day have five or even ten million inhabitants. In his pre-figuring of the Garden Suburb ideal he was, in his way, as visionary as he was famous for his rationality, and seems to have perceived, as none of his contemporaries did, that since London was going to go on growing, it would be better to plan for this than to attempt vain restrictions. However, his views found little support; the City was rebuilt, not on the same style but to the same street pattern, and the suburbs continued their unplanned expansion. (Petty reckoned that London would eventually spread to the Essex coast, to Hitchin in Hertfordshire, almost to Reading in the west, and to Lewes, Sussex, in the south. Two hundred and fifty years later, this very nearly came to pass.)

If anything, the Great Fire probably contributed to the sprawl beyond the walls. It is recorded that afterwards homeless Londoners came and camped in those ever-accessible fields around St Pancras church, and possibly some of them stayed for good in the neighbourhood. In the years following the Plague and the Fire many new names appear in the court rolls. It was then too that Woodehouse came to occupy his 'nearly ruined Mansion of by-gone date', and Randolph Yarwood, a notorious vicar, makes his appearance in those years. He seems to have been a man of decided opinions, and his term of office was marked by chronic quarrels with his vestry. He complained, firstly, that money intended for the poor was being used for other matters (perhaps this included some of the charitable bequests made by parishioners in Elizabeth's and James I's time?) and, secondly, that the trustees of the church lands in the parish were refusing to spend the rents from those lands either in improving his stipend or in paying the rent of a house for him to live in while a new vicarage was being built. (The old, moated vicarage near the church, constructed in the fourteenth century, seems to have been ruinous by then, and the new one was built slightly to the north of the chapel of ease, in the high road.) Yarwood took his complaints to court, and it is thought that the expenses of this litigation were the reason that, in September 1675, he was arrested on three actions for debt, and in the following year was a prisoner in the Fleet prison for a while.

Undaunted, the year after he was opposing the expenditure of the rents of the church lands on the repair of the parish church. His motive for this may not have been entirely selfish. He disapproved, he said, of the manner in which the restoration was being carried out: a gilded cross from the steeple was destroyed in the process and likewise the old screen between nave and chancel and 'so made the Church look like a barne to this day'. (What would he have said of the light, galleried churches that the next century was to bring?) Further trouble followed; he was suspended for three years by the Dean and Chapter of St Paul's for marrying a couple without banns or licence. It is not recorded who took over the parish during this time, but the incumbent who succeeded him on his death, John Marshall, said that he celebrated some services, including marriages, at his own house, and that at other times other priests turned up at the church claiming that they had been sent expressly to marry people 'and it was a perfect scramble who should get to perform ye office'.

The internecine war prolonged itself in 1678 with a dispute about who had the right to nominate the churchwardens: Yarwood wanted John Ives (he of the ancient family and the public house in Highgate) and claimed that the job had been given to another man with fewer votes. He seems to have won that particular round, for Ives did become church-warden for a number of years, but, perhaps in retaliation, his opponents in the vestry locked Yarwood out of his own church. The tale is amplified by Woodehouse, who was evidently one of the pro-Yarwood faction in the parish, so the emphasis is different:

> ... many like myself do not believe the acts laid to his charge ... He attended all the best private families of the parish and received their support and consoling friendship to his last moments, and they had him buried in his own churchyard, indeed there is no doubt that this persecution was carried on by malice and false swearing, as he was a man of utmost humility, and always found by his friends of strict probity and virtue ...

The contention surrounding Yarwood probably reflects not only the man's bizarre personality but also the sensitivity on the subject of religious observances at the period, when only a vicar of Bray could hope to stay continually on the right side of the authorities, and even then would be bound to displease some section or sections of his parishioners in whatever direction he changed course. Yarwood may have been considered by some too dangerously high-church and therefore tainted with papacy – his complaints about the loss of the gilded cross and the rood screen suggest this. Interestingly, the reputation of St Pancras church as a place where irregular things went on outlasted Yarwood's curacy. A report in a newspaper, *The Freethinker*, of 1718, represented it as a church where couples could get married at cut-price rates without a regular licence. The vicar, then and for many years, was Edward de Chair. The following year he made an attempt to let out the church-yard for grazing, but was forestalled by the vestry. Evidently he was having the same arguments with them over his stipend that his predecessor had had, but this time the vestry gave way and let him have an extra ten shillings a year.

It was clearly a difficult parish to look after, not just because of the church and the chapel on two separate sites, but because of the pressures on it, and particularly on its graveyard, from outside forces. It is plain from the sheer numbers of people listed in the marriage register under Yarwood that he must have been marrying couples who had no connection with the parish, and indeed after Marshall took over in 1690 there is a spectacular drop in the figures. But it is harder for a priest to refuse baptism or burial to outsiders, and Marshall's records for both contain many entries concerning people who were just 'passing through' – not a few of them children who were also passing through life and that rather quickly. Winter and summer, there was a constant trickle of strangers up and down the King's Highway, mainly itinerant workers, and some of them found in St Pancras's crowded churchyard their last resting place. People like Richard Waterhouse, who 'was a poor man that came up to haymaking. He came from Clayton in the parish of Gasting nr. Preston, in Lancs. He dyed in one of Mr Gray's houses at the Pindar of Wakefield' (a small and rather scruffy hamlet south of Battle Bridge straddling what is now Gray's Inn Road). Probably Waterhouse was old and already sick when he came south seeking work. Later the same year (1699) another, younger, casualty of haymaking was buried: Thomas Ward, 'son of John and Mary (of Liverpool in Lancs, both lately deceased). It dyed by the way as it was carrying home by its Grandmother who had been at Harvest work in Kent, but had nothing to pay neither for the parish nor King's Duty. No King's Duty.'

At least these people, however humble their condition or brief their lives, were known by name and accorded human dignity (if only in death). Some missed even this. The nameless 'still-born vagrant that lay in Chalcot Barn' was buried without service. The 'unknown person that drowned himself near the Cow and Hare' might count himself lucky to be in consecrated ground at all, assuming that 'drowned himself' is meant to be ambiguous. The 'poor boy found dead in the fields at Tatnam Cort' was merely one of a number of children and adults that roamed these fields and sheltered in the brick kilns. Quite a number of dead children had first names but no surnames, such as 'Elizabeth. A child taken to nurse at the White Hart in Battle Bridge. Supposed to be a bastard child but the parents unknown as also the name' and 'Anne. It was a negro child nurst at widow Shepherd's at Tatnam Cort; the parents were slaves or servants from Barbados, Capt. Griseley Commander of an Indian Merchant ship.' Not that all the 'nurse children' were bastards or indeed fundamentally unwanted. A large number of them appear to have been the offspring of living married parents who were, simply, working at various occupations elsewhere – for example, 'The father is at sea, the mother keeps a publick house in Clare Street, by Clare Market.'

Other bodies that found their way to the graveyard belonged to people who had recently been in other parishes but had died in the St Pancras area, usually in one of several houses that seem to have made a business of taking in the ailing and those in throes of infancy, childbirth or age. But what strikes one particularly is the number of persons being interred who came from London, and are often plainly listed as belonging to such-and-such a parish. Many came from 'St Giles Church End', the overcrowded area round St Giles-in-the-Fields – by then in the fields no longer. What had happened was what, 150 years later, was to happen to St Pancras church itself (see Chapter 7): the graveyards belonging to the town churches were rapidly filling to saturation point and had no room to expand. People had begun to use St Pancras churchyard as a more convenient and suitable place for burial beyond the confines of the town. Thus both the dead and the living spilt out from London proper into the still-rural villages.

The resident population, on the partial evidence of the manorial records, continued to grow, if slowly. A general survey of St Pancras tax-payers made in 1693 lists some 450 names. Nicholas Hawksmoor's sister-in-law moved into a property in Swain's – or Swine's – Lane. (Swine seems to have been the old name, and its transformation to 'Swain' a piece of late eighteenth-century pastoral conceit.) Woode-house, writing in 1699, described as 'deserted' the area near the church, in which his own 'nearly ruined mansion of bygone date' (Bruges's mansion) appears to have lain, but five years later he added a note in the margin of his book – 'Some houses are now building near the church'. It was one of these houses which, within a generation, was 'noted for a mineral spring': the Adam and Eve public house and pleasure garden. Though less famous than the Bagnigge Wells down the road near Battle Bridge, the St Pancras Wells long had a raffish renown. But Woodehouse lived just before the era of the wells and pleasure gardens, and to him the part he lived in was 'a neglected parish' whose chief interest lay in its past, for 'there is such an interest in its lands, its every highway and byeway, that irresistibly urges on my weak pen to draw from oblivion and pourtray to the best of my ability the many claims to notice and attention which it possesses.'

Woodehouse was, as we have seen, a JP for a time (but see pages 239– 40), and at the end of his account of the area appear some of his court papers. These include evidence of several robberies (silver watches, silk handkerchiefs, cheeses waiting in a cart outside the Castle Inn, a pair of plush breeches) and also a couple of cases of attempted rape – or asserted rape. One of these displays incidentally a whole spectrum of attitudes and life styles, all of which are still recognisable:

Elizabeth Bocock: I met the prisoners in a field near Pancras church. They began to be very rude, and put their hands up my Coats, and tumbled me down under a Hedge, but I cried out and then Bateman beat me and so they both went away. I got up and went to Battle Bridge and there they came up to me again, and Bateman asked me to drink and be friends, and so I went with them into the Green Dragon and there they both lay with me, that they did. And there was another man and he lay with me too . . . They all three ravished me, one after another, whether I would or no, for I desired them to let me alone, but they would not, and I was afraid to cry out for there was a thousand men in the house . . .

Court: A thousand men? Remember you're on your Oath, and mind what you swear.

Elizabeth Bocock: I believe there might not be quite a thousand men, but I am sure there was nine or ten, and they all wanted to ravish me, but I would not let 'em, though I don't know but they might have done it too, if Charles Cooke had not been so kind as to stand by me, and fight my way out of the room, for I'll say that of him, he was a mighty civil man, though he was one of the three that ravished me . . .

The Prisoners in their defence said that the girl has a Very Loose character and would not let them alone until they had . . .

Mr . . . : On the very day mentioned in the indictment, I saw this girl lying on the grass behind a hedge and three Boys with her. One of them lay on each side of her and the other upon her.

Elizabeth Laversage: I keep the Green Dragon at Battle Bridge. The Prisoners came in with the Girl, she drank with them very freely, and they put their hands up her Coats and she was well enough pleased with it, but I keep a very orderly house, I assured them that I would not allow any such doings . . .

Mr Theobalds: In July last Mrs Bocock employed me against the

prisoners for assaulting her daughter . . . She said they had beat and
abused her but she made no mention of rape at that time . . . A
meeting was appointed to accomodate the differences, but they came
to no agreement, for she demanded £50 for damages. The Girl came
to me afterwards and said, her Mother would have me indict them
for a Rape. Some time after this she came to me again, and said they
had had another meeting and the Prisoners had agreed to give her
Mother £3 and had put the money into her hands, but, as soon as the
acquittances were signed, Bateman snatch'd the money out of her
hand again. And therefore her Mother wanted to know, if in this case
she could not indict them for street Robbery? I finding by this that
they were a couple of wicked contentious Creatures, I told them: I
would have nothing more to do with the affair. And the next news I
heard was of the prosecution. The Jury acquitted the Prisoners.

Four years earlier a different sort of case occurred in which Woodehouse does not seem to have played any official role but which excited
his interest sufficiently for him to record it in detail. It concerned the
persecution of an old couple for witchcraft, and it is interesting to
compare Woodehouse's enlightened, rationalistic, eighteenth-century
view ('A most dreadful instance of the dismal effect of superstition')
with the credulous and obsessional tone of the pamphlet quoted in the
previous chapter, which dates from sixty years earlier.

An old man living at the Castle Inn gave out that he was bewitched by
one Osburn and his wife living in a cottage in the fields (inoffensive
people near 70 years of age). It was cried in all the neighbouring
Parishes that they were to be tried by ducking on such a day, when,
about noon, a great concourse of people to the number of 1000
appeared in the town . . . The mob demanded these unhappy wretches
at the workhouse, on being acquainted that they were not there,
they pulled down the pales and walls, broke all the windows and
demolished a part of the house. After searching the chimneys and
ceilings without effect they siezed the governor, hawled him down to
the stream, and declared they would drown him and fire the whole
village, unless they delivered these poor creatures into their hands.
The mob ran up and down with straw in their hands, and were going

to put their threat into execution had they not found the two unhappy persons, who were concealed in the vestry room near the chapel. They immediately siezed these miserable creatures, stripped them stark naked, tied their thumbs to their toes and dragged them in this shameful manner to the stream now increased by the rains, and after much ducking and ill-usage the poor old woman was thrown quite naked on the bank, almost choaked with mud, and expired in a few minutes, being kicked and beat with sticks even after she was dead, and the poor man lied long dangerously ill from the treatment he received. To add to their barbarity, they put the dead witch (as they called her) in bed with her husband and tied them together . . .

The account continues with more detailed evidence from the trial, which followed when two men were apprehended for murder (the government, as unsympathetic towards 'superstition' as Woodehouse himself, had offered a large reward for their capture). One of them, Wallis, was hanged with some ceremony on the spot where the murder had been committed, and Woodehouse recorded: 'the infatuation of the people is such that they will not be seen near the place of execution, insisting that it was a hard case to hang a man for destroying an old woman that had done so much injury by her witchcraft.' Belief in witchcraft had evidently, by then, become a matter of class. Wallis's body hung in chains for a while, which must have made two gibbets within a short distance of one another (his and that of Clun's murderer).

Oddly enough, the witch who is remembered as 'the Shrew of Kentish Town', and is commemorated to this day in the Mother Red Cap pub at Camden Town, never seems to have been brought to justice at all. Evidence about the date of her time on earth is conflicting, but one account identifies her with the Mother Damnable who lived through the Commonwealth (when, it will be remembered, witches were discovered everywhere) and states that she was the death of several men who lived with her and that she practised magic both black and white. Her father was said to have been Jacob Bingham, a bricklayer of Kentish Town. A later account, however, identified her with a camp-follower of Marlborough's army (i.e. the period at which Woodehouse was writing), but since this also states that she lived to 120 the one identification does not exclude the other. She was said to have lived in a mud cottage on or near the site of the present public house which, as a meeting place for two roads, was a classic place for a witch's habitation. All that these various stories indicate, no doubt, in historical terms, is that there were a succession of wise women in Kentish Town, as in most villages, and that such outcasts tended to live in the hinterlands between settlements, by cross-roads, gibbets and other unfrequented regions.

Queen Anne's reign appears as something of a watershed in St Pancras between the old world and the new. Scenes like the drowning of Mrs Osburn could take place, with the authorities apparently powerless to stop them, yet at the same time there were families already settled or settling in the area who were to influence its development well into the nineteenth century. The first Morgans appeared in the area then; another prominent local dynasty, whose interests lay partly outside our area but who for many years farmed land round St Pancras church and to the south of it, were the Rhodes. The family name now enjoys a curious afterglow: the same family produced Cecil Rhodes, whose name is remembered in the state of Rhodesia. But Cecil himself had no connection with the parish of St Pancras, except that, in 1890, he had erected a large, collective monument in the churchyard commemorating several previous generations of this proliferating family who had previously been buried there (and presumably – some of them – dug up again when the land was disturbed in 1868 by the Midland Railway workings). The Rhodes family owned the Chalk Farm at one time (outside the parish) and later had a farmhouse in the Hampstead Road just north of where the Temperance Hospital now stands: amazingly, the last vestiges of this farm survived till 1934. Several generations of them were active, not to say dictatorial, in the St Pancras vestry, towards the end of the eighteenth century and the early part of the next; they were probably well-established in the district by the time William Rhodes began appending his signature to vestry documents – in an awkward, unlettered hand – about 1740.

The vestry was by then attracting to itself the power and influence which the manor court had once had, and had allowed to escape in many cases into private hands. In 1725 it was reported in the vestry that the lord of the manor of Cantelowes had sold or given away most of the wastes and commons, and that people had built on them to the injury of tenants and the inhabitants of the parish. It seems to have been Kentish Town Green (up Highgate Road, opposite the Bull and Last, i.e. in the almost separate hamlet of Green Street) which was particularly threatened. The vestry voted rights to its churchwardens and constables to remove any fresh fences. The point was, of course, that once the common lands had been appropriated by individual copyholders, other people, including the many who were not manorial tenants anyway, had nowhere to graze their cows, goats or pigs. Indeed the problems of land use are clear from the court rolls themselves. In the 1730s two copyholders were ordered to refrain from keeping hogs near their neighbours' houses, and at the same period there were repeated and apparently fruitless requests to Widow Lawrence that she should cease to keep her carts on the waste – the earliest example I have found of a parking offence in the area. In 1735 she re-married, and representations were therefore made to her husband. He later became a constable, so perhaps he complied with the request. At the same court Jasper Garland, a brick-layer, was asked to remove a bank he had erected in Swine's Lane.

By then, brick-layers or makers crop up commonly. Contemporary prints show that the brick and tile kilns that were to pollute the air round Battle Bridge and St Pancras church for the next hundred years, were already flourishing. Nor were those with farming interests necessarily distinct from those with building interests. One of the Morgan clan, as well as owning land in Kentish Town, appears to have been a mason of Holborn. The Rhodes family eventually turned many of their 300 acres over to brick-making, and intermarried with the Harrison family of Battle Bridge, who were kiln owners as well as farmers.

The population of London proper in 1700 is variously calculated at 575,000 or 675,000, depending on whether or not one thinks that it increased much between 1700 and 1750. If it did not in fact increase much at that period, then the expansion of the city that certainly took place during those years must have been due to families moving from small to larger premises – an increase, in fact, in living standards and in the numbers of the middle classes rather than a numerical increase. What is undisputed, however, is that much new building and thus actual population increase took place then in districts which only subsequently – and in consequence – came to be regarded as part of London. The pamphleteer Daniel Defoe complained in 1724 that London was becoming 'a vast mass . . . how much further may it spread, who knows? . . . [in] a most straggling, confus'd manner, out of all shape, uncompact and unequal . . . Westminister is in a fair way to shake hands with Chelsea, as St Giles is with Marylebone; and Great Russel Street by Montague House with Tottanham Court.' Two of the districts he mentions, Chelsea and Marylebone-with-St Pancras (as the two parishes were then styled), together with Knightsbridge, Hammersmith and Paddington, were known as the Five Villages Outside the Bills of Mortality. It is known that the combined population of these villages increased from little over nine thousand in 1700 to one hundred and twenty-three thousand in 1801 – by which latter date they were well established as being *de facto* parts of London – but most of that increase probably took place during the last few decades of the eighteenth century. It has been stated that the population of St Pancras in 1776 was still only six hundred souls, and though this may be an underestimation it is known that the real population explosion only began at about this date.

The portents for future growth were there, however, much earlier in the century. Writing in 1742, Ilive, in his *Survey of London*, stated: 'Though the parish of St Pancras-in-the-fields be without the bills of mortality, I have nevertheless thought it necessary to insert an account of that part where the houses are continguous to the suburbs of London, and this part of St Pancras parish, which pays to the poor about £132 a year, contains one hundred and 22 houses, and one person that keeps a coach.'

It sounds as if Ilive was excluding some more isolated portion of the parish, and this I take to be Highgate, which from then on was to assume an increasingly separate identity from the growing village at the foot of its hill; it will therefore figure little, from now on, in this account. Kentish Town proper, as we know it today, was beginning to contract and define itself. It was also beginning to assume a more distinct and special identity.

6

The Rustic Idyll

There is, as Sir John Summerson first pointed out in his *Georgian London*, a fundamental distinction to be made between the suburbia which is just the untidy, sub-industrial fringe of the town – Stowe's garden plottes, teynter yardes, Bowling alleys . . . and such like – and the suburbia of prosperity, the townsman's carefully arranged stake in rusticity. In practice, however, contemporary observers do not always seem to have distinguished between the two kinds: Stowe himself complained of the 'garden houses', which were after all just smaller versions of the richer man's 'houses of recreation' which Norden in the same year noted with approval. Clearly some of the difference must lie in the social class, and hence the eye, of the beholder.

Those who came out to take the waters at 'Pankridge Wells' and to disport themselves in various ways in the fields no doubt regarded this as a nice day out in the country, while to the inhabitants of the 122 houses of the village proper, not to mention the one gentleman who kept a coach, this part of the parish near the church remained, as it had been for some time, the seedy end, dangerously close to the town and contaminated by it. Here, as we have seen, were bodies hung in chains. Here, early in the eighteenth century, was a highwayman shot, and another in 1739. By then, Woodehouse's mansion (once Bruges's, and the pride of Kentish Town) was quite ruined, the remains of many of its fifty chambers overgrown with grass or put to farmyard uses. The siting of the first workhouse in this area, the one from which the Osburns were dragged, in what seems to have been an already ancient building (it was found to be unsafe and ruinous in the 1770s) was probably no accident. Newspaper cuttings in the Heal Collection, and in the Guildhall Library tell a tale of highwaymen and footpads lurking in this hinterland, of horses stolen when put out to graze, of meetings of 'dog-fighters, bullies, chimney sweeps' and other 'low, rough fellows'. There were suicides in these fields, duels – sometimes to the death – and occasional murders. Babies were abandoned there, alive or dead. The man who was vicar of St Pancras from 1750 till he died almost at the end of the century, Benjamin Mence, was, in the tradition of St Pancras incumbents, had up before Doctors Commons for not holding a sufficient number of services in the church proper, but was let off on account of the remoteness of the church from the village and its 'unwholesomeness'. The burial ground was said to be a target for body-snatchers, on account of its isolation.

The smell of the tile kilns tended to create a noxious atmosphere in the area: Louis Simond, a visitor from France, thought at first that it smelt of rubbish dumps, but remarked with his usual amiability that once you realised what was producing the smell you ceased to mind it. Goldsmith, in his ponderously satirical 'Voyage to Kentish Town' in *A Citizen of the World* (1760) describes the road from Battle Bridge to the village proper – that is, the old King's Road – as being full of dust heaps and open drains: an early example of the rustic idyll being derided. In addition, the Fleet was still up to its old tricks of flooding, damaging market gardens and tile kilns alike and occasionally drowning cattle.

The area round the Mother Red Cap (where the second workhouse was established towards the end of the century on the site of what is now Camden Town tube station) was hardly more salubrious: the inn attracted a dubious clientele. There was even a government proposal in 1776 that a public gallows should be set up at the fork, thus converting it into a north London Tyburn, but, although it is frequently stated that executions took place here, I do not believe the plan was ever put into practice. It was probably overtaken by the Jeffreys-Pratt family's development of the area for housing a decade later. Instead, the pound, the stocks and the engine house belonging to the workhouse were erected on the site. The workhouse itself was a 'handsome brick edifice' that had seen better days and in the meantime had been an inn called the Halfway House. It was sold to the parish by Captain Fitzroy, a member of the Southampton family who had been Lords of the Manor of Tottenhall – whose land adjoined Cantelowes' here on the west and who had recently managed to get an Act through Parliament converting their leasehold interest in the lands into a freehold for ever (see page 49).

Meanwhile, half a mile north in the village proper, near the chapel of ease and Hewett's house – now the property of Christ Church, Oxford – away from the poor, the dust, the floods, the fumes and the riff-raff who frequented the Wells and the Mother Red Cap, the inhabitants cultivated a rural tranquillity. A mid-eighteenth-century map of the Environs of London for twenty miles around has a 'gentlemen's houses' sign at Kentish Town. One of the most archetypal of these gentlemen, and in his own way one of the most prominent, was the Rev. Dr Stukeley, the prototype of all early antiquarians and indeed the founder of the Society of Antiquaries. He was rector for many years of St George the Martyr, Queen Square, then a new and fashionable church, and late in life bought and gradually embellished for his retirement his 'Hermitage' at Kentish Town. He wrote in his diary:

> To compleat my felicity after 9 years assiduous enquiry, I found a most agreeable rural retreat at Kentish Town 2 miles and a ¹/₂ distant [i.e. from Queen Square] extremely convenient for keeping my horses and for my own amusement, the hither end of the village [i.e. near end] between the Castle Inn and the (old) chapel, an half-hour's walk over sweet fields. 'Tis absolutely and clearly out of the influence of the London smoak, a dry gravelly soil, and air remarkably wholesome.

The location given would suggest that the house was, like both the Castle Inn and the chapel, on the western side of Kentish Town high road, but other documentation makes it clear that it actually stood at that level on the eastern side of the roadway. It was on land owned since the middle ages by St Bartholomew's the Great on approximately the site now occupied by Bartholomew Place. It was a 'mostly new' house previously owned by Samual Hoggin of the Castle Inn. The following year Stukeley acquired from Bart's for £600 a lease on adjoining property – a stable, shed, cart lodge, yards and gardens, and 2 closes (i.e. hedged fields) one large and one small. He remained delighted with his purchase: 'A vast advantage [Kentish Town] enjoys, before Hamsted and High-gate, is exceedingly soft and good water from the springs at the bottom of the sandy part of Hamsted Heath under Caen Wood. 'Tis brought in pipes to our doors, and by my contrivance makes a little river through my garden.' He also built on a new bedchamber to the

south, and a 'chapel' or garden room, and enclosed two acres from
the larger meadow to make a circular garden – 'a retired place like a
hermitage'. He constructed a 'Druid Walk' and made 'an elegant Eve's
bower'. Later came a 'Mausoleum' with family pictures and also a bust
of Cicero. Over the new room was a Latin inscription he translated in
his diary as: 'Oh, may this rural solitude receive, and contemplation all
its pleasures give, the Druid priest.'

Such were the diversions of elderly gentlemen in the mid-eighteenth
century, when 'the Gothic' was a new and exciting discovery and the
whole pageant of mediaevalism and the ancient world just coming into
focus. It is easy today to laugh at Dr Stukeley's eclectic enthusiasms: his
ideas about Druids or indeed about Caesar's camp at St Pancras (see
Chapter 2) may have been more romantic than soundly-based, but he
was showing a nicer discrimination when he put up in his private chapel
in Kentish Town some broken stained glass obtained from a glazier in
his native Stamford where it had been taken out of churches 'because it
darkened them' (Stukeley was properly shocked by such a Philistine
disrespect for the past). Some of the glass depicted William Bruges, also
a native of Stamford and a benefactor of the church there, so Bruges
came 'home' to Kentish Town after more than three hundred years.
Stukeley was also a genuinely knowledgeable gardener; his diary records
the 230 roots of crocus and gentian he planted and also the fruit trees he
set himself – medlar, service, cornelian, barbery, quince, double blossom,
cherry, crab, non-perel. He wrote of his house in 1761, 'Hither I ride or
walk almost every day. Sometimes I lye there, always enjoying that
incomparable pleasure of the mind delighted with the rural simplicity
and nature, having long since cast off ambition to wish for anything
greater or more splendid.' He was then in his mid-seventies, so these
remarks are not those of a self-conscious philosopher trying to convince
himself that he has chosen the better part, but of an old man savouring a
life that cannot be destined to continue much longer (he died in 1765).
By chance, the Heal Collection has preserved an advertisement from a
newspaper for the year when he was laying out his garden. The seller was
in the New Road (the Euston Road, then indeed brand new), which was
on Stukeley's route from Bloomsbury to Kentish Town. Was this a
source for some of his rarer plants? 'Just arrived, in exceedingly good

order for planting, a great Variety of Trees, flowering Shrubs, Ferns, Gales, Mountainous and Bogg plants, collected in the different Provinces of North America . . . '

By the early nineteenth century, before it was built over, the house and garden at Kentish Town was itself for many years in the hands of a nursery gardener. Dr Stukeley himself is now largely forgotten, but a street in his old parish still preserves his name. By a symmetric quirk of fate, a large portion of this street, its houses demolished, has now been turned into a garden. The creation of such a bizarre oasis in central London would surely have pleased the doctor.

The theme of *health* is one to which eighteenth-century commentators on Kentish Town frequently return. The obsession with pure air, types of soil and pure water, so typical of the period, now seems something of a redundant fancy, but at the time it was rooted in a realistic anxiety. Mortality was high among the working class and even middle-class families were not spared. In his *History of London* (1775), Harrison was able to write: 'At Kentish Town . . . the air being exceedingly wholesome, many of the citizens of London have built houses; and such whose circumstances will not admit of that expense, take ready furnished lodgings for the summer, particularly those who are afflicted with consumptions, and other disorders.'

Indeed as early as 1725 the idea that one came to Kentish Town for one's health seems to have been current. The Assembly House (formerly known as the Black Bull and then, in the early eighteenth century, as the Flask – not to be confused with the one at Highgate) has long possessed an oval, marble-topped table, given to the inn by a satisfied client, Mr Robert Wright. The story is that he had been very ill but was restored to health by a sojourn at Kentish Town which included a daily walk to the public house. Indeed the table still bears round its edge the inscription 'In memoriam Sanitas Restauratae Robertus Wright, Gent. Hoc marmor posuit A. Dni 1725'. It no longer stands in the inn's forecourt under the twin elms, for forecourt and elms have, since the mid-nineteenth century, been gone: the sole relic of the right of way that originally ran through the pub yard to become Assembly House Lane behind (present Falkland Place) was, till 1976, a strip of slanting, redundant roadway at an angle to the high road outside Kentish Town station in front of the news-stands –

recently paved over. But the table is kept inside, a curious relic in a decor where the genuine remains of a florid late-Victorian temple to drink (a second re-building) are married uneasily to 1960s brewers' early-Victorian: mock oil lamps and so forth. I expect Mr Wright chose marble because it was 'handsome' and would resist the ravages of beer mugs and weather; he could not possibly have foreseen that his table would endure when everything round it was utterly transformed (but see page 18).

Another sign of Kentish Town's growing fashionableness at the period was the Green Street races, which were announced for the first time on 'a new track at Kentish Town' in 1733 and were held for many years afterwards. They took place on two fields behind College Lane, the estate held in the seventeenth century by William Platt and subsequently by St John's College, Cambridge (hence the ancient lane's name). Lady Somerset Road, Burghley Road and a new council estate now cover the site, but College Lane itself, slotted through later developments, still winds behind the high road. A few of its cottages are very old, and the walls that line it at one point are remnants – still bearing the ghostly traces of doors and windows – of yet older buildings, put up on the 'waste' between the lane and the high road licitly or illicitly in the seventeenth and early eighteenth centuries. From the courtyard of the Vine (1930s mock timbering) an archway in a small brick gatehouse far older than the present inn leads through into College Lane, but where it originally led was *across* the lane to the Race Fields and thence to a footbridge over the Fleet – another of Kentish Town's many lost or fragmented rights of way.

Green Street – part of which became known now as The Grove, a typical eighteenth-century classicism – continued to be the more select end of the village as it had been since Elizabeth's time. It was here in the later part of the eighteenth century that substantial 'villas' – another classicism, since debased – began to go up, fronting onto Kentish Town Green and probably encroaching on it. The Gordon House (origin of the name is lost, but it is commemorated in the road) belonged to a Mr Cooper, a wealthy man who ran a boys' academy there and died suddenly of apoplexy one day in the last quarter of the century, while in the middle of a lesson. His was the forerunner of a whole crop of private schools which were to flourish in the area in the next hundred years. A little further up was a house lived in by J. Suckling, uncle to Lord Nelson (another Suckling uncle, William, lived down the other end of the village near the Castle, and it was in *his* garden that Nelson was said to have planted trees as a boy). Further up again was 'a gentleman's seat, delightfully situate', and 'a beautiful residence called the Gothic', a name which Stukeley would have relished – indeed he may well have seen it built. On the opposite side of the road 'a most desirable aristocratic residence' occupied what had probably been the site of the Chomondley house in the seventeenth century.

This information is derived from an annotated 'Panorama' of the main roads of the district drawn at a slightly later period by J. F. King, resident of Kentish Town and a descendant of a Huguenot family called Leroy who had settled in St Pancras about a hundred years earlier. Between Mr Cooper's house and the Suckling home, King also shows a large house gutted by fire many years before and known in his day simply as the Ruins. Its identity, however, may be more closely established. In the 1770s there stood next to Mr Cooper's academy a home for the blind called Emmanuel Hospital. As is the way of such institutions on the perimeter of cities, it occupied an old building – perhaps even one of those half-timbered houses built by a well-to-do merchant in Tudor or Stuart times. At all events it must have been combustible, for one night in March 1779 it was burnt to the ground. At first it was thought to have been an accident, for such fires were very common in an age of candles, oil lamps and wooden panelling, but the affair was closely scrutinised by (in the words of a newspaper report) 'some gentlemen who live in town, but have houses in that neighbour-hood and whose confidence is not to be caught by every specious appearance.' Once again, middle-class outsiders were having their effect on the district. They formed the impression that the building had been deliberately fired by the superintendent and his wife, a couple called Lowe, with a view to collecting the insurance money from the Bird-in-Hand Fire Office. Lowe's alibi was that he had ostentatiously left London a day or two before, but the gentlemen unearthed, through cancelled turnpike tickets and inn bills, evidence of a secret return to London by fast post-chaise. Another fast post-chaise (sent by Magistrate Fielding of Bow Street) pursued Lowe, and he was eventually caught in Liverpool, from whence he had hoped perhaps to make his escape to the newly independent States of America.

This Lowe was perhaps a fairly typical example of one type of eighteenth-century social mobility. Starting life as a servant in a livery stables, he later took a public house where he made his fortune 'by usurious means'. He then set up as a gentleman, and one with high ideals and charitable aims. Apparently he was assiduous and skilful in collecting funds for the Hospital, and endeared himself to local Kentish Town society on that account – does the phrase 'gentlemen whose confidence was not caught by every specious appearance' conceal an implication about other local gentry, less fly, who were taken in by him? When cornered at a hotel by Fielding's men he swallowed poison, killing himself. Despite the modern nature of his crime – defrauding an insurance company must have been a relatively new ploy at that date – his end seems to reach back to a pre-eighteenth-century epoch: he was buried without office at a cross-roads, and a stake was driven through his heart.

The part played by fast travel in this story is significant also as regards the development of the suburbs generally. Fifty, even twenty-five years earlier, Lowe could not have hoped to succeed in his ingenious plan, but the general improvement in roads during the eighteenth century and the development of lighter, better-sprung vehicles speeded up travel – not dramatically, as the railways were to do in the 1840s, but to an extent comparable, perhaps, with the motorways replacing old, choked routes through towns in the 1960s. No longer did coaches bound for New-market risk overturning on the King's Road, as they had in Pepys's day. Completely new turnpike roads like the Camden Road and Fortess Road (both following roughly the line of old lanes) and the Caledonian Road in Islington were not built till the early nineteenth century, but the improvement of existing roads and the erection of toll gates had been going on then for some time.

With better roads came better public transport services, and in this Kentish Town was peculiarly well-placed. Indeed its substantial development in the last quarter of the eighteenth century may have been, in part, a direct result of this. Most of the north-bound stage coaches out of London passed through the centre of the village (the by-pass road for

Highgate, the road under Nash's Archway that became the start of the Great North Road, was not built till 1813). In the 1780s there were still only two coaches a day each way, but towards the end of the century houses being sold in the Kentish Town neighbourhood were advertised as having 'the great convenience of coaches to and from London every hour of the day'. First the Vine, but later the Bull and Gate ('Boulogne Gate') public house and the Assembly House on the opposite side of the road, were the pick-up-and-set-down point for local travellers who wished to make use of the first or final stage of one of the long-distance coaches. This circumstance must have helped turn the junction of Highgate Road with the then-twisting Fortys or Fortess Lane into the geographical centre of the village. Later, in the days of horse omnibuses, the Bull and Gate continued to be the stopping point – and terminus – for some of them, and so this was the natural place to build Kentish Town railway station in the 1860s and the tube station in the 1900s. Inertia is a considerable force in town development.

Elliott, a somewhat pompous and sarcastic old person who wrote a brief local history in the mid-nineteenth century which has never been printed, described the newly mobile nature of late-eighteenth-century life thus – with hindsight, he could see the pattern more clearly than contemporary commentators:

> About the period at which we are now arrived, a new system, which has since grown into an established and almost universal practice, began to prevail among the citizens of London . . . Notwithstanding the highly improved measures which in their day were adopted for promoting the salubrity and comfort of the city, a constant residence at their houses of business was not only insupportable but threatened the destruction of their health. [Sic.] . . . In common with its neighbours, Kentish Town partook of the increase of inhabitants occasioned to the suburban villages by this passion for nightly emigration . . .

Commuting was, however, still a gentleman's occupation. The fare into town on the coach was 4*d*. and presently 6*d*. – sums well beyond the reach of all but the middle classes. Ordinary people walked, then and for the next sixty or seventy years. At any rate till the coaches became frequent, many of the gentlemen must have had their own carriages or

chaises anyway. It was not till the middle of the following century that
the commuting clerk, with his cheap mass-transport ticket and his mass-
produced terraced villa to match, became the archetypal Kentish Town
resident.

Indeed some residents were very grand, or had aspirations that way.
In 1777, the Kentish Town House estate – part of the Deaconsfield, with
a substantial house of the Tudor period standing on it – was sold to a
solicitor called Bateman with a smart town practice. He proceeded to
pull the old house down and to build himself a palladian-style mansion
'on the Model of Wanstead House', complete with an ornamental
water-garden, utilising a convenient pre-existing pond fed by the Fleet.
Unfortunately this exercise in the picturesque ruined him and he was
forced to mortgage the property, henceforth irreverently known to the
locals as 'Bateman's Folly', or, more obscurely, 'Annuity Hall'. A more
substantial estate, further up the hill on the same side, belonged to the
Duke of St Alban's.

What such residents were clearly buying was not just fresh air, peace,
Hampstead Water Company amenities and so forth, but the pastoral
idyll – a daydream of a world of milk-maids, shepherdesses, swains
and antique innocence, which developed apace in counterpoint to the
urbanisation and industrialisation going on elsewhere. This was the
period of Marie Antoinette's Petit Trianon and Hameau, and the
English aristocracy were not without similar conceits, though they
escaped paying for them in the way the French royal family paid. In 1787
we find Mrs Barbauld's daughter writing to her mother (an indefatigable
lettriste) from Hampstead lodgings, of the views over Kenwood where
Lord Mansfield lived –

> and the Earl of Southampton's *ferme ornée*. Lady Mansfield and Lady
> S'hampton, I am told, are both admirable dairy women, and so jealous
> of each other's fame that they have once or twice been very near to
> serious falling out in the dispute which of them could make the greater
> quantity of butter from such a number of cows. On observing the
> beautiful smoothness of the turf in some of the fields about this place,
> I was told the gentlemen to whom they belonged had them rolled like
> a garden plot.

The Southampton *hameau* – Fitzroy Farm – was at the end of Millfield Lane, half way up Highgate Hill – a locality which retains even today bosky exclusiveness and some fragments of past farm buildings, though the house itself was a stuccoed 'seat', nothing like a farmhouse. In 1786 the Southampton family had succeeded in securing to themselves in perpetuity the freehold of the Totenhall manor of which they had been the leaseholders (see Chapter 2), and over the next two generations the cows and the green lawns were to become even sleeker on the proceeds of the erstwhile fields of west Kentish Town, which were made to yield profitable crops of bricks and mortar. The large Mansfield dairy farm covered much of what is now Parliament Hill, so perhaps the smoothness of its slopes, on which people now play football, fly kites and take their dogs and children for runs, owes something to the late eighteenth-century use of garden rollers.

Just as, in our own day, the 'gentleman farmer' with an interest in the stock market as well is a feature of the Home Counties commuterlands, so was he a phenomenon in Kentish Town, Hampstead and Islington in the late eighteenth century. Indeed the term was then current: in 1801 a 'gentleman's farm' was advertised for auction, complete with stock, including not only cows but also books. I believe this was the St John's College farm, whose buildings seem originally to have been on both sides of the high road just south of the point where Gordon House Road now enters it: the farmhouse was on the western side where Mortimer Terrace now abuts onto the railway land. The buildings and land on the east were acquired for a while by one Meyer Cohen – a property dealer perhaps? – and then by William Minshall, 'a county magistrate of high respectability'. It is recorded that here he cultivated nineteen acres 'very tastefully'. But the house and possibly some land on the opposite side of the road were bought by a real if less gentlemanly farmer, Richard Mortimer, who already had substantial holdings in the Chalk Farm – Regent's Park area, and had a 'cow lair' and field next to the Castle Inn. (Later this field was bought by J. F. King's father, who turned it into a 'truly picturesque' garden; such transformations were typical of the era.)

The other important local farming family were the Morgans, already mentioned several times in this account. They may have appeared in the area before the end of the seventeenth century, and by the early part of the eighteenth century one of them was bailiff to Cantelowes Manor. By the 1770s his son, William, was established in Hewett's old house in the high street, which became known from then on as 'Morgan's Farm'. William died in 1787, having made a will only a few days before leaving to his eldest son James the farm with its house and contents, which included plate, linen, and a wine cellar. Clearly, even if not a gentleman by birth or education, Farmer Morgan had prospered and acquired many of the appurtenances of one, even to the aforementioned Chinese wallpaper. Two years later another Morgan, Richard, who may have been James's son or may have been his brother, bought the chapel of ease and its plot of ground on the other side of the high street – by this time it was known as the Old Chapel, since a new one had been constructed that year further north, on the site of the present parish church. The vestry were critical of the trustees of the church lands for disposing of consecrated land in this way, and the parishioners in turn criticised the vestry for not looking after their interests better, thus allowing to be 'sold, along with everything else that was found there, the bones and ashes of the dead to be converted into bricks, or to be trampled upon, kicked by man and beast, and shattered to pieces on the roads and fields.' The indignation of the villagers and the terms in which it was expressed would seem to support the theory that the land round the chapel was indeed used for burials at one time, even though it had never been designated for it. (Redevelopment would not have disturbed the deeper graves, then or later. It is curious to reflect that the counters of the present Sainsbury's stand above the bones of ancient consumers of bread, meat and eggs.) It is said that Richard Morgan used some of the old gravestones to pave the yard of his new house, and some of the chapel panelling for wainscotting – '*Old stone to new building, old timber to new fires . . .*'

Writing some sixty years later, Elliott held the belief that the slow but steady growth of Kentish Town at this time was not just due to a favourable combination of circumstances, but had been helped on its way by one particular man. He wrote:

– Nor should we omit to mention that a superintending cause of the great accession it, in the course of a few years, experienced, was to be found in the late Dr William Rowley, a physician of extensive practice, who about this time became a resident of the village. So favourable an opinion did he entertain of the amenity of its situation and the purity of its air – an opinion declared by him to be founded on philosophical experiments – that he denominated it 'the Montpelier of England', and it was his custom in almost every case where he considered a change of air necessary, to recommend most strenuously to his patients a sojournment at Kentish Town.

Rowley (who had the lease of the Fortys Field and lived nearby in a big house in Willow Walk) sounds like a splendid public relations officer for the district, and must thereby have extended his own practice even further, so perhaps Elliott is right to be cynical. But he adds 'Many are the instances in which they who laboured under hopeless and apparently incurable disease have been thus restored to health and vigour,' and adds a note concerning Robert Wright's marble-topped table.

In fact, there had happened to Kentish Town what happened to so many villages just outside big cities at a period of urban expansion and rebuilding: like Islington, Hampstead and Paddington at the same period, and like Montmartre and Montparnasse during the mid-nineteenth-century reconstruction of Paris, Kentish Town was becoming in its small way a 'resort'. No one managed to find mineral springs at Kentish Town, as they did at smarter and richer Hampstead – I am sure it was not for want of trying, but the soil of Kentish Town, which no matter what Dr Stukeley may have said is largely London clay, presumably defeated any such endeavour. But there was the much canvassed 'sweet air' and the river Fleet in its still-rustic beauty. Nor was it only those who could afford to buy or rent, or at least take lodgings there, who wished to profit from the place. A day-trippers' trade established itself, just as it was to do at seaside resorts a hundred years later with the coming of cheap excursion tickets on the railways. Tea gardens and pleasure gardens developed. Kentish Town had always been a village of inns; many are recorded incidentally in the court rolls. Like all places strung out along the main road into a town, the village for centuries enjoyed – or at any rate tolerated – a trickle of strangers passing through. Indeed it probably took the straggling form it did because it owed much of its development

to the inns: a hostelry at some distance from the next clump of houses –
like the Bull and Last in the Highgate Road – could by its very presence
extend the perceived boundary of the village. But now, with coaches
both public and private bringing plenty of custom, and other people
walking out on foot of a Sunday from the newly developed London
districts just the other side of the New Road, the ancient taverns of
Kentish Town enjoyed what was probably their heyday. It was to be an
Indian summer.

The most important of these was the Castle; contemporary prints show
its garden laid out for customers and a rustic bridge over the stream. Its
grounds covered the whole of the space now occupied by Castle and
Castlehaven Roads, Kelly Street, Clarence Way and the disused South
Kentish Town tube station: a horrid spot today, this last. An inventory of
the place taken when Samual Hoggin died (whose house over the way Dr
Stukeley bought) shows it to have been a well-appointed inn as early as
the 1750s. It was presently to be rivalled in its attraction, however, by the
Assembly House, further up the town. This pub was spacious enough for
large gatherings of people, and it was there that house auctions were
held. It possessed two acres of garden (part of which, though this is
irrelevant, later became the site of the house in which this book was
written). About 1780 its landlord, Thomas Wood, was advertising:

> A good trap-ball ground, skittle ground, pleasant summer house,
> extensive gardens, and every accomodation for the convenience of
> those who may think it proper to make an excursion to the above
> house during the summer months . . . A good ordinary on Sundays at
> two o'clock.

Several years later Wood was still advertising his 'larder' in glowing
terms, but appending this advertisement to a public protestation of his
innocence in a recent court case. In 1785 a Sir Thomas Davenport, who
had suffered a highway robbery near the Assembly House, accused
Wood of having been the highwayman, on the identification evidence
of his coachman. Wood was arrested, remanded in gaol tried but
eventually acquitted, and two other men were hanged in his stead.
However Davenport was apparently so convinced that the true villain
had escaped him that he continued what amounted to a persecution

campaign against Wood, who is said to have 'died raving mad' (in 1787) as a result of it. He is also said to have been a relative of the Sucklings and therefore of Nelson – but Nelson, like the Old Farm House (Morgans, Hewetts etc.) seems to have been something of an obsession with nineteenth-century commentators.

Despite all the protestations about 'healthful tranquility' highway robbery was a feature of life in Kentish Town. At night, the high road was almost as unsafe as it had been in Clun's day, a hundred years earlier: there was a particularly bad outbreak between the years 1775 and 1785. Newspapers of the period contain frequent reports of hold-ups – money and valuables were almost always handed over by the victims to escape a worse fate – and also advertisements of armed patrols leaving the main public houses at set hours, so that those who wished to seek the safety of numbers could do so.

The Vine, higher up Highgate Road, also had a garden and skittle ground, and it is recorded that the landlord, Odhams, 'being civil and obliging', did very well and saved money. He appears in a short list of the principal landowners in the area of 1804. The Vine, the Bull and Gate, the Bull and Last – all these taverns which, like the Assembly House and the Castle, are still there today in name, had then the aspect (if no longer quite the character) of country inns. Most of them were houses that were old already, timbered constructions with wide yards in front of them. The only public house in this whole area that escaped rebuilding during the nineteenth century was the Flask, still to be seen up at Highgate. Every one of the numerous Kentish Town taverns was to be changed, over the next two generations, into an urban public house, the Victorian 'gin palace' that came in for so much abuse both deserved and undeserved. The gardens, paddocks and bowling greens disappeared under streets, and with them went the last vestiges of Kentish Town's innocent pretensions to health and country virtues. They were much regretted. As so often, it was only once the area was irrevocably transformed into something else that its earlier qualities were fully appreciated. The changes which, individually, had each been regarded as an 'improvement' or a 'refinement' were, cumulatively, destructive. Moreover the destroyers were the very people who had come to the district in appreciation of it, and it was what they actually sought there that they destroyed, by their sheer presence and numbers. The paradox is a familiar one today. Elliott, writing when it was too late, could point the moral:

> The villages surrounding the metropolis . . . were filled with an extraneous population, to which their means of accommodation were altogether inadequate. Hence arose the necessity for the erection of new dwellings, and hence all the charms of nature were compelled to give place to the gratification of the caprice and avarice of man.

Thus was Eden lost. But it was only subsequent generations, such as Elliott's, who saw the matter in this light.

By the time Elliott was writing, Kentish Town Road had become 'a continual street of closely ranged dwellings'. This, as King's 'Panorama' shows, did not happen all at once. But it is true that the building explosion that it underwent in the last quarter of the eighteenth century was largely ribbon development – not, like its name, an unpleasant twentieth-century invention, but simply the natural way expansion takes place unless deliberate efforts are made towards some other pattern. A commentator, Aiken, writing soon after the turn of the century, remarked that 'the hamlet of Kentish Town consists of a long street ascending to the high ground near High-gate, and chiefly composed of boxes [originally 'hunting boxes', and hence by vulgarisation any holiday house] and lodging houses for the accommodation of the inhabitants of London, with boarding schools and public houses etc.' Certainly the very detailed map of 1796, which enables one to walk about the place almost as in life noticing every cottage, stable, cow-lair and vegetable plot, shows the road from a little below the Castle northwards as far as Bateman's Folly at the foot of Highgate Hill entirely fringed with properties of one kind or another, though many are spaced out with gardens and paddocks in between. The first lateral development – Mansfield Place (now Holmes Road) and Spring Place – had also appeared.

A very few of the houses built in these years are still there, hacked about and disfigured, disguised behind inappropriate modern shop fronts, their twelve-paned windows usually replaced by sheets of later glass. One stands just below the (rebuilt) Castle, sideways on to the road, hiding behind a fish-bar, some advertisement hoardings and a coat of dark red paint. Another stands, similarly sideways on to the main road (the later terraces always fronted the road) with a sweet shop in front of it, facing what is now a cobbled alley – Leverton Place – but was once one side of the spacious cobbled yard of the old Assembly House. It is clearly recognisable on King's 'Panorama', and he comments that it 'was formerly called Village House and occupied by Captain Finch . . . it was very pleasantly situate with a commanding view to and fro.' No longer, poor house, no longer, as the clogged traffic at that well-known north London bottle-neck sits exuding fumes, and chip papers blow into the remaining segment of what was once its front plot. In its side wall the slot through which 'night soil' would once have been discreetly tipped to men who came at dusk with carts has been bricked up. Behind, where its walled garden once ran, is now – after an interval of several generations covered with small houses – a garden again, of a sort. There is grass, and trees, but they are often damaged, and small parties of harmless but bleary drinkers frequent the place.

Another eighteenth-century house survives, with a mansard roof, and a second-hand car dealer on its ground floor, on the corner of Fortess Walk, once Willow Walk. Its memory goes back not only to willow trees but to the days when Willow Walk, now cut off short by Fortess Road, curved round in a crescent to meet the main road again, enclosing a paddock where Dr Rowley kept his horses, and passing *en route* another so-called Old Manor House – in reality, another eighteenth-century gentleman's abode.

Further north up the Highgate Road there is the Bridge House, hiding behind a later pebbledash facade, and several cottages in College Lane, including a doll-sized pair with a triangular scrap of garden (appropriated from the public way by stealth, undoubtedly) and a sign saying 'Ancient Lights' nicely painted yellow to match the rest of the woodwork. Then, just before the point where the lane runs under its own specially-constructed arch beneath the Hampstead Junction Railway, it crosses a remarkable and now carefully preserved survival of Kentish Town's late eighteenth-century prosperity in the shape of a row of bow-windowed shops, fronting a cobbled lane running between College Lane and the high road. It is called Little Green Street – the only reminder left that the main road at this point used to be known as Green Street – and the shops no longer sell coffee, ribbons and mouse-

traps but have become carefully modernised homes. Next to them, on
the high road, are two more houses which are probably also eighteenth-
century, but they have been altered almost out of recognition. One has
a pleasant rose garden in front: the other, blinded by ill-shaped modern
windows, is fronted by a wilderness of overgrown plants, bits of broken
plastic, wall paintings, slogans and other signs of radical decay. A decent
tallow-chandler once made his candles here.

But the finest survival of this era is Grove Terrace, at which point
College Lane emerges from its tunnel and runs openly along the facade
of the terrace between it and the lawns stretching down to the main
road – a bit of waste which managed *not* to get squatted on in the
eighteenth century – before losing its identity irrevocably in Woodsome
Road. The terrace has twenty-seven houses, all much of a kind but not
uniform, varying in detail within a gentlemanly consensus of opinion
about what a town house should look like – for these were some of the
first houses built in Kentish Town which conformed to the prevailing
recipe for a town residence rather than aspiring to be a Gothic cottage,
picturesque retreat or villa fit for a retired Roman general. They were a
portent of things to come but, with the exception of a run of pleasant
houses built soon after near Jeffreys Street at the other end of the town,
few of the later Georgian, neo-Georgian or Victorian terraces that were
to swallow the fields of Kentish Town were constructed with Grove
Terrace's fine detail as to iron-work and cornices. Within are elegant
staircases, fireplaces and ceiling mouldings. Yet this terrace, now pointed
out as a noteworthy example of what the eighteenth century could
do when it tried, was, like much architecture of that period, put up by
a builder without benefit of architect. Indeed perhaps its delightful
irregularity is due, in part, to the rule-of-thumb techniques of
uneducated men, who didn't have much use for grand plans like Thomas
Nash's but knew what the genteel public liked: a nice Grecian style
doorway, a nice balcony to show themselves on on summer evenings, a
convenient iron holder for a lamp over the front gate, a walled garden
behind and a mews for their chaises and traps – nothing opulent, no
palace-facade over-all such as the great squares of London; just three- or
four-storey family homes for people who liked decent brick combined
with fresh air.

J. F. King's depiction of the terrace is a particularly good example of the method he employed throughout. He shows several houses built, with scaffolding up, and the rest of the view is of the field that was there before. For the 'Panorama' does not embody what Kentish Town was actually like in (say) one given day in 1810, but is a retrospective record, made rather later in the century, presumably with the aid of previous sketches, and showing concurrently buildings which did not, in fact, co-exist. It is clear from the notes accompanying it that King's intention was commemorative and valedictory. As a lifelong resident of the village he wanted to record it at a phase which he could remember clearly but which was passing by the time he was adult. But it is not to be supposed that he necessarily deplored the changes he saw in his life time – or, to be more precise, he probably deplored them emotionally, but felt that this was an unworthy attitude, that one must move with the times, that after all these new terraces were very fine and a sign of progress. For example, 'That portion where the trees and Barn stand, Six excellent houses are built. House No 25 is where farmer Holmes lived; the whole space is known as Holmes Terrace.'

The population of the whole of St Pancras parish in 1776 was stated to have been only 600 people, and though this is now thought to have been an underestimation the overall dimensions of the total would not allow for a very large error. By 1801 the number of people had increased to 32,000. Admittedly a large part of this huge increase would be accounted for by the 1790s development of Camden Town – which from now on we allow to fall away from our account of Kentish Town, as a place with a separate life of its own – and by the new and crowded development of Somers Town to the south of it. But it is plain that Kentish Town proper had grown too, if less spectacularly. The decision in the 1790s that the old chapel would no longer accommodate the populace was a sign of what was happening, and in 1817 the one that had been built to replace it further up the road had, in turn, to be enlarged.

By chance, this crucial period in the village's development has been documented not only by King but also in a little book – the only one of its kind ever written till now – entitled *Some Account of Kentish Town showing its Ancient Condition, Progressive Improvement and Present State.* It was printed and published in Kentish Town by a J. Bennett who probably also wrote it – and is not to be confused with Elliott, who wrote later in the century and in a quite different, florid style. Writing in 1821, J. Bennett seems to have been a modest, conscientious person, much more inclined to admire the 'Progressive Improvement' of the area as evinced by its increasing gentility than to lament it. Here he is on the town's growth:

> It has been calculated that between the years 1775 and 1795, the village increased in its buildings one half – Within that period the Terrace, Upper and Lower Craven Place, Prospect-row, New Chapel-row, Hayman's-row, a part of Mansfield-place and Spring-place, and Camden-row, were erected; besides other houses either detached or not particularly named. And subsequently to the last-mentioned year, a still greater increase has taken place; Mortimer-terrace, Pleasant-place, Cottage-row, Fitzroy-terrace, Fitzroy-place, Francis-terrace, Gloucester-place, Montague-place, Inwood-place, York-place, Holmes's-terrace, a very considerable part of Mansfield-place, part of Spring-place, Crown-place, Eden-place, part of Old Chapel-row, Alpha-place, Southampton-terrace, Trafalgar, Bartholomew-place, Providence-place and Cane-place, very much exceeding in the number of their houses one-third of the whole of the village, having risen on land which had previously been chiefly unoccupied by dwellings.

Kentish Town was reflecting what was, in fact, a general building boom between 1816 and 1826. Some of these new runs of houses led off, like Mansfield Place and Gloucester Place (present day Leighton Road) at right angles to the high road, making literal 'in-roads' into the fields, but most were in-filling developments lining the main road, each given a separate name according to the whim of the ground landlord or the year of its construction (*e.g.* 'Trafalgar'). It was then considered quite acceptable to have a street name which changed every few houses up the same roadway, and these old names for the different sections and different sides of what is now all Kentish Town High Street persist on maps till the middle of the nineteenth century. A few fragmented sections of the terraces themselves remain to this day, dwarfed by higher late-Victorian or twentieth-century replacements, their doll-sized upper floors peering out over the top of inappropriate modern shops.

It took a foreigner at that period to define the curious and indeed unique spectacle which the outskirts of London then presented. London was spreading outwards along all its main arteries with an essentially *urban* growth. The fields behind the new terraces might still be as rural as ever, sprinkled with cows and barns, but they were no longer visible to the passing traveller. Instead, he saw rows of pedimented, stuccoed facades as uncompromisingly urban as any in the new planned developments like Bloomsbury or the Cavendish Estate. Yet places like Kentish Town, still improperly paved and lighted and innocent of drainage, were not really part of the town yet; the houses along the main roads were in every sense a facade. Louis Simond, visiting in 1812, perceived that there was something anachronistic about all these new houses, improbable even:

We have spent several days in the County of Hertford, twenty miles to the north of London. One travels half the distance between two rows of brick houses. New ones get themselves built every day [*Ils s'en bâtit de nouvelles tous les jours*]; the walls are so thin that you tremble for them. . . . One feels that the leases of these spectral houses must stipulate that no dancing is to take place there. London is stretching out her great arms on all sides, as if to embrace the whole countryside. Yet her population is not growing in proportion, it is simply displacing itself from the centre to the outskirts. The centre has become a trading counter, a place of business. Instead, the people live more spaciously in the suburbs, with better air, and more cheaply; the public coaches which pass by every half hour make it easy to travel back and forth.

The whole idea, so tenaciously English, of a separate small house for each family, was new to Simond; however his tolerant readiness to accept the virtues of a new way of life which was totally new to him is a marked contrast to the bitter detestation of the suburbs shown by several English writers a generation later. But about one thing he was wrong. He thought that London had already had her major spurt of growth, and would soon reach her maximum size and population level. How wrong he was the rest of this book will show.

7

Country into Suburb

Three years after Simond's visit in 1812, another observer, an Englishman
called John White, wrote:

> It is not a little singular that with very few exceptions as to small spots,
> the whole gravel district will be built upon, when that space of Crown
> estate which lies within a few hundred feet of the New Road is covered
> with buildings. The gravel strata there approach their terminations, as
> if to say to builders 'Thus far shall the town extend, but no farther.
> Here is the limit of local springs of fresh water, and here health and
> comfort require you to stop.'

Such pronouncements make odd reading in conjunction with the
map of London that developed – and went on and on developing – as
the century went by. But there was this much truth in them: the line of
the New Road (Euston and Marylebone Road) more or less coincided,
perhaps by design, with the ending of London's 'Taplow terrace' of river
gravel, which gives way at this point to worse-drained London clay. And
the New Road did indeed mark, by the end of the eighteenth century,
the limits of the grand building schemes, such as those on the Portland
or Portman Estates or in Bloomsbury. It remained a boundary. There
were pockets of high-class development north of it: Nash's terraces all
along the edge of Regent's Park are the obvious example of this. But on
the whole developers seem, like John White, to have been of the opinion
that 'here health and comfort require you to stop'. Not, of course, that
they actually stopped building, but they didn't build north of the New
Road for the same class of person, and didn't therefore nurse the same
comprehensive schemes.

A piece of minor town planning was the Polygon – later called
Clarendon Square – built on land originally part of the St Pancras

Manor, subsequently owned by the Charterhouse and then by the Cocks family, one of whom became Lord Sommers or Somers. However, Somers Town (as the area is still called) simply failed to appeal to the sort of occupants for which the Somers family may originally have hoped. As the *Gentleman's Magazine* put it in 1813, 'everything seemed to proceed prosperously, when some unforeseen cause occurred, which checked the fervour of building, and many carcasses of houses were sold for less than the value of their materials.' Later, and in consequence of this débâcle, Somers Town became over-crowded, and rather squalid.

Was the cause really so 'unforeseen', or were the administrators of the Somers Estate over-optimistic? Lord Camden's estate next to it (the old Cantelowes manor lands) does not seem to have made the same error, in that their expectations were all along lower. The early streets of Camden Town on the east of what became the High Street – Pratt Street, Bayham Street, Royal College Street – were laid out not with fine houses but with modest ones: Dickens's impecunious family lived here when he was a boy. Similarly the early houses on the Southampton (ex-Tottenhall) lands on the western side of Camden Town were described – in the official building leases of 1809 – as 'third-rate', and Nash (whose own Regent's Park development adjoined them) called them 'mean'. John White called them 'miserable, modern erections'. It has been suggested that the resolutely lower-middle-class nature which Camden Town seems to have assumed from the first was due to the fact that the leases from ground landlord to builders were only for forty years and this discouraged speculative builders from putting up good class properties, but it is possible that the short lease was a symptom rather than a cause. A short lease would be cheaper to acquire than the 99-year one which had by then become standard in 'better' areas, and therefore would attract the smaller builder who would be likely to speculate only in modest runs of houses on a modest scale. The big landlords such as the Southampton and Camden families were not financial fools (that much is quite clear) and if they deemed that an area 'ripe' for building was only likely to attract a rather commonplace populace, they would tend (whatever they said in their initial brochures) to try to secure the sort of speculators who were at least *likely* to build in such a place. It was, you may say, a self-fulfilling prophecy.

The southern part of St Pancras parish, for so long marginal urban land, was hardly virgin territory. It had numerous water-filled pits, the result of brick-earth diggings. There were the kilns themselves. There were a number of burial grounds and a sprinkling of light industries such as soap-boiling works. These must have combined to make the celebrated wells and the tea-gardens less attractive than they might have been, and certainly seedier than the relatively select establishments up the road in Kentish Town. There were plenty of cow-lairs still, for this area was, with Islington, one of the main milk-producing districts for the metropolis, but on the 1796 map of the district the old names of fields like 'the Murrells', 'Church Field' and 'Figs Mead' have disappeared, to be replaced by 'Lower Brickfield', 'Upper Brickfield' and 'Dustground'. Farmer Rhodes and others were engaged in the lucrative business of turning pastures into bricks. It is true that brick-making is an essentially transient industry, which invades an area, despoils it, but then moves on to other fields. Sometimes the land passed straight from meadow to brickfield to acreage of terraced housing (as in Cruikshank's famous cartoon in *Punch*), but sometimes, when the brick-earth was exhausted, it was allowed to return again to pasture. Much of St Pancras therefore retained for decades a partly-green, partly rural air. Building, in fact, was rather slow, because builders were not over-confident of the area's potential, and this, paradoxically, helped to keep it more pleasant than it might otherwise have been. The population of St Pancras parish did, however, go from 46,000 in 1811 to almost 72,000 in 1821, over 100,000 in 1831 and almost 130,000 in 1841. But this is looking ahead.

It has been calculated that a good half of London was built by this odd, indeed unique, 'building lease' system. The landowner sold leases of parcels of land on the understanding that the lessee of each parcel would build on it a house or houses which, at the expiry of the lease, would become the property of the landlord. The ground rent which the lessee paid to the landlord would normally be only a peppercorn for the first year or two, after which houses might be expected to have been built on it and the amount demanded would increase. But the lessee – the builder – usually had considerable freedom in the way he chose to use his land and thereby offset the amount of the ground rent against his profit in letting or selling the houses. Sometimes, in the more prestigious estates, the ground landlord would lay down rules about the size and general appearance of the houses, since, if the area declined into a slum during the period of the building leases, he would be the loser at the end of it. But this only occurred in comprehensive, planned developments, whereas in St Pancras in the early years of the nineteenth century most building was piecemeal – a terrace here, a line of detached villas there. Many of the speculating builders – and indeed the ground landlords – were, like the builder of Grove Terrace, quite small men, local masons and bricklayers who only ventured a few houses at a time, in the hope of being able to rent them quickly and then, but only then, use the rent to finance a little more cautious building.

In Kentish Town, many of the short terraces fronting or adjacent to the high road, which Bennett listed, were built in this way. Holmes Terrace, for instance, was built by 'Squire Holmes', a local farmer, tenant in turn of Farmer Morgan – in fact his descendants are landlords of that piece of Kentish Town property to this day. Evans Place (soon to be renamed Gloucester Place – the high street end of Leighton Road) perpetuates the name of the man who owned the livery stables opposite the Assembly House. Certainly a large number of the inhabitants listed in local censuses in the following generations declare themselves to be 'owners of house' or 'living on rents from property', and many of these were clearly, judging from their neighbours and from the street they lived in, people in relatively humble circumstances themselves. 'Owning houses in London' was not then, nor indeed until the 1950s, the golden nest-egg it subsequently became: it was the security of the more insignificant and cautious classes. The commodity of real value – the land – still remained in most cases vested in a ground landlord who was not the house-owner, and land ownership was very often a matter of luck and chance. Fenimore Cooper, the early nineteenth-century American novelist who was Consul in Switzerland in the 1820s, visited London then and dined with English relatives. These people had, two generations earlier, innocently bought a small property in the vicinity of London to give their children the benefit of country air, but when Cooper visited them he found himself in the midst of streets built upon the property, which were providing the grandson of the original purchaser with an *income* of between fifteen and twenty thousand pounds per annum.

The English ideal home, then as now, was a detached villa, but only a landlord or builder without an eye to the main chance, or else with a very definite expectation of being able to let or sell the finished villas for high amounts, could afford to use land in such a prodigal way. Parts of St John's Wood and Nash's Park Villages are the classic surviving examples of building to fulfil an ideal rather than for the immediate profit motive, though no doubt profits were made. Another such area – now almost all rebuilt – was The Grove at Kentish Town Green (opposite Grove Terrace): a solitary double-fronted house of the period remains, shorn of its garden, surrounded by cliffs of flats of both 'mansion' and council variety. There is a pleasant early nineteenth-century villa with decorative eves still standing at the corner of Prince of Wales Road opposite the Mother Shipton, and a few more, semi-derelict and spectral, at the junction of Kentish Town and Hawley Road. But most of St Pancras was not developed in this way except where individual landlords built individual dream homes, big or small, for their own habitation. In the places where it did occur the detached nature of the houses was either destroyed by subsequent in-filling (as in Gloucester Place, Leighton Road) or the houses were pulled down later in the century for a continuous terrace to be built – this was the fate of 'Bellina Villas', which went up along the newly opened Fortess Road around 1820, but were replaced later in the century by a dreary run of houses, when lower-grade housing swamped that quarter after the coming of the railways.

The typical ribbon-development in St Pancras parish, and indeed all over London, around 1820, was already the terrace. This was the form of building that made most economical use of the land available along a given road-frontage. In fact this peculiarly English type of house, found nowhere else in the world except in places to which the English exported it, is thought to have been due, to a large extent, to the prevailing building-lease system. The road frontage would be divided into narrow but often quite long strips, running back from the roadway at right angles. At the front, each house would occupy the whole of the cramped width, commonly no more than about sixteen feet. The spare space was (and is) all at the back, on land that was no use to the builder because there was no road access to it – at least until another street was planned, parallel with or at right angles to the first. Here the houses, so cramped-looking from the front, could extend into back-additions – which are called that even when the 'addition' has not been subsequent to the house's building but is an integral part of the design. Here were – and are – yards, lawns, vegetable gardens. Even today one terrace house in Leighton Road has a garden of 200 feet, and gardens of 80 or 100 feet are common in the district. Yet houses of this type have, typically, only two or at most three rooms on each floor. The conception is radically different from that of the Continental 'house', in reality a substantial tenement block with multiple lodgings grouped around an interior courtyard; its oddity struck Louis Simond and produced a memorable image: 'The small houses in London are very narrow and high with a number of small storeys, one for eating, one for sleeping, a third for entertaining company, a fourth underground for the kitchen, a fifth right at the top for the servants. The speed, agility and ease with which the whole family hops up and down between these different floors makes me think of a bird-cage with its perches.'

As family homes today, these houses do not fulfil modern concepts of good design: four sets of stairs to service no more than eight or so rooms obviously date from an extinct era when there was no shortage of people to fetch, carry and sweep. But the design is otherwise less inconvenient than outsiders suppose. The numerous separate strata, initially reflecting the socially stratified nature of nineteenth-century life, adapt well to the disparate needs of a modern family, who do not necessarily wish to gather in one large circle round the parlour lamp of an evening, or even round the television set: modern lighting and heating systems render such unity unnecessary. The larger terrace houses have also proved very suitable for multi-occupation, with a separate household to each floor and the stairs (where the lavatories were normally situated anyway) as common territory. Post-war local councils, in their wisdom or folly, have destroyed acre upon acre of such multi-occupied houses in areas like Camden and Kentish Town, in the belief that such 'shared, sub-standard accommodation' was not good enough to be used as homes any longer. It is only now that the errors of such wholesale, high-principled destruction become apparent, when it is observed that the carefully purpose-built accommodation which has replaced these traditional terraces simply lacks, in most cases, the flexibility and privacy which the old houses, whatever their shortcomings, were able to provide. But this is a melancholy theme to which we shall be returning.

Within a very few years of their building, many earlier nineteenth-century terraces fronting main roads were already in fact proving their adaptability; their ground floors were being converted into shops. A number of the Kentish Town terraces Bennett listed in 1821 as being new housing were, within a decade or so, to lose their small front gardens to a 'front-extension', with the old front room becoming the back parlour of the shop. You may take this as a sign of England's overall industrial prosperity and growth of consumer goods during this period, or as a portent of Kentish Town High Street's decline. Doubtless it was both.

But in Bennett's era the keynote of the district was still selectness: otherwise his little book would hardly have been written, or not at any rate with his note of quiet pride. He was pleased, for instance, that the residential building of recent years had resulted in a proportion of public houses to private ones 'more equitable than it formerly was.' Also, 'Besides the chapel of ease to the parish church, there is a meeting house of the Independents, which was opened in 1807, and another of the Wesleyan methodists opened in 1817 . . . The village is watched throughout the year, and lighted from the 1st day of September to the last of May, pursuant to an act of Parliament obtained in 1817.' He speaks of highway robbery as a thing of the rustic past: this was another epoch. And yet people looking back to Bennett's time a generation later were, in turn, to remark how tame Kentish Town had become since those days. In 1820, the often-flooded road (Water Lane) between Camden Town junction and the start of Kentish Town proper, was still unpaved and unlighted and mostly unbuilt. The Regent's Canal, which crosses under the road at that point, was opened that year, and pre-sumably the coal merchants and the small industries, many of them connected with the building trade, which soon clustered themselves round its wharves did nothing to improve the immediate neighbour-hood. A canal was not then, or for more than a hundred years, considered a social amenity, but an industrial one. A correspondent to a local newspaper in the 1860s, looking back to these years, recalls that this stretch of roadway was felt to be dangerous at night. The inhabitants at the southern end of Kentish Town (the Jeffreys Street area) used to fix bells to their shutters to act as a warning if anyone should try to tamper with the fastenings. There were no police then, only 'old Lorimer, the Constable . . . and of course there was a sense of insecurity then'. A rural kind of insecurity. There was still a duckpond on one corner, and a village cricket ground on the edge of what later became Hawley Road. But Bennett wasn't interested in ducks (unless confined within the 'model farm' then attached to Bateman's Folly, which he notes approvingly) and probably considered the chickens which then still stalked and pecked in every side lane as something Kentish Town could well do without. Here he is on the area's developing amenities:

. . . we now turn to the gratifying task of recording the benevolent institutions of Kentish Town, for which, whether they be viewed with regard to their number, their extensive usefulness, or the practical good resulting from them, the village may proudly vie with any other in the kingdom.

A school for the education of the children of the poor, bearing the name of 'The Kentish-Town and Camden-town National School' was opened at Kentish Town-town on the 12th of August 1815.

The inhabitants of both villages had contributed to it by public sub-scription, and

The melioration which the advantages conferred by this institution have effected in the manners and morals of the children of the lower classes, must be visible to the most casual observer . . . the inhabitants see even in the streets, decency where they encountered disorder, and civility where they experienced rudeness . . . a large proportion of children among the inferior classes attend the established church, and contribute with their voices to the devotion and pleasure of its service . . .

These schools then occupied a plot of land on the eastern side of Royal College Street (named for the Royal Veterinary College in Camden Town), near the top, just above the fork with St Pancras Way. Later, in 1849, they moved to a new building in what became Islip Street further up the town – part of which remains to this day, with its bell on top, as a Church of England primary school. The old school building in Royal

College Street became a laundry for many years, but the site passed in
due course to the Board of Education and a board school was established
there in the 1870s. It was rebuilt and enlarged in 1908, and is there today
as Richard of Chichester Roman Catholic secondary school – a circumstance which would doubtless have shaken the original subscribers of
Kentish and Camden Town, through whom the site was acquired in
those anti-Papist days.

Bennett mentions a 'Dispensary for the Relief of the Sick Poor',
a 'Ladies Working Society' for making clothes for the poor, a newly
established Auxiliary Bible Society and a Religious Tract Society; both
these last were presumably dedicated to the dissemination of those great
avalanches of moral print which deluged the nineteenth century, drifting
down into every odd corner, silting up behind items of furniture or
wedged into the draughty gap between floor boards – so that even today,
when a house is demolished in an area like this one, grimy tracts issue
from between the house's joists, just as broken tea-seats and clay pipe
bowls surface perennially in its gardens. The establishment of tract-
producing organisations in 1821 was a sign of the deluge to come, and
presumably it would fall to Bennett to do much of their printing. But his
favourite local charity was 'The Lady's Society, for the relief of the
industrious female poor of Kentish-town and Camden-town,* during
their lying in' – a charity which, as he says, 'must more particularly
obtain the most powerful advocacy in the breast of every mother'.
The prevailing note of Victorian charitable enterprise, genuinely com-
passionate yet intolerably patronising by twentieth-century standards, is
already audible in his writings. It is clear too that the institutionalisation
of social organisation, mainly through the Church of England and
various non-conformist sects, was already, in the early nineteenth
century, superseding older, *ad hoc* village organisation.

All in all, with plenty of people like Bennett around, and others with
more substantial resources living up at Green Street and The Grove,
Kentish Town does not sound a bad place to have been poor in during
the early nineteenth century, even if you did get tracts along with your

---

* As with the National Schools, these two localities were then grouped together;
of the two, Kentish Town figured first, as the more established centre.

baby clothes and your hot soup. Despite a succession of bickering Poor Law officials, your lot was likely to have been far more fortunate than that of similar families in places that had never had much of a middle-class population, like Somers Town, or quarters like Spitalfields and Whitechapel from which the wealthier citizens had moved away.

But it should not be supposed that an oppressive Victorian earnestness had wholly overtaken Kentish Town even before Victoria came to the throne. It still retained, until the middle of the century, enough of those characteristics of a 'village retreat' – superficially – to attract the sort of talented, mildly bohemian society that either cannot afford or does not want to live in a more imposing district. Lady Hamilton is said to have lived for a while in a house near the Castle, where – one hopes – Nelson's garden-loving uncles made her feel welcome. Mrs Serras, the illegitimate daughter of the Duke of Cumberland, was living in a house in Trafalgar Place (opposite present day Sainsburys) during the protracted law suit which she instigated against her natural father in order to claim her rights. One can see that Kentish Town would be just the place for people who required a fundamentally quiet and respectable life without actually being 'respectable' in the most conventional terms. Doubtless, a number of the summer lodgings to let there came in discreetly useful for ladies wishing, for natural reasons, to be out of the public eye for a little while, and not all those allegedly there for the sake of their 'consumption' were actually suffering from anything as lethal and permanent.

John Keats, that archetypal and genuine consumptive, lived for a while in a house in the then newly built Mortimer Terrace off the Highgate Road (named after Farmer Mortimer) where Leigh Hunt also lodged. The house is still there, hemmed in by railway arches. Later in life, Leigh Hunt lived in another house on Highgate Hill 'the corner of Bromwich Walk' – that is, near a footpath which ran across what is now the Holly Lodge Estate. It has several times been claimed that Shelley lived in Kentish Town, but this is not true. What *is* true, however, is that in 1824 when Byron's funeral cortege passed in the rain through Kentish Town, Mary Shelley and her friend Mrs Williams, both recently widowed, watched it from the windows of the lodgings they then had in Trafalgar Place and marvelled bleakly on the effects of time and chance and on the premature deaths of their own husbands. Mary Shelley, incidentally, was not impressed by Kentish Town's famous healthy atmosphere: she considered it an 'odious swamp'.

A number of artists and engravers lived in Kentish Town during these years – the sort of names which, though well enough known in their day and eulogised on their passing, were not, in the final analysis 'known to the man in the street of the next generation' – that is, not in the blue plaque class. One, Burford, even had a special circular building there – the Rotunda painting rooms, where he painted the Diorama exhibited in a similar though more opulent building in Regent's Park. The Rotunda stood behind the National Schools, and later became an organ factory. Another artist, an engraver called Grignion who lived for many years in Grove Terrace, was, as his name suggests, a French *émigré*, one of those who had taken the north-west passage from Somers Town, where they first settled, just as Irish immigrants were to do a couple of generations later. Another French immigrant – or so I assume – was a gentleman called the Baron de Beranger, who lived in a place called 'Target Cottage', which I have not been able to locate but which must have been up the Highgate Road – Green Street end of the village: it has a rural sound to it, and so do the goings on there in 1827. The Baron had a running feud with his neighbour, George Mason, who claimed that the Baron's ducks used to cross the ditch that separated their two properties and eat his cabbages. One morning, he took out a shot gun and shot twenty-seven ducks and ducklings – the Baron was particularly outraged at the massacre of the 'innocent' ducklings, and perturbed because his children had also been running around while Mr Mason had been taking his pot shots. To this, Mr Mason said that yes, indeed, the Baron's children had been annoying him too. He also threatened to shoot the Baron if he suffered any more trespass. For this threat, he was brought to court, where the judge opined that he was quite unfitted to be trusted with a gun and bound him over to keep the peace – which perhaps he did, as no more is recorded on this subject. It might be thought that this was one of the last examples of such country-style feuds in Kentish Town before the encroaching houses drove ducks, cabbages and fowling pieces further off, but not a bit of it. Full forty years later two people in adjoining houses in Leighton Road, right in the centre of the built-up area, had a bitter quarrel which centred on the unruly behaviour of a set of chickens (see page 159).

Similar violent goings-on involving animals – dogs – between people otherwise leading a peaceful and law-abiding existence, occurred in the second decade of the century in Mansfield Road (now Holmes Road) between two tenants there: a Mr Cummings, aged about sixty, and a Mr Holmes aged about forty, whom I take to be the son of the Richard Holmes who laid out the land in houses. Holmes assaulted Cummings, and Cummings was finally awarded £100 damages by a sympathetic jury who would have liked to have given still more. The going rate for crimes of violence had increased considerably since the days of the manor courts in the fifteenth century. It was commented ambiguously in court that 'the parties were both persons of respectability'.

The same, however, could not be said for a Captain Borthwick, who in 1818 was residing at Village House, the 'very pleasantly situate house' by the Assembly House which J. F. King noted as having been earlier the home of a Captain Finch (see page 111). The coincidence of professions and rank does suggest a connection between the two men, but it is a little surprising that in his notes King makes no mention of Captain Borthwick, as one would have expected the scandal of his behaviour to have rocked the village. According to a contemporary newspaper report he

represented himself as a professor of music, of great talent and celebrity, to article a young lady [Elizabeth Henrietta Aubrey, aged thirteen] to him for seven years, upon the understanding that he was to provide her with board and lodging, perfect her in music and dancing, and, at the expiration of the term, she was to be brought forth in public, and the emoluments of her performance were to be divided between the teacher and her friends.

Evidently then as now gullible families were prepared to go to any dubious lengths to see their progeny shine on the stage. Not everyone will be surprised to hear that, the agreement having been signed by both parties, 'it was afterwards discovered that Mr Borthwick had no pupils, as a teacher of music, and that his respectability did not answer the expectation of Mrs Jones (the girl's mother). Nor does it come as a great shock to learn that 'his ultimate designs upon the young lady were of an improper nature.'

The 'taking in pupils' ploy was temptingly easy in those days: anyone and everyone could claim to be running a school. It was as simple as setting up a laundry business – that other, more lower-class expedient of people who found themselves in possession of some accommodation but without any visible means of support. All you had to do was have a few brochures printed and put up a brass plate. The Dickens family tried it on at one time in Camden Town, just as the Brontës did in their Yorkshire vicarage, and at neither of these 'schools' did any pupil ever present themselves. The first Census records for Kentish Town, dating from a little later in the century (1841) have literally dozens of 'schools' recorded, some of them with a respectable number of pupils in quite spacious villas but some in ridiculously tiny quarters – houses, or even parts of houses, in narrow terraces. Some of them cannot have been schools in any more than name – really no more than establishments for boarding out, at minimal cost, children with vaguely middle class connections whom no one particularly wanted: the many Jane Eyres and Smikes of that period of no birth control and a high maternal death-rate.

The places J. F. King mentions as schools were clearly among the largest and better known of the district, but even among these it is evident that eccentricity and private school keeping tended, then as now, to go hand in hand. Near the Gordon House Academy (see page 100) was 'a French Academy kept by a gentleman of the name of Jollie, who, on the breaking out of the French Revolution in the year 1789, introduced the manual exercise and had his pupils regularly drilled and dressed in uniform, all conducted in military order according to French nationality.' Whether it was the Old Regime that was to be defended by these boy soldiers or the new one to be advanced, is not clear. This was probably the same place which, in the next century, was known as 'St John's Park House School' (it was originally next to St John's Farm) and which was still in the hands of the French: its owner was a lady called Henrietta Koene. She is buried in Highgate cemetery and her gravestone bears the words: ' "Encore un peu de temps et je vous reverrai." St Jean XVI:16.'

A correspondent to *St Pancras Notes and Queries* at the end of the nineteenth century remarked that 'The name [St John's Park House] still remains on the gate posts, but the house, which lay back from the road, was pulled down many years ago. I am told that it was very old, belonging probably to the seventeenth century.' The land this house stood on was part of the Chomondley estate at the end of Elizabeth's reign, so here, we have a very strong hint, was one of the vanished 'gentleman's houses' of Kentish Town at a far more distant date. A second-hand car dealer's now occupies this particular segment of malleable London clay.

One of the early nineteenth-century schools still stands. This was Southampton House Academy, once run by a Captain John Bickerstaffe, slightly to the south of the Gordon House, on the Kentish Town side of what was then a cart track and is now Gordon House Road. It has lost its side wing and its once-spacious playground to the North London Railway bridge that crosses the Highgate Road here, and the word 'Academy' has been erased from its facade. But it is still 'Southampton House' (alias 137 Highgate Road) and still possesses its fine, pillared doorway and fan-light. After a shadowy period in the 1960s, when the GCL believed themselves about to pull down the whole run for road-widening, and it was inhabited by squatters, it has now been rescued: its inside has been gutted and reorganised into modern units of accommodation while its outside has been restored to a careful simulacrum of its former looks.

Poets' widows, artists, boarding schools – actors too: poor Clun, who established his wife and children in Kentish Town, at a safe distance from his mistress in London, and died because of this, was the forerunner of a number of Kentish Town actors. A late eighteenth-century one, John Palmer, was famed for his impersonation of none other than Dr Stukeley, by then dead but not forgotten. King says that the Kemble family lived for a while not far from Bateman's property; and shows a four-square house close to the road uncannily like, yet not quite like, the present 'Croft Lodge' which is owned by the Sainte Union Convent School. The next house down, now gone, described as a 'pretty villa', was lived in for years by Joseph Munden, a well-known comedian of the early nineteenth century and a leading local light; he chaired a Harmonic Society which met at the Assembly House. Another comedian, Charles Matthews, renowned for comic monologues, lived at the same period

about half a mile to the north on the other side of the road, on the edge
of Millfield Lane. Did they visit each other for uproarious tea-parties?
George Daniel, in a book called *Merrie England*, described Matthews's
house as 'a pleasant thatched cottage at Kentish Town, rising in the
midst of green lanes, flower-beds, and trellis-work, fancifully wreathed
and overgrown with jasmine and honeysuckles . . . ' But Daniel's own
fancifully wreathed and overgrown description probably need not be
taken too literally. He was writing at a time when the vanished gardens
of London represented Lost Youth, Lost Eden, 'Merrie England' indeed,
a debased and popularised version of Traherne's 'orient and immortal
wheat'. Only labourers' cottages were still thatched at that period, and
Matthews would not have lived in one of those, since they were still
(rightly) considered comfortless dens full of 'low fever'. Anyway the
small picture of the 'cottage' (in reality rather spacious) which appears
in Howitt's *The Northern Heights of London* shows a tiled roof with
pretty barge-boarding under the eaves. Howitt, writing in 1869, spoke of
the house as still standing then but as if he fully expected that within
a few years terraces of drab bricks would march all over it – 'the
engulphing ruin of the advancing tide of population. What the last
generation saw we see only in isolated fragments – a stump, a piece of
ancient wall here and there. What we see our children a very few years
hence will see no more.' But in fact this gloomy prophecy, however
accurate in general, did not in this particular case come to pass.
Parliament Hill Fields, with the ponds which Millfield Lane faces, were
finally secured as part of Hampstead Heath in 1889 and the 'engulphing
ruin' was consequently arrested. Millfield Lane today, complete with a
house which I rather think is Matthews's somewhat altered, is one of
those curious pockets of land (like parts of Hampstead, or Black-heath)
which are not really like the country but which preserve a townsman's
idea of the country at a particular date, and which therefore develop a
special interest in their own right.

    In the late 1820s both the Southampton residence and another large
house on Highgate Hill, the country seat of a one-time Lord Mayor,
were demolished – a sign of London's inexorable advance, not yet fully
visible from their windows but perhaps perceptible in the smoke and
smuts which increased in the atmosphere from year to year. On the site

of the latter house St Michael's church, Highgate, was built, and Highgate Old Cemetery was laid out on the house's gardens, incorporating a cedar of Lebanon that once stood on its lawns and now is the centrepiece to the famous catacombs. The opening of one of the London Cemetery Company's big new grounds here was in itself significant of an inexorable progression. As we have seen, in the late seventeenth and eighteenth centuries St Pancras, then known as in-the-fields, became a popular burial place, despite persistent tales of body-snatching. Another two burial grounds, nominally the property of St George's, Bloomsbury and of St Giles (once 'in-the-fields' itself) were added on to the St Pancras churchyard in the later part of the eighteenth century, but even so by the first part of the nineteenth century the ground had, like the City grounds of old, become so stuffed with corpses that it was difficult to fit new ones in. Horrid tales were told in the 1840s of residents in the workhouse nearby seeing partially decomposed bodies dug up and shovelled unceremonially onto bonfires, and of the unpleasant stench of burning, putrified flesh. In any case the area – the old St Pancras manor – was by then inexorably set on the downward path into urban industrialisation. In 1822 the Imperial Gas Light and Coke Company had established its works a little to the south of the church, and the same year St Pancras New Church, Inwood's Grecian effort, was opened in the New Road, just over the border in upper-middle-class Bloomsbury. After this, the old church was seldom used, and it must have seemed as if it might be only a matter of time before it disappeared from the face of the earth. It was derelict for a while – just as it had been hundreds of years earlier – but after St Paul's relinquished its long control over it in 1845 it was extensively rebuilt and reopened. No more burials took place in it after the early 1850s and indeed in the late 1860s a large section of the ground was lost to the Midland Railway (see Chapter 9). The era of the new, big cemeteries further out had come in the 1830s: Highgate, Kensal Green and Nunhead were then the acme of hygienic modernity, their green expanses as yet uncluttered with stones and impeccably gardened. In their turn, these overspill new towns for the dead were also to become semi-derelict places of Gothic gloom; in our own century new lands have had to be sought still further out, in Finchley or Southgate. Today, Highgate cemetery is shut for burial and subject to vandalism – the St

Pancras churchyard story repeating itself. Such are the patterns of urban development (but see page 19).

What has been called 'the full declension – meadow land to slum' (Dyos) does not usually occur in one generation. It did in Somers Town, and more strikingly in Agar Town (see below) and in some parts of west Kentish Town when that came to be developed in the 1840s, but classically the progression is from farm-building and scattered cottages, to 'gentleman's seats', to the individual villas of aspiring gentlemen, to rows of terraced housing for the commercial middle classes, to the same housing multi-occupied by the working classes. Similarly, for land that manages to remain unbuilt the progression is from unenclosed open country, to arable fields, to meadows to provide hay for the approaching town, to small 'gentleman's dairy farms' or private gardens, to market gardens and cemeteries. With cemeteries, a dead end is reached, so to speak. One of the ironies of the legislation on the subject that took place in the later nineteenth century, in an attempt to ensure that the bones of the dead should be better respected than they had been in St Pancras, is that today the dead have far more security of tenure than the living. A cemetery is the one place that no individual or authority can redevelop – short of a special Act of Parliament and wholesale exhumation. At the most, it may be turned into a garden or playground, but it cannot be built over. Chance, and the determination of early nineteenth-century public health pioneers, took the garden of Ashurst's one-time mansion house and stuffed it with the flesh of dead Londoners, many of them distinguished. Today, the Duke of St Albans' garden to the west of it is covered with suburban houses and could, in another hundred years, be occupied by something quite else again – but in their plot the dead Londoners remain, with or without their distinction, immoveable, by their unseen presence turning the land into a petrified wilderness. Many of the tombs now overgrown and collapsing were originally endowed with a sum of money to assure their upkeep 'for ever' – sums of money which time and inflation have now rendered derisory, as obsolete as the monies left by pre-Reformation inhabitants of the district for masses to be said for their souls 'in perpetuity'.

In its early, pristine and prestigious years, Highgate cemetery co-existed not only with the Duke of St Albans' Property towards Highgate

Kentish Town and Highgate beyond, viewed from the Chalk Farm area c. 1800. It looks very rural, but in fact was already becoming a fashionable suburb.

Opposite   The Fleet, with a footbridge, at the back of the Castle Tavern, *c.* 1830. Within a few years, both fields and Fleet were to be covered over and the ancient tavern rebuilt as a 'gin palace'. Today it has even lost its ancient name.

Hewitt's fine Jacobean house (*see page 63*), drawn in the early nineteenth century by which time it had descended the social scale to become Morgan's Farm. The artist of both this and the preceding picture was a local man, A. Crosby, who fortunately was on hand to record the last years of Kentish Town's countryside.

'Bateman's Folly' (*see page 104*) at the foot of Highgate West Hill. By building it, complete with ornamental water gardens to the rear, its owner bankrupted himself. St Alban's Road now occupies the site.

'London going out of Town – or – The March of Bricks & Mortar'. Cruikshank's famous cartoon about the nineteenth century growth of the metropolis, first published in 1829.

The Christchurch Estate (*in heavy outline*) – once Hewitt's estate – in 1804.

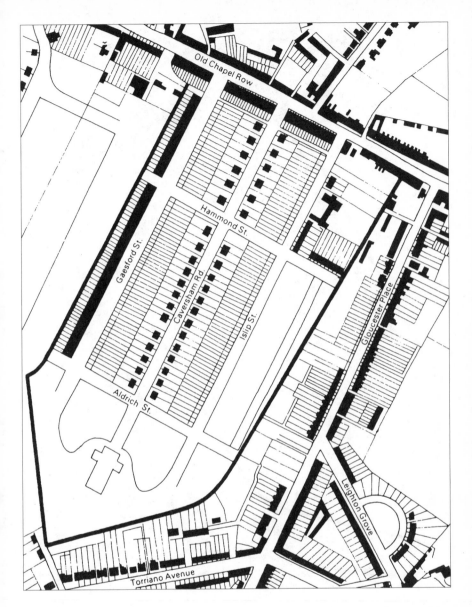

The Christchurch Estate (*in heavy outline*) – once Hewitt's estate – in 1849. The remains of Hewitt's house and moat are visible, not far from the high road.

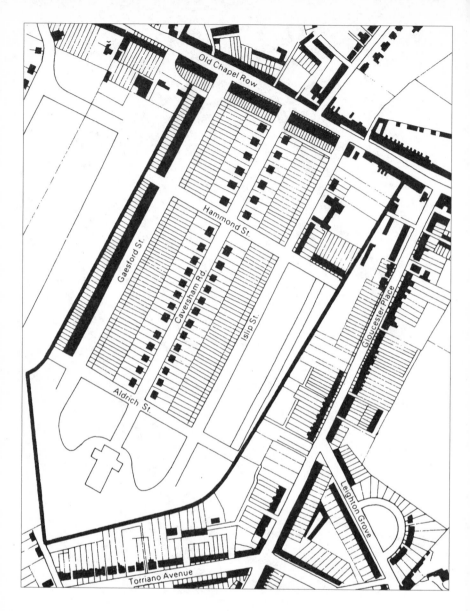

The development of the estate as projected in 1860.

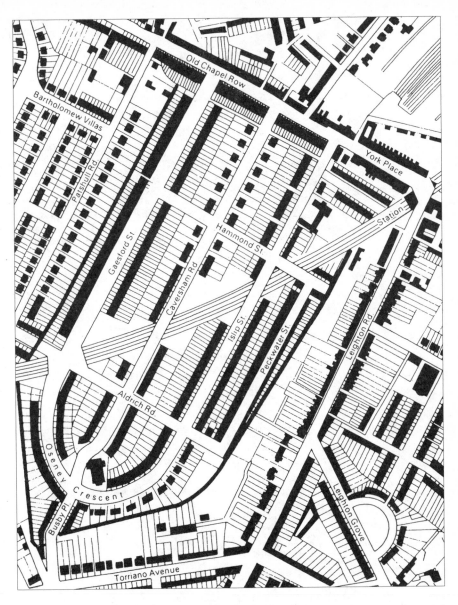

The development of the estate as actually completed by 1880. Both plan and reality show the way in which the old field pattern became fossilised in the lines of the back garden walls, and affected the street plan particularly in the buildings of Oseney Crescent. What the planners of 1860 do not seem to have envisaged, however, is that the main Midland Railway would carry its line through the estate before the end of the decade.

The old Assembly House tavern, where Leighton Road today joins Kentish Town High Street. A segment from King's panorama of the district. Note Mr Wright's oval table (*see page 99*) beneath the trees. Village House stands on the left (*see page 111*).

The Assembly House just before being pulled down in 1853, after the collapse of the coach trade with the coming of railways. Note the oval table still in evidence.

Village House, as was, *c.* 1900, with a shop built out in front of it but surviving, in a townscape where everything else, including the Assembly House, had been rebuilt and changed.

Village House in the 1970s (the shop still selling the same sort of things). The narrow street in front of it and alley to the side are a vestige of the right-of-way that originally ran through the forecourt of the old, country-style pub.

The 'terrace, blackish brown' of Betjeman's poem (*see page 237*), complete with 'Zwanzigers, the bakers', taken shortly before Betjeman's childhood in the years immediately preceding the First World War. The terrace still stands.

Opposite above An old (i.e. pre-nineteenth century) house surviving just south of the Castle, embedded in later shops (*see page 110–11*).

Opposite below One of the few surviving examples (this one is in Leighton Road) of the kind of gentleman's houses still being built in Kentish Town in the 1820s and '30s. The side-porch is a later addition, dating from when the house was divided into two dwellings. Originally it stood detached, in its own garden.

The sort of building that was appearing in Kentish Town in the early 1800s (*see page 123*). It stood more or less opposite the block in the previous picture and the heart of it, including a hammerbeam roof, is still there, concealed behind a modern facade.

Opposite   Daniels', the big shop of Kentish Town, part of the urbanisation and modernisation of the 1860s (*see page 166*). The building, though not the store, survives. It occupies more or less the same site as the chapel-of-ease occupied between the mid-fifteenth and the late eighteenth century. Today part of it is occupied by Kentish Town's independent bookshop.

'Improvements' 1960s-style – Kentish Town in turmoil. Note the pre-Victorian village-style shops (two of the three remain today), the re-building taking place round them, and the presence of a tower block (Monmouth House) behind. Note the name too on the estate-agent's board, and see page 186.

(soon to become the Holly Lodge Estate, home of the redoubtable philanthropist Angela Burdett-Coutts) but with the closing era of another *ferme ornée* down the hill in what was still then considered part of Kentish Town – later to be euphemised into 'Highgate Rise'. This was the erstwhile Bateman's Folly, till 1831 the property of Phillip Hurd, rich lawyer, vestry-man and bibliophile. He planted a grove of oaks, stocked with deer, and his dairy, piggeries, poultry yard etc. were said to be of the most up-to-date kind. A correspondent to a local paper later in the century marvelled in the same breath over Hurd's deer and his illuminated manuscripts, as if both belonged to the mythic and remote past where Kentish Town was concerned. The estate was later sold to Miss Burdett-Coutts, the adjacent landowner, and part of St Alban's Road and Villas were built on it *c.* 1850.

But what of the real farmers in these years? Their time was running out. Much of the land was still there, behind the houses, let for grazing, but the old farm houses themselves were disappearing. St John's and Mortimers had gone. In 1831 the current William Morgan left the Old Farmhouse, Hewett's House and ceded his land to the ground landlord, Christ Church, Oxford, declaring that if he continued farming he would end either in gaol or in the workhouse. Clearly farmers then tended towards the same sanguine optimism which characterises them today, but it does seem that Morgan had been less successful than his father and grandfather were: the house was said to be in a very dilapidated state (see pages 64–5).

Crosby, the water-colourist, records that the barns and grasslands pertaining to the farm were rented by a Mr Silversides, a butcher of London with a ridiculously suitable name. Butchers at that date still butchered their stock themselves: they had not yet been emasculated into retailers. Indeed, in those days before refrigeration, all animals were commonly preserved 'on the hoof' until the latest possible moment. They were still killed at Smithfield, and flocks of sheep and cattle were to be seen being urged through the streets near the City in the early morning as they had been from time immemorial. Later, the Metropolitan Cattle Market was established a little further out, in Islington, just over the border from Kentish Town, with the result that herds continued to parade through Kentish Town for decades. The

beasts were unloaded from railway trucks at the goods yards that
developed in the 1860s behind Highgate Road, and were driven along
Leighton Road towards Islington. This still occurred within living
memory and is, I believe, the basis for most of the wild stories told by
elderly residents about there having been 'farms in Kentish Town' in
their youth. Nearly all the so-called 'old farm buildings' surviving today
are in fact bits of railway stabling and stock sheds. Talking to old
people in the course of compiling this book, I was again and again told
'Cows were grazed at Gospel Oak when I was a girl', or 'It used to be all
fields around here, dear; I remember before such-and-such a street was
built.' Reference to a map of the period shows this not in fact to have
been the case. Every street in central Kentish Town was there before
the birth of the oldest person now living – indeed large parts of the
district are now so old that they have reached the rebuilding stage; the
crop of houses has been sown anew. What appears to be significant
about these 'reminiscences' (which are regularly reproduced by gullible
local newspaper editors) is not their objective truth but the fact that
people of all ages *wish* to believe that they are true. The desire to
disinter the fields that lie sleeping underneath, or to believe that these
fields still exist in the safety of memory, is a very widespread one.

Kentish Town did, however, retain some grazing land, and some
cows to graze it, into the 1860s. Most famous of the nineteenth-century
cow-keepers in the area was Brown, whose dairy occupied a strategic
site in the junction of the roads at Camden Town (the site of the
workhouse till 1817) and whose cows grazed on west Kentish Town
until that area began to be laid out as a building estate in the 1840s.
(Building booms in the area, as in England as a whole, succeeded one
another at roughly twenty-year intervals: between 1816 and 1826, in the
early 1840s, and in the 1860s after the Midland Railway had come.)
Brown's Dairy in its early days was a no-nonsense place of scrubbed
deal tables and wooden forms, but in its latter years it developed a
certain self-conscious allure: 'the interior of the shop was handsomely
fitted up, and contained some elegantly carved oak frame work with
costly embossed and engraved plate glass, the work of an eminent
west-end firm and manufactured expressly for the premises. Large
glass cases of gaily feathered stuffed birds, including cranes, humming

birds, parrots and toucans, enlivened the windows . . . ' Outside was a rockery and a crenellated facade, in debased Strawberry Hill gothic, the whole edifice being known as 'the Cows' Cathedral'. In other words, it had developed all the *folie de grandeur* of a late Victorian public house, even to the engraved glass, but such was the nostalgic appeal of milk as opposed to beer and spirits that the very same people who were quick to stigmatise the rebuilt taverns of Kentish Town as 'gin-palaces' long regarded Brown's as a proof of Kentish Town's continuing – if tarnished – rustic virtue.

The Castle Tavern was rebuilt in 1849, losing its gardens and being transformed into a square, three-storey building that stands today, an archetypal large, grubby, town pub. The same year the Assembly House suffered severe damage in a storm which also struck one of the elm trees in its courtyard. The place had become run-down and seedy since the abrupt passing of the coaching era; it was rebuilt in the early 1850s, and Leverton Street swallowed what was left of its garden. (The present building, however, with its cliff-like exterior and neo-French turrets, dates from the second re-building, in the great pub boom of the 1890s, when licensed houses changed hands for larger sums than they have ever done before or since.) The tea-garden trade had by the 1840s moved away from the centre of the village to its periphery; the Brecknock Arms, at the still almost deserted junction of Camden Road and Maiden Lane, was then the place for assignations, wrestling and similar faintly dis-reputable delights. There were balloon ascents in the field attached to it just as there had been at Pancras Wells a generation earlier, and the 'last duel in England' is said to have taken place there. But this is one of those indigestible statistical facts which sends one to gaze in vain at the shabby, paper-strewn forecourt of the present late-nineteenth-century public house, at the dry-cleaners, Greek grocers and Irish butchers that surround it, at the thundering traffic in the Camden Road, and think – in what sense can this be said sill to *be* the spot? In what essential quality is the meaning of place invested? In any case last duels are like last wolves killed and last highwaymen hanged: there are many such in different places.

There was also at that time, in the vicinity of the Brecknock Arms, a turnpike, a floor cloth factory, and a newly if belatedly built 'gentleman's country retreat' named Montpelier House,* the property of a retired varnish manufacturer. Such was the hybrid nature of Kentish Town in the 1840s.

The *Topographical Dictionary* of 1842 stated that Kentish Town was a 'pleasant and populous village' of 10,000 inhabitants some three miles from London. But this way of seeing such an area was already out of date. To clearer-eyed men from abroad, London, then unique among cities, seemed already almost impossibly enormous, a geological structure rather than a town.

London conveys the idea of unlimited space, filled with men incessantly and silently displaying their activity and their power. And in the midst of this general greatness, the extreme neatness of the houses, the wide footpaths, the effect of large panes of glass, of the iron balustrades and of the knockers on the door, impart to the city an air of careful attention and an attractive appearance, which almost counterbalances the absence of good taste. (Guizot, 1840)

What careful fairness, what damnation with faint praise.

Another observer, J. F. Murray, in a book aptly titled *The World of London* (1843) described the suburbs of London as clinging to one another 'like onions on a rope' –

[The houses] delight in a uniformity of ugliness, staring you out of countenance with three windows in front, and a little green hall door at one side, giving to each house the appearance of having had a paralytic stroke; they stand on their dignity at a distance from the road, and are carefully defended from intrusion by a body-guard of spikes bristling in a low wall. They delight in outlandish and ridiculous names: a lot of tenements looking out upon a dead wall in front, and

* A contemporary map shows this apparently standing in one corner of a private 'park' spanning York Way/Maiden Lane and thus the borough boundary: Tufnell Park, which was later to give its name to the area. William Tufnell was an eighteenth-century builder who earned £30,000 working for the New River Company – the Islington equivalent of the Hampstead Water Board – but his 'park', apparently houseless, only figures on maps for a brief while in the mid-nineteenth century, and I cannot discover the history of it.

a madhouse at the rear, club together, and introduce themselves to your notice as 'Optic Terrace': another regiment is baptised by the christian and surnames of 'Paradise Prospect' . . . [People] live here for the benefit of their health – and fortune. When you visit them, they are eloquent upon the merits of an atmosphere surcharged with dust, which they earnestly recommend for your inhalation, under the attractive title of 'fresh air' . . .

This, incidentally, is *all* he says on London's suburbs in a two-volume work, but it is enough: the damning image was clearly fixed. Henceforth, from being the delight of country-loving gentry, the suburbs were to be presented more and more as an aunt sally for those lucky enough not to live in them. Inconspicuously, individually, the suburbs of London went on providing homes, satisfying dreams, being *themselves* in intricate, private ways, loved for themselves. But no one realised this any more except for those actually living in them. As places in their own right, they became invisible.

8

'Black Snow'

No one in the middle decades of the nineteenth century depicted the ex-rural hinterlands of London at that period better than Dickens. Best known, perhaps, is the account in *The Old Curiosity Shop* of the flight of Little Nell and her grandfather north wards from the Tottenham Court Road area which has variously and wrongly been described as a journey 'through Islington' or 'to Hampstead' but which clearly passes through Camden and Kentish Towns, Dickens's own boyhood haunts:

> These streets, becoming more straggling yet, dwindled and dwindled away, until there were only small garden patches bordering the road, with many summer houses innocent of paint and built of old timbers, or some fragments of a boat, green as the tough cabbage stalks that grew about it, and grotted at the seams with toadstools and tight-sticking snails. To these succeeded pert cottages, two and two, with plots of ground in front, laid out in angular beds and stiff borders and narrow paths between, where footsteps never strayed to make the gravel rough. Then came the public house, freshly painted green and white, with tea gardens and a bowling green, spurning its old neighbour with the horse-trough where the waggons stopped; then fields and some houses, of goodly size, with lawns, some even with a lodge where dwelt a porter and his wife. Then came a turnpike, then fields with trees and haystacks, then a hill.

This would be a fair description of Kentish Town in the 1830s or 40s, travelling up the Highgate Road till Parliament Hill was reached, and indeed Phiz's engraving of Little Nell and her grandfather, resting under a bent hawthorn tree on a hill with a view of St Paul's dome in the distance, could hardly be anywhere else: you can sit under just such a grown-out hedgerow today, and still the mass of London spread out below will seem close yet quite separate from the green hill – oddly foreshortened, as if viewed through a telescopic lens. But precise identifications of places miss the point: what is significant about the above description is not how exactly the public houses, turnpike, lodge gates etc. can be made to fit with the map, but that it is at the same time a description of everywhere. By the same token his description in *Dombey and Son* of Harriet Carker's house seems to locate it somewhere up the Finchley Road (a new road built by the Turnpike Trust), but the location is less important than the general message of geographical and social change which it bears. It could equally relate to the Camden Road, another new turnpike laid across open fields in the 1820s and only gradually colonised, with its bizarre conjunction of Montpelier House and an oil-cloth manufactury:

> The neighbourhood . . . has as little of the country to recommend it as it has of the town. It is neither of the town nor country. The former, like the giant in his travelling boots, has made a stride and passed it, and has set his brick and mortar heel a long way in advance; but the intermediate space between the giant's feet, as yet, is only blighted country, not town . . . here, among a few tall chimneys belching smoke all day and night, and among the brickfields and lanes where turf is cut, and where fences tumble down, and where the dusty nettles grow, and where a scrap or two of hedge may yet be seen . . . the bird catcher still comes occasionally, though he swears every time to come no more . . .

Dombey and Son is also Dickens's railway novel, and the descriptions in it of the devastation the coming of the London and Birmingham Railway caused to Camden Town in the 1830s and 40s are famous. But at that period Kentish Town's railway trauma lay in the future, and if the still-green area was gradually becoming dirtier and less salubrious it was not then the trains that were to blame but merely the smoke from all those thousands of new brick chimneys rising in the fields near at hand.

We traditionally associate smoke and its consequent grime with the Victorian era, as if the standard black garb of the Victorian clerk was simply a form of protective clothing and his 'stove-pipe' hat a symbol of the cause of it all. But in fact smoke was no new thing to London. John

Evelyn in the seventeenth century was already complaining about it. The eighteenth century was preoccupied with escaping from it; indeed the burgeoning of tea-gardens and spas just beyond its reach was in part a reflection of the increasing dirt of the town and people's consequent obsession with clean air. But as the nineteenth century went on these same tea-gardens and spas fell victim to the smutty blight of the encroaching town. It is hard today, when that particular type of pollution is a thing of the past, to imagine just how formidable the smoke nuisance had by that time become. As early as 1812, Louis Simond already felt a certain problem in conveying the idea to his foreign readers: 'It is difficult to imagine the type of daylight which the town of London enjoys in the middle of winter. The smoke from coal fires creates above it an atmosphere which is visible from several miles away, like a large round cloud attached to the earth . . . The air is positively loaded with small flakes of soot in suspension . . . This black snow attaches itself to clothes, to shirts, to one's face.' London at that time was using 1,200,000 tons of coal a year. Another Continental visitor a generation later, Max Schlesinger, contributed the memorable image that 'the English houses are like chimneys turned inside out; on the outside all is soot and dirt, in the inside everything clean and bright.' Doubtless the English middle-class preoccupation with a clean and comfortable interior was, in part, a reaction against the increasing dinginess of the streets beyond the carefully shut windows.

Although throughout the nineteenth century the connection between smoke and fog was much discussed, many people refusing to believe 'London particulars' could really be just the result of the cheap, bituminous coal burned in all its open grates, the problem did indeed grow steadily along with the consumption of coal. Louis Simond's million-odd tons per annum had developed, by 1880, into five million tons, fairly representing the enormous expansion of the town during that period. Over the same space of time the average number of days of fog per year went from 18.7 to 54.8, and it was within those years – about the span of one man's life – that the image of London became fixed in the imagination of the world: the City of Dreadful Night, where the urban landscape had acquired a mystery and romance all its own, a place where caped policemen flitted in pairs between gas-lamps aureoled in a sulphurous haze, where men worked all day at counters and ledgers by artificial light and in winter never saw the sun, where riches unimaginable in most parts of the world produced for the masses smoke, fog, stench, dirt and a loss of contact with their origins. The population of London increased six-fold during the century and by the 1870s the great majority of adult Londoners had not been born in London. They had come there, and had changed it from a basically traditional city ringed with semi-rural suburbs into a vast metropolis stretching for mile after unchanging mile, a phenomenon then unique in the world. Only in the twentieth century have other countries emulated it.

It seemed as if the creation of this new urban habitat, once started, could not be stopped, however much people might lament the loss of the landscapes of their youth. And people did lament. Typical of many was the florid complaint of one Edwin Roffe, who grew up among leaves and streams such as Crosby depicted, but in middle age found himself in a different world:

> Bricks! are becoming the bane of the Pancredgian being . . . In Oak Village there is not even a sapling of that sturdy representative of English hearts to be found. Maiden Lane has lost all virgin simplicity: – the grateful modesty of woman has departed from the face thereof, and the expression of that once green-tinted lane is now all but completely Brick-brazened. Highgate Rise has raised new rows of houses. Pancras Vale [the Chalk Farm Road] is now more like a Valley of Dismal-dumps than anything else: – coal shoots pollute its once fragrant air, and locomotives puff odours far away.

But this is looking somewhat ahead. Although, no doubt, the telescoping memory of later life leads people like Roffe to feel that the changes in their parish had been effected almost overnight, like a transformation scene in some satanical version of a Victorian pantomime, the houses did not all grow up at the same time or at the same rate. There were periods of many years when, particularly in Kentish Town itself, development was almost at a standstill. After the great building burst noted by Bennett, which petered out about 1825, nothing much happened to the village for some fifteen years. Camden Town, to the south of it, was eviscerated with enormous railway workings, but Kentish

Town managed to retain – and indeed confirm – its character as a Nicer Area. Not till the 1840s did the inexorable in-filling of the fields behind the main-road houses begin on any large scale, and this period also sees the beginning, in Kentish Town as elsewhere, of comprehensive suburban development rather than ribbon development and piecemeal erosion.

In 1840 the Southampton family, evidently deciding that the time was auspicious for transforming west Kentish Town from a rural to an urban landscape, produced a brochure and plans. It was typical of many at that period, but whether it was ever seriously regarded as a practical scheme for the area is open to debate. All round London landlords were convincing themselves, and attempting to convince prospective buyers, that this or that area was just the place for spacious, elegant streets of detached or at worst semi-detached 'villa residences', all standing in their own ample gardens. Prospectuses showing land so divided were published in profusion, and survive today with some of the 'lots' already booked by inked-in names, but most of them still blank and hopeful. The fact was that, then as always, the demand for such a superior type of development was limited, and the fact that such a thing was successful in choice spots like St John's Wood was no guarantee that it would succeed elsewhere too – rather the reverse. At the same time there had been much criticism of 'third rate' development such as had flourished in Camden Town. There was a generalised, if rather illogical, feeling that in providing houses for the masses rather than for the upper classes the great landowning families were letting down the side and 'not acting in London's best interests', as if you could turn a field into a good class neighbourhood just by wishing to do so.

At all events, whatever their declared intent, the Southampton family fairly speedily laid out their Kentish Town lands in quite another form from that on the original plans. Or rather, the *form* was much the same, in that the main skeleton of roads was constructed as planned but what was put along them and between them was different. Prince of Wales Road, Malden Road, Queen's Crescent, Marsden Street – these wide streets sweep in generous curves across the neighbourhood, but their interstices were filled not with villas but with continuous terraces, and extra streets were slotted in between the lots in what should have been the villas' large gardens, with cul-de-sacs and narrow alleys (see maps).

Other plans of the same period were still more spectral. The Southampton Estate were also responsible for a tentative map showing the lower reaches of Parliament Hill Fields, with a row of detached houses and gardens on what are now the tennis courts alongside Highgate Road, and Salisbury Plain (the old name of the fields where the Hampstead Lido now lies) 'proposed for making bricks'. There is a morbid charm about such never-executed designs, as if somewhere, in some other version of time, these things, so confidently depicted on paper, actually exist. Kentish Town and a thousand other places like it may now be buried fields, but so, by the same token, are areas like Parliament Hill Fields and indeed Hampstead Heath itself phantom townscape. They might very easily have disappeared under a covering of bricks and mortar had local conditions in the mid-nineteenth century been only a little different, and indeed Hampstead Heath still contains today the phantom carriageway for the landlord's projected estate – the viaduct over a marsh called the Red Arches, isolated now and forever in scrub and woodland.

Only in such individual and celebrated cases was the march of what was then and for long after called 'progress' turned aside. In most places, for most of the nineteenth century, ground landlords did exactly what they wished, just as factory and sweat-shop owners did what they wished too. (Indeed the ingrained belief, which is feasible in a rural environment but not in a densely urbanised one, that if you own a piece of land you should be allowed to do more or less what you like with it, long outlasted the nineteenth century and only finally ran out of steam in the 1930s, by which time 'suburban sprawl' had reached unimaginably far into Middlesex, Essex, Buckinghamshire, Hertfordshire, Surrey and Kent.) In one generation, between roughly 1840 and 1870, Kentish Town was substantially altered from a suburban village, surrounded by fields, into the townscape we see today. To believe that change, and in particular the *speed* of change, is something peculiar to the twentieth century, is an error, at least where the physical environment is concerned. Except in a few specific places, like New Town sites, the changes seen by many people living today are as nothing compared with the paroxysms of alteration and despoliation weathered by their great-grandparents. The old man who, in the 1890s, was wheeled in a bath-chair down grimy, walled Angler's Lane and marvelled to think that he was passing over the spot where, as a boy, he had bathed naked from the deserted, grassy banks of the Fleet, was one of a legion.

The new industrialisation, which was making England the richest country in the world, was also making this extraordinary building explosion possible. Bricks were still fired locally, but no longer did people stealthily cut down oaks on the common land to provide themselves with beams and bannisters: indeed most of the oaks had by then gone. Instead hard wood came from the other side of the world, chiefly from the West Indies, and fir for doors and window frames was shipped from the Baltic. The new canals and newer railways brought in brassware from Birmingham and iron grates and railings from the expanding industrial cities of the north. Marble for mantelpieces was imported from Italy, even for relatively ordinary houses, while the roofs of the new London were almost universally provided by the mountains of Wales. Lord Penrhyn had begun to export slate from his quarries in the late eighteenth century; by the end of the century twelve thousand tons a year was reaching London and there was much more to follow. It had become *the* cheap roofing material of the era, and even today after much rebuilding the view of London from a high place is a vista of slate roofs and innumerable disused chimney pots. Yet slate has become, like the York stone that once graced every pavement, a rare and expensive commodity. It may be, as is said, that the luxuries of one generation become the necessities of the next, but the converse is true also.

If the people who sweated to cut slate and deal and make brass and ironwear, usually far from London, were the new industrialised proletariat, those who made sure that the system worked were the new middle class, and there were relatively more of these in London than in any other large city. Their grandfathers and fathers had been small-holders or country tradesmen, but they themselves were part of a new, vast army of white-collar workers, and their expectations and modes of life had altered accordingly. The 'decent clerk', whose father had been perhaps a corn-dealer content with wooden chairs and a sanded floor, beautified his own stucco-fronted nest in Camden, Kentish Town or Islington with padded upholstery, chenille tablecloths and engravings of uplifting scenes. The extraordinarily cluttered and over-furnished look of the average Victorian parlour, by modern standards, was simply a natural response to the unprecedented number of consumer goods which, through mass-production, then came on the market for the first time. The housewife whose ancestors had used the same few iron or copper pots all their lives and left them in their wills to their descendants, now used and discarded worn-out tin pans almost as housewives do today. Or, more likely, she sat in state in her heavily-garnished parlour while in the basement kitchen the pans were burnt or dented by a succession of very young, very ignorant servant-girls.

For the keeping of servants – or *a* servant – by people of no great means or education themselves was yet another symptom of the real if unequal wealth of the age. No other European country at that time could afford to keep so many middle- and even lower-middle-class women in virtual idleness for the greater part of their lives. The French housewife even at quite a high social level did her own cooking, the German *hausfrau* remained very much that even where other help was kept. But the English housewife sat and practised being a lady, while English standards of cookery and domestic economy descended to the level for which they were long notorious. In London and the suburbs, in 1851, there were 115,000 females between the ages of fifteen and twenty, of whom almost 40,000 were in domestic service. The sheer number of houses that were built with basement kitchens even in relatively modest areas are themselves testimony to the ubiquitousness of servant-keeping. Such a plan makes no sort of sense unless the basement is envisaged as a habitat for a separate race of people. In the smaller houses that were actually built for working-class habitation, the kitchen, with wash-house-scullery beyond, is traditionally at the back of the ground floor, the front being reserved for the little used 'best room'. Yet nineteenth-century census records show that even houses of this type quite commonly housed a living-in skivvy. Did she sleep under the kitchen table, perhaps?

The commuting clerk who, by the end of the century, had become *the* archetypal denizen of the suburbs, was already a feature of places like Kentish Town by the mid-century. But it is a moot point what percentage of ordinary clerks – office workers, in modern terms, but all male – actually commuted before the 1860s. We have seen that from the late eighteenth century people living in Kentish Town availed themselves of the long-distance stage-coaches, which conveniently stopped there, simply to go to and from London. By the early part of the nineteenth century these were supplemented by many short-stage coaches run primarily *for* just such a public. Although they still looked like the traditional stage-coaches, they were the fore-runner of the omnibus. By the 1820s Kentish Town, which was peculiarly well-provided in this respect, benefited from seven coaches making between them a total of fifty journeys a day in and out of the City or West End – more than Islington and far more than remote and countryfied Hampstead. But the coaches were the two-horse variety, carrying only four to six passengers inside and seven at most on top, so this can hardly be regarded as a form of mass travel. In any case the single fare to town had risen to between 1s. 6d. and 2s. (it varied with the price of corn and indeed the whims of the owners), clearly a rate far beyond the means of the more ordinary sort of clerk, let alone the working man.

The omnibus proper, with no room for baggage but rather more for passengers was introduced after several false starts *c.* 1830, when the coaching era was in any case coming to its end with the introduction of railways. The standard omnibus fare was 6d., still a not-inconsiderable sum, but it seems to be, nevertheless, from this era that the image of the commuting clerk dates. Periodicals of the time commented on it, as a new mass phenomenon: ' . . . decent clerks, fagged and harmless and going home to their tea . . . six and twenty sweating citizens, jammed, crammed and squeezed into each other like so many peas in a pod' (*New Monthly Magazine*, 1833). Another 'Observer' of the same decade, quoted by Barker and Robbins in their *A History of London Transport,* analysed the situation in greater detail:

> In the mornings from the hours of 8.10 to 10.0 the various short-stages and omnibuses are pouring in, bearing with them the merchant to his business, the clerk to his bank or counting house, the subordinate official functionaries to the Post Office, Somerset House, the Excise, or the Mint, the Custom House or Whitehall. An immense number of individuals, whose incomes vary from £150 to £400 or £600, and whose business does not require their presence till 9.0 or 10.0 in the mornings,

and who can leave it at 5.0 or 6.0 in the evenings; persons with limited independent means of living, such as legacies or life rent, or small amounts of property; literary individuals; merchants and traders small and great; all, in fact, who can endeavour to live some little distance from London . . .

In other words, although an 'immense number' by the standards of previous, less commercialised and bureaucratised generations, these omnibus users were still exclusively people above a certain level in society; the humblest of them were living at a near £3-a-week level, which was much above the wages of the ordinary run-of-the-mill clerk toiling over ledgers for long hours in his detachable collar and cuffs. Bob Crachitt, it will be remembered, had only 15s. a week on which to keep his family, and it is made clear by Dickens that he did not take the bus but walked – or occasionally ran – all the way from Camden Town to the City and back again at night, a total of about six miles a day. Obviously, even if most employers were not as mean as Scrooge, there must have been many others like Bob Crachitt.

But as omnibuses became more numerous and took more passengers, fares gradually went down to 2d. or 3d. Certainly there was a general belief in the mid-century that the horse omnibuses had been responsible for the development of many of what later generations would regard as the 'inner suburbs' – Clapham, Brixton, Hammersmith, Kentish Town, Islington, Holloway, Highbury. It was even stated in evidence laid before the Committee on Metropolitan Turnpikes that 'builders and parties in the district raised money to get the omnibuses up there'. A similar growth pattern took place further out in the late part of the century, when housing followed the railways after the introduction of cheap workmen's tickets.

Nevertheless the importance of the commuter, in Kentish Town and all the other places like it in the mid-nineteenth century, should not be over-rated. Most omnibus users, after all, represented several other persons, usually unemployed, sitting at home. In addition, it is clear from Census records that the new suburbs had plenty of those people 'with limited independent means of living, such as legacies or life-rent, or small amounts of property' who only occasionally needed to go anywhere at all. If your standards were not too high, it was relatively far easier to amass enough private income to live on then than it is now. Many people must have simply existed, doing nothing very much since that was what a 'genteel' life implied, taking to piety, laudanum, charitable works or the reading of three-volume novels according to taste, perpetually and thankfully aware of the vast gulf between themselves and the classes below them.

By the mid-century an *average* working man's wage in London was about 21s. a week, which means that very many industrious and respectable members of the working class must have received less. In consequence, the working classes either walked long distances to work – as their agricultural forbears had often done before them – or lived near to it, which in practice usually meant closer to the centre of London than the middle classes now cared to live. From this dates the beginning of the 'decayed inner ring', which is still with us, merely displacing itself a little further out each time some energetic municipality attempts to deal with it. In St Pancras parish, areas like Somers Town, which quickly became rather poor, and Agar Town, which could never have been intended to be anything else, were part of this pattern.

At the beginning of the 1840s, when the Southampton family were maturing their plans for west Kentish Town, in the one-time manor of Tottenhall, the ground landlord of part of the old manor of St Pancras decided to do likewise. This was Councillor Agar, who lived in a turretted house slightly north of St Pancras church standing approximately where St Pancras Manor House had once stood, and is remembered now in Agar Grove. J. F. King, who depicted Mr Agar's house ('Elm Lodge') on his 'Panorama', described him as a hospitable man: indeed the picture shows a tea-party in process upon the lawns of the estate, but it was for bad landlordism that the name Agar later became a by-word.

The streets that were laid out south-east of Elm Lodge adjoining Somers Town and the new Euston railway terminus, had not even pretensions towards middle-class aspirations, being without drainage, paving or lighting, and this development effectively sealed the fate of the southern end of St Pancras parish, so long blighted, which from then on was fit for nothing but a takeover by the railway. Indeed Agar Town only existed for about twenty years, before being swept away for the construction of St Pancras Station and goods yards in the 1860s. But in its brief time it became famous, or rather infamous: Charles Dickens published a piece on it in *All the Year Round*, calling it 'A Suburban Connemara' – a title which gives one a clue to the nature of immigrant life in London in those years. A little later (1861) another popular writer, Hollinshead, the author of *Ragged London*, wrote of the six or seven thousand people in Agar Town, crammed into just a few streets

> built of old rubbish, on a 21 years lease. Some of the builders still live in them, happy and contented, dreading the time – about 1866 – when their term will expire. They are always ready to rally round the place, and to call it a 'pretty little town' . . . An old inhabitant, who holds property in the district, and keeps one of those comfortable chandlers' shops . . . thought Agar Town would be a delightful settlement 'if it wasn't for the drink'.

There was nothing new in such places: large parts of mediaeval and even seventeenth- and eighteenth-century cities were very much like this. It was a rural kind of squalor, abounding in chickens and donkeys: as Hollinshead himself said, 'here is Dorsetshire itself under our very walls.' It only seemed shocking by the new standards of the rising middle classes. But just as the image of suburban respectability – privet, net, stucco etc. – jelled in the nineteenth century and has remained petrified ever since, so the image of the slum then assumed the definitive form which it still has today, in people's minds if no longer in reality. In the words of *Punch* (1845), the slum had by then become the place of 'awful little by-lanes of two-storied tenements, where patent mangles are to let, where the street is encumbered by oyster shells and black puddles, and little children playing in them . . . Grim looking Methodist chapels, schools, churches and asylums innumerable.'

It is interesting to note that here places of worship and charity are no longer seen as objects for congratulation in a neighbourhood, as they had been in Bennett's day, but as signs of poverty. The portents for Kentish Town, by this reckoning, were not good.

Essentially, slum areas were those in which the inhabitants lived cheek by jowl with the industrial enterprises in which they worked, which by their nature were often smelly or noisy or both. It must have been partly a genuine objection to noise and smell which drove the middle classes to seek the new dormitory area further out, but it was also a matter of hardening lines of class demarcation. Unlike their immediate ancestors, 'gentlemen' in the nineteenth century did not live over the workshop, did not soil their hands, did not even contaminate their vision by *seeing* the means of production to which they owed their comfortable position in life. The late eighteenth-century 'master's house' standing right next to its factory in stern pride, as the Wedgwood mansion did at Etruria, had given way to a carefully segregated existence. The mediaeval cottager who hung around at the back door of Bruges's mansion hoping for the leftovers from the feast may have lived a very different life from that of his social superiors, but they inhabited the same landscape. 'Hovels' stood quite near to fine houses, farmyard smells might bother both impartially, often the same well supplied everyone. But the mid-nineteenth-century inhabitant of one of the new suburbs, with his paved roads, his piped water, and water closet linked – after about 1850 – to one of the new main drains, might have been living in a different country from the inhabitant of one of the slum-pockets nearby. Agar Town, with its open street drains, fringing the banks of a canal by then scummy and smelly with industrial effluent, became notorious for its knackers yards, bone boiling, manure making, soap manufacturing, refuse collecting – all the trades which expanding London needed but would rather not recognise. Attempts by people like Dickens and Hollinshead to describe such districts to their genteel public were partly, no doubt, a sign of awakening conscience but they were also a sign of the apartheid that had grown up during the century between rich and poor, to the extent that the former *needed* to have the lives of the latter indicated to them – the 'glimpses into another world' situation.

Agar Town, and the substantial houses set among lawns and trees in the north of Kentish Town, represented two extremes. Between them, both geographically and socially, lay Camden Town and Kentish Town proper, and quite early in their urbanisation both these areas developed a speckle of local industries. Mann and Sargon's Floor Cloth factory, established on the Camden Road around 1830, and at first regarded as distinguished enough to form a fit subject for a print, was a sign of more to come. By the later half of the century Kentish Town, and in particular west Kentish Town, had metal work shops, suppliers to the building trade, a glass engraving and painting works, numerous laundries and a manufacturer of artificial teeth (in Angler's Lane). Here, and still more in Camden Town to the south, skilled trades predominated: telescopes and other scientific instruments were made in small workshops, but the big trade in the area was the manufactory of pianos and organs.

In the late eighteenth century the Tottenham Court Road area had become a centre for furniture making; when increasing trade and the advance of the town displaced the manufacturers, they moved north-wards. They thus found themselves in the Camden Town, Regent's Park, Kentish Town area just at the period when a piano was becoming *the* symbol of home comfort and respectability, and when their trades could readily be applied to this end. At one time there were literally dozens of piano works in the area, some general, some catering to a specialised branch of the manufacture such as key-board construction or french polishing. Burford's Painting Rooms (see page 128) became the Rotunda Organ Factory – and later the scene of one of those disastrous and under-insured fires that characterised the trade. As time went by some factories were even designed as two twin buildings with iron doors in between, so that when one side was gutted business could go on as usual in the other. Derelict or converted factories still abound, standing like extinct beasts against the skyline, as rich in wooden beams as mediaeval tithe barns, and much bigger. Even today, if you ask elderly people in the area what work they or their fathers used to do, the answer is extremely likely to be either 'worked in a piano factory' or 'worked on the railways' – both occupations at the more prosperous end of the working class scale. With the exception of Somers Town and Agar Town, much of which had been extinguished by the railways by 1870, no part of the borough, even at its grimiest, ever developed that desperate poverty which came to characterise the East End and parts of south London. The middle-class myth, current between the wars and even up to about 1960, that St Pancras was 'all slums now' tells one quite a lot about the traditional English obsession with the virtues of rurality and the consequent fear of the 'dismal city', but very little about the true state of affairs.

The piano-making trade, incidentally, is also said to have been responsible for the very large number of public houses which flourished in Camden and Kentish Town, to the disgust of many middle-class or chapel-going inhabitants. Evidently Bennett's remark (1821) that the provision of public houses was more equitable with the number of the inhabitants than it had been in the past did not remain true for long in the eyes of many. Piano workers had the means to treat themselves to beer, and they also had the excuse that they worked in a hot, dry atmosphere. *The Builder* wrote in 1854:

> On the pastures lately set out for building you may see a double line of trenches with excavation either side . . . and a tavern of imposing elevation is standing alone and quite complete, waiting for the approaching row of houses. The propinquity of these palaces to each other in Camden and Kentish Towns is quite ridiculous. At a distance of two hundred paces in every direction, they glitter in sham splendour.

By a symmetrical twist of fate, this scene was briefly recreated in many streets in the 1960s, when whole sections of west Kentish Town and other similar parts of London were demolished for the then-fashionable 'comprehensive redevelopment', but the pubs – whose licence-holding demanded that they did not close – were allowed to remain standing, at any rate until a replacement was built. For the second time the 'palaces', now become rather faded and cavernous, found themselves standing in isolation amid acres of churned mud.

Perhaps one man may represent the many who, in the nineteenth century, moved from a rural setting and modest origins, via industry, to urban wealth, and whose lives thus paralleled the transformation of vast areas of what became London. John Brinsmead was born in north Devon in the year before Waterloo, the son of a farm-worker, but went into the cabinet-making trade. He came to London in 1836, when he was twenty-two, and presently set up a small piano-making business off Tottenham Court Road. By the time he died in 1908 he had been for half his lifetime proprietor of a huge company whose main workshops were in Grafton Road, Kentish Town. He owned a fine house near Regent's Park and, in the phrase of the period, was 'widely known for unobtrusive philanthropy' as well as being for some years Chairman of the Board of Poor

Law Guardians. He had been married for seventy years, and when his wife died a month before he did, the doleful news was successfully kept from him. Clearly, he was born under a lucky star, for his death more or less coincided with the end of the Great Piano Era. Pianolas and other early forms of the gramophone had begun clicking away in drawing rooms; no more fortunes would be made, and after the First World War the piano was swiftly relegated from being the universal prestige object to a symbol of all that was now despised and derided in the Victorian era. The ill-educated and under-employed daughters of clerks and tradesmen, who had thumped their way through five finger exercises in a million stuffy front rooms, now thumped typewriters instead. Keys yellowed, apricot silk panels faded, walnut veneers became cracked and dried. What happened to all the pianos in the end? It is almost impossible to believe that the twentieth century could simply have absorbed and dissolved the vast numbers of pianos produced in the nineteenth, and yet it has apparently done so, just as it has absorbed iron ranges and tin baths and countless gas-light fittings which were a similar essential feature of Victorian terrace housing.

Naturally the traditional rural occupations were not displaced by industrial ones overnight, or even over the course of a decade or two. Until well into the second half of the century Kentish Town retained its coachmen, its gardeners, its cow-keepers, its agricultural labourers. Nevertheless, between the years 1841 (the date of the first effective Census), 1851 and 1861, even in areas that were already built up by the earliest date, some interesting changes are apparent and serve as pointers to the way Kentish Town was going.

From the wealth of unprocessed material the Census returns contain, one can only select a few streets, a few factors, to indicate much. Let us, for example, take Harmood Street, which was at least *there* by 1841: most streets in Kentish Town post-date this. Harmood Street was one of the first side-developments of the Chalk Farm Road ('Pancras Vale') and thus on the south-western fringe of Kentish Town. John and Mary Harmood owned the field that was here c. 1800 on a lease from the manor of Tottenhall. When it was built during the 1830s, first one side and then the other, fields separated it from the Kentish Town Road and nursery gardens stretched towards Haverstock Hill on the north. The houses in it were – and are – extremely small, the two-up, two-down-and-a-wash-house variety, with tiny back gardens. The presence of quite a number of large old fruit trees in the gardens even today suggests that the land was in use as an orchard immediately before being built upon. They can never have been intended as true middle-class dwellings; nevertheless they must have been, originally, extremely pleasant places to live in.

In 1841, by which time Harmood Street had forty houses, it had 251 inhabitants. Among heads of households, the largest group of all was those of 'independent means' – some sixteen people and their families; clearly Kentish Town was still a place to which to retire and live out your days modestly on your modest savings. There were eight clerks; five people employed in various capacities on the railway, which had then newly arrived in Camden Town, just down the road; a surveyor and a builder. The rest of the population represented a fair cross-section of the skilled lower-middle, upper-working class of that date: there was a coach-builder, three printers, two binders, an engraver, a milliner, a carpenter, a gardener, two carver-gilders, a tailor, a schoolmaster, a surgeon and several shopkeepers. There was a 'music student', an engineer, a 'merchant', two governesses but only one laundress. In an adjacent cottage was a blacksmith.

By 1851 the picture had changed somewhat. The street was becoming surrounded by others, both on the Southampton Estate to the north-east and the Hawley-Bucks Estate to the south. There were now double the number of houses in Harmood Street itself – eighty-two to be exact, including a pub and a few shops – but the number of inhabitants had more than doubled, from 251 to 561. In other words the average number of people per house had gone up from six – already quite a lot in a four-roomed house – to seven. But the most noticeable thing is that many more professions are listed, since more of the wives were employed than had formerly been the case, and more of the houses were in multi-occupation. One house actually contained a 'solicitor's managing clerk' (a frequent claim in Census records), his wife and five children (fortunately small), a railway messenger, a monthly nurse and – at any rate on the night of the Census – a casual lodger whose name was unknown. One must assume that the clerk and his family, having fallen on hard times, had let two rooms out of the four, and that the railway messenger and the 'monthly nurse' were their lodgers. I also suspect from the unnaturally frequent appearance of 'monthly nurse' on the Census records, here and elsewhere, that the term was in fact a common euphemism for an even older profession and that the nameless lodger was therefore one of her clients.

To be fair, not all households showed such signs of social decline. There were still twenty-four people variously described as being of independent means, though this represents, proportionally, a considerable drop on the previous decade. There was a sprinkling of artist-engravers (a genteel form of sweated labour at the period), governesses, a landscape artist, a 'portrait painter in oil' (his sisters went in for landscapes and modelling in clay), and a missionary. There was even a 'ladies seminary' run by the wife of a surveyor: it had four pupils. Out of eight laundresses, four were in the same household and three of these were teenage girls; there was also a 'wife who takes in mangling' (shades of the *Punch* writer's 'patent mangles to let') and quite a few 'dressmakers' or 'needleworkers' with both husbands and children to occupy their time in addition. There was even an 'artistic florist' aged eleven. Few households kept a living-in servant. No less than thirty-two people were now employed in some way on the railway, either building it or running it, and there were half a dozen piano-makers. There was also a person exercising the new art of daguerrotypes.

By 1861, by which time west Kentish Town was largely covered in houses, the number of houses in Harmood Street was still eighty-two but the population had gone up again, not spectacularly but slightly, to 578. The number of persons of independent means had gone down to nine; two of these were pensioners and two were visitors not normally living in the street. In other ways also the composition of the street appears more working-class, not dramatically but significantly. There are proportionately fewer clerks, and rather more people of un-equivocally humble station in life, such as a coal porter, bootmakers, a dealer in earthenware toys and a widowed mother and daughter who made baby-linen. There were now four photographers, a typical living-by-your-wits trade. The artists, engravers and governesses seem largely to have abandoned the place, and indeed few of the tenants of ten years previously were still in occupation. Evidently Harmood Street was a place for people on the way up – or the way down. There are actually rather more children listed as 'scholars' than there had been in 1851, but presumably this reflects the general increase in school-going in all classes but the poorest at that period, rather than a local social fluctuation.

For comparison, let us look at Gloucester Place – the High Street end of what later came to be called Leighton Road. Older than Harmood Street, it participated in some of the piecemeal villa development that made Kentish Town attractive in the early years of the century. The map of 1796 shows a footpath following the line of it alongside the bowling green and paddock belonging to the Assembly House, to a stile and to a further path leading across the fields to Islington. There were no houses as yet. By 1804, however, the path had been widened and paved as far as the stile and was dignified with the name 'Evans Place'. The ground landlord of this whole slice of land, running back from the Assembly House towards Maiden Lane, was a gentleman with the exotic name of Joshua Prole Torriano, who was nevertheless a descendant of a perfectly English soap-maker called Cox. He is remembered in Torriano Avenue up the road, built rather later in the century. The land on the north side – the public house land, that is – seems to have been early sold off in small freehold lots, whose purchasers built houses for their own occupation, and the houses on it are freehold to this day. Several of the houses were large enough to have stables, but those have disappeared, swept away either by the construction of Leverton Street on the north post-1850 or by the advent of the Midland Railway on the south in the 1860s. One substantial one remains, built as a large single family house, its porch graced by delicate ionic columns: later in the century it was divided into two houses and another, more ordinary porch was added at one side. But before this occurred the decent garden space between it and its original next-door neighbour had already been filled by a small double-fronted house standing on a plinth with the air of a doll's house, needing only a brass hook on one side to complete the illusion.

During the 1820s and 1830s the street, now known as Gloucester Place,*

---

* 'Gloucester' in a street name denotes a date after 1816, when the Duke of Gloucester married Princess Mary.

gradually prolonged itself beyond the point where the stile had stood. Terraces appeared, containing houses of a more modest type than the original ones. In 1840 a six-roomed house which effectively became part of a terrace but stood on a single freehold plot, was sold by Mr Crowe, its ground landlord and builder, to one Henry Hugh Pike, who styled himself 'barrister at law' and claimed to be a member of Lincoln's Inn, though in actual fact he was a former member of Gray's Inn. The house, with a large garden whose length corresponded to the breadth of the erstwhile Assembly House grounds, was sold to Pike for £900, a then substantial sum of money which reflects the continuing desirability of the neighbourhood. Pike did not at first live in the house – 94 Gloucester Place – himself, for the Census the following year finds it occupied by a widow of independent means, a lodger who may have been a relation, and two servants. Ten years later, in 1851, the Pike family (of whom we shall be hearing more in a moment) were still absent, the rent of the house presumably providing them with some sort of an income, and the place was occupied by an architect, his wife, two children, a nurse and a servant. Among their immediate neighbours were two solicitors, an accountant, a landscape painter, a clerk in a fire insurance office, and a family called Edwards, clothiers who had bought a plot of land and built several houses some thirty years earlier. At Bower Cottage next door, one of the largest and oldest houses in the street, lived an auctioneer and his family. It was hardly a grand neighbourhood, but it was evidently still an agreeable one.

By 1861 the picture had changed somewhat. Although the gardens of the houses on the north side still backed onto fields, on the south side (the Christ Church lands) a substantial new estate was planned, and further up the road houses branched out to right and left in Torriano Avenue and Leighton Crescent. At the High Street end the Assembly House had been rebuilt as a town pub and had lost the remainder of its garden to Leverton Street, at that date still a cul-de-sac. These tiny houses, each with its scrap of garden and its pretentious stuccoed facade, could never have been intended to attract a middle-class ownership, and its general social level, from the first, was not much above that of Harmood Street. A goldsmith lived there, and a 'water-colourist', two governesses, a confectioner, a gardener, a piano-maker, and clerks both in and out of work. They were family houses – there were not the nameless lodgers and four-to-a-room railway workers who had appeared in Harmood Street by this date – but there were few servants.

In Gloucester Place itself, Bower Cottage was at this time lived in by the large Crane family, who were local builders responsible for many of the new constructions in the area including the National Schools in Islip Street (1849). Other people along that run were the Edwards, still present; a jeweller's assistant with a wife, five small daughters and no servants; a solicitor's managing clerk with two grown-up sons, clerks to the Western Railway and the Submarine Telegraph Company respectively; a professor of drawing with a wife, three small children, a lodger and one servant; a retired ironmonger with two servants; a commercial traveller called Thomas West with a wife, a seven-year-old son and one servant; and an elderly warehouseman living with his wife, assorted elderly relatives, his son and his son's wife.

There was also Mr Pike, now in residence in No. 94. Things had happened to Pike in the intervening decades, although from the Census record, in which he still styled himself 'barrister-at-law', you would not have known it. In 1844, six years after being called to the bar, he had been disbarred for colluding with a solicitor to share the profits of cases with him. He appealed against the disbarment, but the order was confirmed. Where he went in the following decade I do not know – judging from the birthplaces of his children, to south London and Great Yarmouth – but his enforced retirement from his profession was presumably the reason why, by the age of fifty, he had retreated to his Kentish Town property to cultivate his garden. His household in 1861 comprised himself, his wife, daughters of twelve, eight, six and four and a son of two. He had no servant, though living in a house of a size where one would normally be kept and a road where most people did keep one, and the future cannot have looked bright to him. Five years later he was involved in an unseemly court case, the details of which were sufficiently piquant to find their way into the *Daily Telegraph* for 21 June 1866 under the heading 'Neighbourly Relations'.

Against these three of his neighbours Mr Pyke [sic] brought the action for trespass and conspiracy, and the perpetration of numerous petty annoyances, which were described as follows: During five or six years he had been annoyed and sneered at by the defendants, who looked impudently at him and did other acts to cause him pain. Dead cats and defunct chickens were thrown into his garden. The flowers and vegetables there were destroyed by the defendants' fowls. On the 5th November there was a bonfire in the adjoining garden; squibs and crackers were wantonly thrown over his wall. On one occasion a pole was erected, on which was tied a stale mackerel, and underneath it was put up the effigy of a pike with this inscription: Beware of the pike – he is a most voracious fish. . . . There were continual noises in the adjoining houses late at night, which prevented the plaintiff and his family from taking rest, and on the death of one of the plaintiff's children the glass was broken, and a disturbance created. There were also hooting, yelling, and cock-crowing, West being so good an imitator that Mrs Pyke said he used to set all the cocks in the neighbourhood crowing. The children were unable to go into the garden without being subject to annoyances of this kind, and were told that they were starved, uneducated and ill-clothed. A stuffed owl was put up on one occasion. Dirty water was thrown over plaintiff's children. On Sundays, some of the defendants and others used to sit upon the wall, drinking and smoking . . .

The defendants, on their part, deposed that they had not annoyed the plaintiff and his family, or given them provocation . . . Mr West said that his wife had been grossly insulted by the Pyke family, and the lady herself testified that they had constantly addressed her as 'beast' and 'Old Scraggy'. . . . Mr Boyes confessed to having imitated the crowing of a cock, the grunting of a pig, and the mewing of a cat; but averred it was only to amuse himself and Mrs Crane's children. The other assertions of the plaintiff were generally denied . . . After a conference of the learned counsel on both sides a juror was withdrawn, and an agreement entered into for abstention from all further annoyances.

The ludicrous details of this case captured the imagination of a feature writer for the same paper, who made it the subject of a long, facetious article, distilling all the lofty scorn which the upper-middle classes had by then developed for lower-middle-class suburbia – the theme which George Grossmith was to exploit with more skill a generation later in *Diary of a Nobody*. He concludes:

> Had all these worthy people only managed to control their temper, they might have lived a happy and tranquil life. It is soothing to think that they may yet be reconciled, and our fancy dwells with pleasure upon a picture of their future existence. Let them fraternise; let Mr Pyke and Mr Crane exchange presents of vegetables; let Mrs West forgive the aspersion cast upon her form; let Mr Boyes invite them all, if not to a *thé dansante*, to a ventriloquial choclate, with imitations of animals interspersed; let them but do this, and Kentish Town will be Arcadia. At present, we confess, it is not.

Evidently the very idea that Kentish Town might ever have been considered Arcadia had, by the 1860s, become highly laughable. Alas for Dr Stukeley's Eden of a hundred years earlier.

While it is, of course, impossible to tell where the rights and wrongs of the matter lay, there are several details in the saga which suggest that rather more may have been involved than ever came out: in particular, the gibes – real or imagined – about the Pike children being uneducated, ill-clothed and half-starved, and the curious slogan about a pike being 'a voracious fish', suggest some monetary issue. Pike was no doubt in direly straitened circumstances, living as he and his family did without visible means of support, and it is possible that he may have been attempting to use whatever capital he possessed to practise a little money-lending in the neighbourhood – hardly the way to endear himself to his neighbours. However it is clear that, whatever others thought, he considered himself a person of the utmost rectitude. In 1870, we find him writing to the local paper, the *Kentish and Camden Towns Gazette*, on the 'height' of the service held at the new St Luke's church in Oseney Crescent on the Christ Church Estate: 'Sir: As a parishioner, I neither like the outside of this building nor what is going on within it. To my mind both appear to me un-English and foreign to its church . . . ' He also objected to the innovation of gaslight in a church. He signed himself 'Formerly barrister-at-law'. The letter was answered the following week by an extremely snappish one from 'A Churchman', who claimed that

until Mr Pike's style improved 'he may fairly be deemed to be outside
the pale of gentlemanly controversy'. Another reader wrote in to point
out that, living as he did on the north side of Leighton Road, Pike
was not in St Luke's parish anyway. The argument about the services,
however, continued for weeks.

In pursuing Pike, I have moved ahead in the tale of Kentish Town,
into its railway age, and will have to return. But, to conclude the saga
and to underline its implications, I will add that 1871 finds Pike and
his wife still living in their house (now mortgaged, and also entirely
surrounded by others) with their unmarried and uneducated daughters
and their son. Pike, incidentally, was styling himself 'solicitor' in 1871!
Nine years later the mortgage was foreclosed: the debt, because of unpaid
interest, now amounted to £400. When the house was resold in 1880,
although its big garden was still intact and it had been improved with an
upstairs drawing room, it fetched only £500, as against the £900 Pike
had paid for it forty years earlier. These figures are a graphic illustration
of the decline of Kentish Town during that period.

Mr Pike's garden is once again growing potatoes and lettuces as well as
flowers, and one or two of his fruit trees are still standing, though past
bearing fruit. The one which provided the rotten plums that were thrown
at Mrs West, fell during a storm a few years ago. The Wests' house still
stands, still 'unimproved' (i.e. bathroomless), as does the garden wall on
which he and his cronies gathered to drink and smoke. But the house
adjoining on the other side has long been empty air, the space serving as
a driveway to a residential local authority nursery. Bower Cottage, where
the Crane clan lived, was by the 1870s a soup kitchen and Outdoor
Relieving Station, and today is embedded like a fossil in later buildings
belonging to the nursery.

What makes Pike irresistible as a subject is the combination of
eccentricity, vague loucheness and intense external respectability which
seem in retrospect to have typified the Victorian period. His house, with
an embellished sitting room but no proper domestic help, no bathroom,
and the only lavatory in the back yard; his daughters living at home in
unschooled idleness – these things are eloquent of a whole system of
values. Add to that the fact that, when further works were done on the
long-enduring house in the 1960s, the space between the floors disgorged

countless dust-embalmed pamphlets on religion and teetotalism, and you have a very model for Matthew Arnold's famous strictures on the Victorian suburban middle classes, which were published the same year as Pike's unfortunate law-suit:

> ... Drugged with business, your middle class seems to have its sense blunted for any stimulus besides, except religion; it has a religion narrow, unintelligent, repulsive ... What other enjoyments have they? The newspapers, a sort of eating and drinking which are not to our taste, a literature of books almost entirely religious or semi-religious, books utterly unreadable by an educated class anywhere, but which your middle class consumes, they say, by the hundred thousand; in their evenings, for a great treat, a lecture on teetotalism or nunneries ... Your middle-class man thinks it is the highest pitch of development and civilisation when his letters are carried twelve times a day from Islington to Camberwell, and from Camberwell to Islington, and if railway trains run to and fro between them every quarter of an hour. He thinks that it is nothing that the trains only carry him from an illiberal, dismal life at Islington to an illiberal, dismal life at Camberwell; and the letters only tell him that such is the life there. (*Friendship's Garland*, 1866)

The coming of the trains, running indeed to Islington and back again among many other places, and in doing so transforming Kentish Town finally and irrevocably into an urban area, is the subject of the next chapter.

9

'Railway trains run to and fro'

It must not be thought, however, that Kentish Town in the middle decades of the nineteenth century was inhabited exclusively by people leading 'a dismal, illiberal life'. The northern part of the area, at any rate, was still a good address. T. J. Barrett, later an inhabitant of Hampstead and celebrated for his local history of that place, lived at the foot of Highgate West Hill as a young man, near the Howitts (see page 25). The Holly Lodge Estate on the east side of Highgate Hill passed around the mid-century to Angela Burdett-Coutts, Thomas Coutts the banker's granddaughter and heiress and a close friend of Dickens; through him, she met Hans Andersen, who visited her there and admired her rhododendrons – then a foreign novelty. She gave big garden parties in the summers; the local paper for June 1867 gives an account of hundreds of coaches going up there for a *'conversazione'*, and all through the year friends and acquaintances received presents of fruit and flowers from her greenhouses. Even today, when Holly Lodge Estate, a twentieth-century suburban development, covers the site, some of her rhododendrons and other, still uncommon, foreign plants are to be found in many of the gardens. Later, when she had acquired the Kentish Town House Estate further down the hill, she ran a stud farm there, where Sultan, one of the most famous steeplechasers of all time, was bred. The main stable block is still there in St Alban's Road, disguised as Brookfields Garages. A little further north is Holly Village, a collection of spacious gothic cottages, with much ornate woodwork, which she built for her servants. They are grouped round communal green lawns, like a vision of Oxbridge rebuilt by Ruskin or William Morris.

Moving down towards Kentish Town proper, we have the poet Coventry Patmore living in The Grove (now Grove Terrace) in early married life during the 1850s. His best-known work, *The Angel in the*

House, is a distillation of the Victorian idealisation of the Home, and was very much to the taste of the period. Ford Madox Brown, the pre-Raphaelite painter of the same generation, was Patmore's neighbour for a while in The Grove and then moved to a nearby house in Fortess Terrace. Dr Southwood-Smith, the eminent public-health authority, also lived in Fortess Road; he was a friend of Angela Burdett-Coutts (slum-improvement was one of her chief interests) and the grandfather of Octavia Hill of housing-trust fame. The family was also connected with the Lewes family, from which came George Henry Lewes, George Eliot's companion, and it was George Henry's son by a previous marriage who, later in the century, joined with the Southwood-Smiths, Miss Coutts and other like-minded people to secure Parliament Hill as part of Hampstead Heath. Had it not been for the presence of people like this in the district, those fields would certainly have been built upon and Kentish Town would have lost its green lung.

Nearer the centre of Kentish Town, in Lower Craven Place (immortalised by Betjeman as 'the terrace blackish-brown' and not demolished till the 1960s), lived Douglas Jerrold, a well-known contributor to *Punch* at the period and the author of 'Mrs Caudle's Curtain Lecture'. This was a comic monologue very popular as a turn at the amateur concerts which brightened Victorian life in places like Kentish Town: it sometimes used to be delivered (as a sweetener, no doubt) at the improving 'penny-readings' that were regularly held through the 1860s at Milton Hall, which stood on the edge of Hawley Road where a cricket ground had formerly been. Less famous than Jerrold then, but far more now, was another local inhabitant – Karl Marx. Marx first came to London in 1849, and moved to Kentish Town eight years later. With his family, he lived in bourgeois but somewhat disorganised poverty, first in Malden Road in west Kentish Town and later – with a slight upturn in his fortunes – at the more airy and bosky Medina Villas off Haverstock Hill (subsequently called Maitland Park Road and now expunged by a housing estate). Picnics on the Heath were one of the brighter features of their family life. It is nice to think that even in death Marx remained faithful to the unpretentious area of north London that had sheltered him in life, but in fact his presence in Highgate Cemetery is simply due to the fact that this was the general, non-denominational burial ground of north London. By an ingenious twist of fate, present-day Marxists are still a feature of Kentish Town's borders: the Russian Trade (sic) Delegation occupies premises in a large house near the top of Highgate West Hill, and the Holly Lodge Estate, mentioned above, is the home of a number of their families. They are reported, however, to keep themselves very much to themselves.

During the 1840s, when the Southampton Estate (see previous chapter) was in process of building, the Hawley-Bucks Estate, a smaller parcel which adjoined it on the south running down towards the canal and Camden Town, was also laid out with streets. This was the 40-acre property next to the Castle, on part of which J. F. King's father had made his garden; but gardens were at a discount by then (the Castle's gardens disappeared at the same period) and the estate was quickly developed, mostly with rather horrid little houses, probably because of its proximity to the Chalk Farm railway yards.

In the 1850s the segment of land between Southampton Estate and the older development around Holmes Road and Spring Place was filled in with a vest-pocket development of very small houses. The names of its streets – Inkerman, Alma, Raglan etc – date it precisely and the local pub bears the name Crimea. It soon filled up with pianoforte makers, wood engravers, dressmakers and railway workers, all helping to swell Kentish Town's industrial proletariat, which was now threatening to swamp the middle-class inhabitants. Brief as they are, some of the entries for the first Census after its building – that of 1861 – speak volumes. What, for instance, is one to surmise of the failed life of a 'retired grocer' and his wife, both aged only 49, he born in Islington and she in Kentish Town itself, who were living in Alma Street with their unmarried daughter, a governess of 23, and another daughter aged 10? Did that one governess's scant wage support the entire household? And what of Clara Brooker, a widow in the same street, herself a governess, living with one son of 15 apprenticed to a printer, two daughters of 17 and 13 who were down as 'dressmakers', two more of 8 and 3 and another son of 10? The proliferating back streets of the period received these people, who had fallen through the inadequate security nets then erected, just as they received Henry Pike and Karl Marx and many thousands of others who might once have hoped for better things, but it is doubtful if they assured them a life worth living.

But attempts to create a substantial amount of upper-middle-class housing in Kentish Town were still continuing. In the late 1850s and early 1860s, first the Christ Church Estate and then St Bartholomew's Estate, adjoining it, laid out their land as streets (see page 58), thus transforming the eastern side of the district and creating an area known – at any rate for a while – as 'New Kentish Town', presumably to mark the social divide between it and the already tarnished Southampton Estate developments on the other side of the main road. The roads were wide, the houses mostly spacious and officially described as 'superior class'. Here, it was envisaged, would live the sort of people who would counterbalance the less desirable elements that had invaded west Kentish Town, people who would shop not at street stalls or obscure general stores in converted front rooms but at Daniel's in the High Street – a chain of shops which Mr Daniel the draper had recently unified into a department store. This was the forward, prosperous image of Kentish Town which was being invoked by the anonymous writer to the *Gazette* (1867) on the prevalent nineteenth-century theme of change: typical is his evidently ambivalent attitude to all this improvement:

A stranger passing through Camden and Kentish Towns at the present time, and observing the vista of large and magnificent shops, the busy appearance of the principle streets – well paved and well lighted – and the miles of superior Villas, Crescents, Squares and Avenues, could not fail to be attracted by the appearance of prosperity and health presented . . . The changes have been so swift, the progress so rapid and sudden . . . Still, a feeling of regret will arise when the pleasing pictures are destroyed, and the regret at the uprooting of an old tree or the destruction of a field by its conversion into bricks, plainly shews an inherent love of nature which is implanted in the human breast . . .

The writer went on to draw a comparison between the sweet innocence of rurality and the 'vice' which flourished, according to him, like weeds, in the city. Here, in a nutshell, you have the Victorian moral dilemma: the concept of progress, with all that implied, coming into direct conflict with the growing awareness of the evils which urbanisation was bringing in its train, and the consequent sentimentalisation of rural life even as the last shreds of it were retreating towards Highgate, Highbury, Fulham or Kennington.

Yet despite the hopes and expectations of the builders of 'New Kentish Town', there are signs from the first of its having been an insufficiently-considered venture, 'speculative building' in the worst sense of the term. Indeed one is irresistibly reminded of Cruikshank's cartoon 'The March of Bricks' (see illustrations), with its terraces cracking and subsiding even before they are finished, when one reads in contemporary newspaper reports that a run of houses in Gaisford Street collapsed before they were up:

> . . . the stacks of chimneys were so far completed as to have the ceremony performed of hoisting the flags, made by workmen's handkerchiefs, . . . so as to entitle the men to the usual regalement of beer on such occasions. The stack of the third house from the corner is stated to have been much higher than those of the adjoining houses, and whilst one man was fixing the last chimney-pot thereon, the entire stack fell, dragging with it a great proportion of the upper part of the party wall, together with the whole of the scaffolding and their occupants. Many of the poor fellows, who had fallen from a height of between fifty and sixty feet, were got out, and the worst cases were conveyed to the University College Hospital . . . (1859).

A further report the following week states that 'Mr Temple Elliott, the ground landlord and owner of that portion of the estate . . . caused a rigid investigation to be instituted, in order to ascertain the circumstances which led to the occurrence.' In point of fact Elliott was not the ground landlord but, presumably, the person who had taken a building lease on that parcel of land from Christ Church. He also seems to have been the person who, a few years earlier, had written an unpublished book on the area (see page 110) lamenting its decline from a country village to a suburb. Ambivalence, as I say, was a characteristic of the times.

But a further hazard awaited the Christ Church Estate, and that was the coming of the Midland Railway, whose main line into Euston (constructed in the early 1860s) passed right through the centre of the estate. It seems extraordinary that the developers did not foresee this imminent eruption into the area, but the complete absence of planning permission in those days, in the modern sense of the term, no doubt made such short-sighted construction easy. It is also possible that the laying out of Islip, Caversham and Gaisford Streets was less short-sighted than wily: perhaps the administrators of the Estate *did* indeed realise that the railway was coming, and reckoned that there was more money to be made out of the Midland if the Company had to purchase houses for demolition than if they purchased open fields. But in that case it was not sensible to plan such a superior class of estate, for the fact that the line came through, cutting off corner houses, almost before the plaster on the walls was dry, could only have a deleterious effect on the area. True, the line there was slotted discreetly through a cutting, with a tunnel under the grander houses across Camden Road, in Camden Square; it was not allowed to become a barrier and eyesore as the North London line (see below) had in west Kentish Town ten years earlier. But the coming of the main-line railway does indeed seem to have spelt the end – though not in any sudden or dramatic way – of aspirations for Kentish Town as a distinguished address, and when the remainder of Bartholomew Estate was developed alongside the Christ Church one the streets on it were narrower and the houses mostly smaller. By 1871 over 50 per cent of all the houses on the two estates were shared – that is to say, they were lived in by an extended family rather than by a nuclear family with servants, or the owners took in lodgers. There was also a falling off in the number of people from Class I, judging by occupation.

Another part of the Kentish Town district, which, from its nearness to Hampstead and the Heath one might have expected to become favoured, seems to have been blighted by the railway before it was even built. This was the Gospel Oak district and the area immediately to the south of it, where several small landowners had interests besides Lord Southampton and Lord Mansfield, whose lands adjoined there. By 1851 the street pattern around what became Lismore Circus was laid down (at any rate on maps) but not yet built with houses. By 1853 there were still only 'some 12 or 13 houses with a beershop at the corner' – apparently 'the favourite resort of navvies and quarrelsome shoemakers'. This same year an enquiry was held concerning the designs on the area entertained by the Hampstead Junction Railway. This was an offshoot of the company which had built a line from Bow to Camden Town (Camden Road Station) three years earlier, intending it as a freight line to carry goods from Regent's Canal to the London Docks. It was quickly realised, however, that the line had a potential for passenger traffic, and it was with this in mind that it was envisaged extending it up through the west side of Kentish Town, through Gospel Oak to Hampstead. William Tite, the architect retained by the railway, gave evidence to the effect that west Kentish Town (particularly the Hawley-Bucks Estate) was already a third-class area and therefore could not be much further damaged by the railway ('I should not like it myself, but there is a great difference between abuse in Lowndes Square and this class of house'). He went on to summarise the few properties already standing at Gospel Oak as 'humble', adding, rather speciously one may feel, 'I do not mean to say they are to be disregarded because they are humble, but they are very humble . . . some of them are very inferior, very ill-built and wretched.' Was this fair comment, or special pleading?

It is, in fact, a moot point whether the coming of the railways blighted the areas through which they passed, or whether the railway companies had a marked tendency to select routes through areas which already had little prestige or value. Obviously it was easier for railway companies, both financially and in terms of appeasing public opinion, to route a line through west Kentish Town or to efface Agar Town with a main line station, than it would have been to take a line through St John's Wood or to build a station on Regent's Park. Significantly, when the Midland Railway had to put their line through Belsize Park in the 1860s, they buried it in a tunnel. The lie of the land is relevant too, but several engineers at the time specifically advocated choosing the cheapest route even if it did not necessarily offer the most direct access to the desired point. In *The Impact of Railways on Victorian Cities*, Kellet comes to the conclusion that the pattern of the railway, as it evolved, was subordinate to estate holdings and land values: the presence of three major termini in a row (four, if you count Marylebone) all sitting along the Marylebone–Euston Road and glaring at the select Bedford and Portland Estates to the south, is testimony to the ultimate power of money and prestige to keep undesirable things at bay.

Nevertheless, one can think of a number of instances where an apparently salubrious neighbourhood was, seemingly, 'spoilt' by the railway: one half of Nash's Park Village East was demolished to accommodate the London and Birmingham line only a generation after the houses had been built. And there is a good deal of circumstantial evidence that people in an area like west Kentish Town did see the railway as a despoiler – as well they might, since it was carried through the already-built area in the 1850s, on a viaduct, rooftop high. The Governesses' Institution, for instance, which had been established in Scottish baronial grandeur in the newly-developed Prince of Wales Road in 1849, as an 'asylum' for aged and infirm governesses, found by 1865 that 'the increasing encroachment of the railways, disturbing this once peaceful home with shrill shrieks at all hours of the day and often of the night, besides shutting out the access of the sweet air that used to come from Hampstead and Highgate, has caused the removal of the old ladies to be seriously contemplated.' (Removed they were, in the early 1870s, to a place further out; the building became Miss Buss's North London Collegiate School. Later it was inherited by her sister-school, the Camden School for Girls, and today is part of the senior school of St Richard of Chichester's RC school.)

Probably the truth about the effect of land on the railways or railways on the land is to be found in a complex interaction between reality and perceived expectations: a district might be – as so much of Kentish Town was pre-1850 – perfectly respectable and pleasant, yet lack that cachet of smartness, that upper-middle-class character which would ensure for it special consideration. So it would be claimed as a 'third rate district' and a railway or railways would be put through it – which, of course, had the effect of a self-fulfilling prophecy. Gospel Oak is a case in point. It had always been a rather inaccessible spot, isolated from both Hampstead and Kentish Town, away from the main roads. There was, in theory, no reason why it should not have been laid out handsomely. But the various small landlords were evidently unable to get together and agree on such a project, and meanwhile the first railway came and placed its seal on the place. Ten years later no one had yet bothered to build a proper carriageway from Highgate Road, and its remoteness, instead of being rural, was becoming squalid. In 1867 Lismore Circus, planned years before, was still a 'mud island', and a letter to the local newspaper the same year complains of 'the dank, pot-holed state of the roadway lying at the back of Oak Village . . . we are completely isolated from the civilised world. Vehicles can only approach our dwellings by a long and roundabout detour.' The letter went on to speak of garbage, puddles of dirty water, dead dogs and squads of children playing in the street – the mark of a poor area, even today. Another letter from a different correspondent, later the same year, complained that the dis-possessed poor of Agar Town, then newly demolished to make way for St Pancras Station, 'are crowding, and lowering in character, the once-promising locality springing up known as 'Oak Village'.

It appears to be true – though it would take a lot of comparative work with different Censuses to prove it – that many of those who settled in the greyly-expanding areas of north Kentish Town in the 1850s and 1860s did indeed come from the districts nearer the centre of London which had been disrupted by the railway: Euston had been built in the early 1840s (the line in the late 1830s ended at Camden Town), King's Cross in 1852; St Pancras followed in 1868. Certainly, by the beginning of the 1860s, the demolition and destruction caused by the railway companies, which a previous generation had been inclined to regard complacently as a form of desirable 'slum-clearance', had become some-thing of an open scandal. Lord Derby declared in an impassioned speech to Parliament in 1861: 'The Poor are displaced, but they are not removed, they are shovelled out of one side of the parish only to render still more over-crowded the stifling apartments in another part.' Professor Dyos has calculated that between 1859 and 1867 alone, 38,000 people were displaced in London by the railways.

Whether the coming of the railways simply exaggerated and made patent a social decline already insidiously overtaking Kentish Town, or whether it was *the* important factor in the transformation from semi-rural village to urban semi-slum, their ultimate physical effect on the geography of the area is indisputable. For a railway, particularly one on a viaduct but even to some extent in a cutting, is a physical barrier in a way that a road is not: it cuts off streets, truncates estate patterns, and even where there are arches under which people and vehicles pass it con-stitutes a visual barrier. Thackeray, writing in 1860, ingeniously used this image of the railway barrier to symbolise the barrier between past and present which the coming of the railways effectively raised: indeed it would be hard to overestimate the enormous change experienced by people, like Thackeray or Dickens, who were born in the fifteen-miles-an-hour stage-coach era and who lived on into a time when long journeys between, say, London and Liverpool, took the same amount of time as they do today: 'Your railroad starts the new era, and we of a certain age belong to the new time and to the old one . . . They have raised those railroad embankments up, and shut off the old world that was behind them. Climb up that bank on which the irons are laid, and look to the other side – it is gone' (Thackeray, quoted by Richard Altick in *Victorian People and Ideas*).

A literal taste of what Thackeray meant can still be obtained today down by St Pancras Old Church. If you approach it from the west, it stands on its grassy knoll just as it has for centuries, an unchanging island in a world that has transformed itself not once but several times. But mount the knoll and cross it – on the far side, instead of a vista of cows and trees, another hillock rears up, a railway viaduct, and beyond it one of those *terrains vagues* that are the curse of railways: a wilderness of derelict goods yards, a disused canal, gas works, the rear of London's most exotic station.

Such wildernesses were another reason for the railways' disruptive effect on a neighbourhood. For railway land is not flexible or piecemeal. Unlike the mews, garages, tram depots, bus yards and the like generated by road traffic, the ancillary services for a railway line cannot be scattered about. The shunting yards, goods yards, workshops, loco sheds, coaling bays etc. had to be grouped together, usually on large wedges of land which previously might have been open field crossed by footpaths, but which then by virtue of their new use became inaccessible to the general public and invisible behind high walls of sooty pink brick. Moreover these wedges of land were often larger than was strictly necessary, even in the heyday of steam trains, since, by the middle of the century, companies had adopted the policy of buying up more land than they immediately needed, to be on the safe side. The results of this policy were sometimes curious. In Kentish Town, until very recently, there existed a small copse and part of a field in a totally untouched state, appearing much as it must have over a hundred years earlier. This was because the railway company concerned – the North London Line, Tottenham branch – had acquired a large segment of land behind College Lane in the 1860s (the old Green Street race fields of eighteenth-century days) but in the end had only used a part of it, for sheds and a railway hostel. The rest had remained untouched, wood violets and all, except for generations of marauding local children, delighting in its wildness. All in all, by the end of the nineteenth century, in that part of London which lies north of the Euston Road, over three hundred acres of land had disappeared into the hands of the railway companies, including most of the old manor of St Pancras, a large slice of northern Kentish Town and a similarly extensive chunk of northern Camden Town – Chalk Farm.

The distorting effect of this on local communications, and indeed the whole shape of districts, is considerable. The railway dominates Kentish Town today like an unseen presence, for the wedge of railway land north of Holmes Road and west of the Highgate Road is far larger than most people living in the area realise. They are so accustomed to making detours around it that it does not, for instance, strike them as odd that there is no proper route westwards from the High Street but Prince of Wales Road in the south and Gordon House Road in the north on the fringe of Parliament Hill. But viewed from a passing train, or from the top of one of Kentish Town's few tower blocks (Monmouth House, Raglan Street, for instance) the scene comes into perspective – a swathe of open but inaccessible land half a mile wide and nearly a mile long, much of it now derelict and empty. This was the land which, in the early 1860s, fell into the hands of the Midland, who were bringing their main line through to the projected new station at St Pancras and were looking for a suitable site for their workshops.

Their first choice was St Pancras Old Church and graveyard, which they confidently attempted to purchase. But public concern for ancient monuments was beginning sluggishly to assert itself by the 1860s and the church was denied to the Midland Company; they were, however, allowed to buy much of the eastern portion of the graveyard (i.e. most of what had been the original graveyard). It was supposed that a tunnel 12 feet deep would avoid disturbing any graves, but so much had the height of the ground risen with burials in it over the centuries that bodies were found to lie at that level. A cut-and-cover method, with removal of coffins, was therefore adopted. It was done in considerable haste, at night and behind screens – the young architect Thomas Hardy was one of those present, and was perturbed by the manner of its doing. A much later poem of his is based on that youthful experience.

Mr Agar's old house, where tea parties had been given on the lawns earlier in the century, became railway offices. Agar Town itself was wiped out. But, balked of the amount of space it needed for all its ancillary services, the Midland turned their eyes to the area further to the north, and the first bit of open ground they found was this Kentish Town wedge behind Highgate Road – the estate of a Mr Harrison, descendant of the farming and brick-making family. Indeed the land was said to have been used for brick-making and gravel-digging earlier in the century, and to be rather low-lying and marshy in consequence. Two tributaries of the Fleet ran through it, and there were watercress beds where the streams converged, just north of the present junction of Holmes Road and Spring Place. (To deal with this, clay spoil from the diggings further south in Camden Town was later dumped there – a good example of the indestructibility of matter. Is *that* where the pulverised fragments of the old manor houses finally went?) It was also quite expensive: out of the £35,000 the Midland had to pay out in compensation to various parties for their extension to London, £20,000 was spent just on acquiring Harrison's estate. But presumably the Company reckoned this still came cheaper than buying up a comparable acreage of houses – the only other alternative.

The coming of the Midland after 1864 really constitutes the invasion of Kentish Town by the railway. The London and Birmingham Line into Euston constructed in two stages during the 1830s and 1840s convulsed Camden Town, but did not touch the older suburb up the road; nor did the construction of the Great Northern Line across the fringe of Islington to King's Cross in the early 1850s, though this greatly altered the southern part of St Pancras Borough. Even the extending of the North London Line ('Hampstead Junction Railway') in the late 1850s did not at first seem to threaten great changes for the area, since much of the track north of Prince of Wales Road and the Governesses' Asylum at first ran through open fields. A disastrous railway accident that took place on the line in 1861 occurred in this open terrain: a crashed train fell off the viaduct, but onto open land, not houses as it would have further south. In any case the new branch line to Hampstead was an amenity for the area, opening new possibilities for commuting to the City and for day-excursions to places as daringly distant as Richmond. A school teacher on a working trip to London at that period was enchanted with this new means of getting about – 'making my way to the Railway Station, from there I soon was carried along by that large Tea Kettle called An Engine to Camden Town . . . ' (from an unpublished MS diary). But the Midland, because of the size and central nature of its invasion, was another matter. Kentish Town was once again filling its historic role as a place on a great route north – but the new road was not stone but iron, and the buildings it brought in its wake were not inns and hunting lodges but 'quite a little town in itself, with offices, dwellings, workshops, stables etc.' – in the words of a fulsome Midland Railway circular to shareholders.

There was a good deal of opposition to the Midland Railway Extension to London Bill when it came before Parliament in 1864. The days of total *laissez faire* over expropriation had already passed, and, as already mentioned, the company had to spend a substantial amount in compensation, as well as £12,500 for a new church in Oseney Crescent on the Christ Church Estate, designed by Basil Champneys, to replace the old St Luke's demolished with Agar Town. (It was the new St Luke's that Mr Pike objected to.) The Bill was opposed by the Great Northern Railway Company, the North London Railway Company, the newly-formed Metropolitan Board of Works, St Pancras vestry, the Regent and Grand Junction Canal Companies, and the Imperial Gaslight and Coke Company whose gas works had been on the St Pancras site since 1822. It is, however, obvious that most of these, except the vestry, were opposing the Bill not out of any high-minded concern for the amenities of Kentish Town but out of self-interest: in any case the Bill was eventually passed.

In 1864 the fields of Harrison's estate were mown for the last time. The railway workings began, and continued through 1865 and 1866, though with some setbacks. The first contractor turned out to be under-capitalised and had to be replaced; relations with the St Pancras vestry were not easy and a bond of £15,000 had to be entered into to indemnify them for possible damage to the Fleet sewer. Indeed the cholera epidemic which occurred in the district in 1866 was widely believed to be due to disturbance of the Fleet in its bed of long-lying filth. In the spring and early summer of the year Agar Town and a large chunk of Somers Town disappeared, and the crowding of their population into the northern parts of the parish ('the poor are displaced, but they are not removed') may have had as much to do with the outbreaks of fever as any sewer. A special team was organised by the Medical Officer of Health, who visited 7,000 families in St Pancras parish and found their 'sanitary arrangements were mostly defective'. Many cases reported were probably due to simple dysentery rather than cholera, but several hundred died including the MOH himself. The sewers were sluiced with disinfectants – then a relatively new discovery – and the Metropolitan Board of Works took the opportunity to insist that the Fleet should be cased in iron pipes for the whole of its underground journey. Although these facts are usually quoted as evidence for the insalubrious state of London in the mid-century, they are equally a witness to the gradual rise in standards of public health that had been going on. A hundred years earlier, outbreaks of 'low fever', with deaths, hardly occasioned comment.

Agitation about the waste-disposal arrangements of the vastly expanding metropolis had in any case been going on for over a decade, ever since the major cholera epidemic of 1849, which was generally attributed – probably correctly – to underfloor cess pits. A lot of main sewers had already been laid in the 1850s, though connection to them was voluntary; house-owners paid a sum of money for a connecting drain usually shared with a neighbour. The summer of 1858, with a phenomenally low rainfall, had brought the Great Stink, when the Houses of Parliament found the smell rising from the river Thames – still the common drain for London – almost intolerable. The newspapers of the late 1850s and 1860s are full of discussion on the subject of drains, some people upholding Edwin Chadwick's idea that a comprehensive waterborne sewage system was the only solution for London (and much cheaper in the long run than paying men to empty cess-pools) while others held fast to the belief that such a system would inevitably end by contaminating the drinking water.

Under the sheer pressure of numbers, the social organisation was, of necessity, changing in these years: old parishes like St Pancras were soon to be scissored up into smaller, densely populated parcels, old landmarks were every month being lost. Between 1851 and 1871, the population of St Pancras rose from 166,000 to 221,000. Half way through this period the population of Kentish Town alone was given as 23,000. The old village was all but drowned in a flood of anonymous urbanness, yet through this anonymity a new identity as an urban district was struggling.

The newspapers, particularly the local ones, reflect all this seething growth, but in an inevitably dazed and myopic way. Thus the momentous coming of the railway yards to Kentish Town appears in the *Camden and Kentish Towns Gazette* only as a series of querulous details: new, poor people, it was complained, were crowding into Kentish Town; the railway workings attracted 'riff-raff' and spawned illegitimate babies, some of whom were subsequently to be found dead at the bottom of cuttings or abandoned in convenient railway carriages – the classic no man's land of the late Victorian novel. There were complaints that the noise of the new line was scaring horses in Camden Road (under which the line ran), and an intermittent grumble about lost footpaths and inadequate compensation. The footpath question was in fact debated by the vestry in November 1867, and one could wish they had taken the matter further. Present day Carkers Lane, a dank inlet between two factories on the Highgate Road opposite College Lane entrance, is the rump of a once respectable and useful right-of-way that crossed the fields there in the direction of Hampstead, passing near the Gospel Oak itself. An early plan for the Lismore Circus development allowed for its inclusion and development into a road, but this seems to have been conveniently forgotten by the Midland Railway when the time came.

The Company also suppressed the traditional Gospel Oak Easter Fair, and indeed probably did for the actual Gospel Oak, though a certain mystery surrounds this venerable tree. Various claims have been made for it – there is evidently something about oak trees which makes people lose their sense of the probable – and a motley and fundamentally unlikely selection of people are reported to have preached under it, starting with St Augustine (*c.* 590) and going on to Wycliffe, Wesley and Whitefield (of Whitefield's Tabernacle, Tottenham Court Road). You might well think there would be local consternation when the actual day came for its removal, but in fact the ending of the oak fades into imprecision. On a detailed map of 1834 it is shown very clearly lying near the present Southampton Road (the borough boundary with Hampstead), approximately on the site of the present-day Wendlings Council blocks. Yet the development plan for the Lismore Estate (*c.* 1850) shows it inked in and labelled considerably farther east, in the middle of the present railway land. Had its very existence, by that time, become a matter of myth and romantic conjecture rather than of existential fact? If so, that seems in itself a measure of how far events, unchecked by any responsible overall plan, were overtaking the inner suburbs by the middle decades of the century. Little wonder that, by the 1870s, reminiscences from 'An Old Inhabitant' and 'Glimpses of the Past' had become a regular feature of local papers: local history was by then acquiring the appeal of the fairy tale. References to cow-keepers and hay-fields took on a mythic, visionary quality. The phrase 'railway milk' (which meant milk brought by the new trains and stored in the new refrigeration depots) was spoken with meaning: in practice, it was probably more healthy than milk from cows kept in confined city quarters, but it was regarded as being in some high moral way less desirable. In the same way the new public houses, traditionally stigmatised as 'gin palaces' though the days of ferocious gin-drinking were then past, were regarded as less moral than the old inns had been. Even the ancient 'dwellings of the labouring poor', the huddles of wooden shacks that pre-dated the new streets, were seen, once they had been swept away, with a sentimental eye. The squalidly rural Camden Town dwelling of the chimney sweep in *Dombey and Son* seems regretted by Dickens once it had 'vanished from the earth'. The sweep now lived in 'a stuccoed house three storeys high, and gave himself out, with golden flourishes upon a varnished board, as contractor for the cleansing of railway chimneys by machinery'.

The railways may not have exactly brought the new commercial style, but they typified it. The correspondent who wrote to the *Gazette* in February 1868, the year St Pancras station was finally opened, hit more than one nail on the head. He complained about the new advertisements on the railway arches in Kentish Town Road (the viaduct of the North

London Railway) and went on 'it is most unjust . . . that these great companies should be allowed to disfigure our neighbourhood in this wanton manner. What a storm there would be if a railway company were to attempt to carry a line of arches over Belgravia!'

What indeed. But Kentish Town was not Belgravia, and the proliferation of railways had now ensured that it would never become so. Indeed if all the railways proposed during the boom year of 1863 had actually been built, virtually the whole of the district, the east side as well as the west, would have disappeared under rails and heaps of cinders! There was even a line suggested to Highgate Cemetery, like the Necropolis Company's private line from Westminster Bridge Road to Brookwood in south London.

It seems that the effect of the new acreage of shunting yards on the houses in Highgate Road, and on the terraces off it like Mortimer Terrace and Prospect Place, must have been similar to one of those Victorian scrap books where different pictures are stuck next to one another to create a composite but often ill-matched landscape. One year, the people in the good-class terraces and large, select villas on the west of Highgate Road looked out at the back on fields, hedgerows and elm trees with a clear view towards Hampstead. Two or three years later the frontage of the houses was just the same, the road was just the same – but the back-land had become a landscape of shunting trains. Prospect Place now had a prospect of coal bays. Pleasant Place was a travesty of its name. Except where actual garden space was lost, no one compensated the inhabitants for this grim transformation in their habitat, but it is clear that the bottom fell out of the property market in this particular area. For instance, throughout 1867 and 1868 a big house was interminably advertised in the local paper as being to let for £50 per annum (a price above the mean level, but suspiciously cheap by upper-middle-class standards). It was described as having ten rooms and a conservatory and as being 'three minutes from the Bull and Gate', where the omnibuses stopped – a fulsome phrase which obscured the fact that this placed it squarely in the railway-blighted area, but evidently did not obscure the fact enough to tempt any tenant. Later, the price was reduced further. By the end of 1868 tactics had changed, and similar large houses in the neighbourhood were being advertised with the proximity of the railway as an inducement to purchase: it was suggested that their site would shortly be needed for yet more railways, and that therefore they represented an investment.* But it was not to be. That year, the North London availed themselves of some of the Midland's land to insert a branch-line to Tottenham which crossed Highgate Road. It carried away with it the playground of Southampton House Academy and St John's Park House opposite, but did not involve much demolition of houses. Highgate Cemetery never got its necropolis line, perhaps because it would have had to cross the land of Angela Burdett-Coutts. The railway had come, had done its worst and then swept on, cutting off streets and lanes leaving behind a permanent legacy of smuts, fumes, noise, vibration, but leaving also houses, gardens, people stranded in its wake.

Those who could, obviously moved out. Ford Madox Brown the painter left Fortess Terrace in 1866. Comparison of Censuses for the Highgate Road area in 1861 and 1871 is instructive. In Lower and Upper Craven Place and Francis Terrace, ascending the Highgate Road, people with several servants lived in 1861, including two doctors with resident apprentices. There was another doctor in Bridge House opposite. There were the ubiquitous small academies. Further up, in Fitzroy Terrace, was the entrance to a remarkable late example of the pleasure garden – Weston's Retreat. Mr Weston only opened the place at about that time, converting his own garden and gradually adding grottoes, fountains and cascades; he advertised firework displays, the traditional balloon ascents and other delights, all readily accessible by omnibus from central London. He claimed that his gardens covered seven acres and were lit by 100,000 gas jets, neither of which is believable. The vestry, who had at first been opposed to his venture on the grounds that it opened on Sundays, later commended him for keeping 'howling cads' out of his premises, but this did not save his Retreat. The whole chimera was swept away by the railway within five years, so Mr Weston may have been a

---

* It rather looks, from the newspaper reports of Pike's law suit, as if at this period he unsuccessfully attempted to get the Midland Railway to include his little plot within their plan, and that this was yet another bone of contention with his neighbours.

compensation-hunter; but, if so, he was not a successful one: the news-paper of 1868 records his bankruptcy, by which time he was working as chairman at the Bedford Music Hall, Camden Town. Fittingly, several years later Weston's house was being lived in by a Mr Wedderburn, Railway Superintendent.

The overall picture in 1871 is of a far greater number of houses in multi-occupation than before. Some, as you would expect, retained middle-class tenants, but others had become crowded: that is, the social mix was now considerable. For instance, at 53 Highgate Road were living, in 1871, a coachman, his wife and four sons, all of whom, down to the six year old, were listed as 'locomotive cleaners'. An engine fitter, his wife and son lived in the same house. Further up again, at 103, a cow-keeper still lived, but in the houses on either side of him were engine-fitters. In 109, a substantial Georgian house whose three-storey bay at the back had previously commanded a fine view to Hampstead, lived a widow of forty-five and one servant. Next door lived a sixty-one-year-old comedian and his family. Further north again, in the section of the road formerly known as 'Green Street', which was par-ticularly badly blighted, the social decline was more pronounced. Labourers, charwomen, hawkers of china and many other ephemeral trades of the Victorian era, had moved in. And this, it should be remembered, was less than five years after the railway's establishment. I suspect that the Census for 1881 may show a more pronounced decline and a progressive thinning of the numbers of middle-class tenants still hanging on, but at the time of writing (1976) that Census is not yet available to be consulted. By law, one hundred years has to elapse before the possibly scandalous secrets of people's domestic arrange-ments may be casually exposed.

Several new churches were built to minister to the supposedly urgent spiritual needs of the greatly-increasing population: rather fortunately however, as it has turned out, the scheme enthusiastically submitted by Canon Dale (the vicar of St Pancras) for *ten* new Church of England churches in the old parish was firmly opposed by both vestry and parishioners on the grounds of expense. The churches that did get built mostly stand today forlorn and quiet, their expensively rough-hewn stone darkened by a hundred years of soot, houses in which God Himself can no longer afford to live. In their day, they were crowded, particularly the non-conformist   ones where popular preachers (including Spurgeon) promised their pleasantly titillated congregation hell-fire and damnation – but it should not be supposed that 'everyone went to church then', either in Kentish Town or anywhere else. Universal church-going is one of those golden age myths: 'everyone' never went to church. It was mainly indulged in – often indeed to excess – by middle-class families such as the Pikes, by the more respectable working class with middle-class aspirations, and by the not-quite-so-respectable who went for what they could get out of it in the way of Sunday School prizes and boots for the children. But as social institutions and foci for local life the importance of the churches in newly urbanised areas like Kentish Town would be hard to overestimate, and charitably-minded clergymen were among the most prominent and powerful of local figures. Two ragged schools were opened in Kentish Town in the late 1860s, one in Reeds Place near the Rotunda Organ factory and another off Hawley Road. A mission hall was presently opened in Warden Road – Lyndhurst Hall, a mission-to-the-slums administered from the new church at the corner of Lyndhurst Road, Hampstead, a fact which tells one much about what was happening in Kentish Town at this time. Soup kitchens and free dispensaries were opened in Leighton Road and in Holmes Road, supported by voluntary contributions – the buildings still stand, now under the aegis of the all-benevolent Council. Bags of coal were distributed. Penny readings were held in the church schools, which were almost invariably described by the local press as having been 'a great success despite the inclement weather'. Ladies, from Baroness Burdett-Coutts downwards (both socially and geographically) held perpetual sales of work at which the proceeds of their ample leisure hours were sold to raise money. 'Berlin woolwork' was the most favoured form of pastime, and there were shops in Kentish Town devoted to selling solely the materials for that, at three-pence farthing the dozen skeins.

The management of St Pancras workhouse (down by the Old Church)

---

*   One of these, the Wesleyan Methodist church by Tarring in Lady Margaret Road (1865) has recently re-populated itself by becoming an RC church. What *would* the original congregation say?

and its local relieving stations, where grudging handouts were made to people who were not workhouse inmates, was the subject of continual dissension through the 1850s and 1860s. In 1868 a running battle was going on between Harding, the Medical Officer to the Board, and Chapple, a relieving officer of 'over-bearing manner'. It was said in the vestry meeting that Mr Harding was kind to the poor but that 'some considered him too meddling'. It is not clear whether he won his battle with the Relieving Officer, or whether the same quarrel was still continuing two years later. In the January of 1870 a girl of nineteen with a baby in her arms walked about the streets all one bitter December day, because an old man in the relieving office at Grafton Hall (west Kentish Town) told her when she came in the morning that the officer was not there and told her the same thing again in the late afternoon: in neither case was it true. The girl finally collapsed on the doorstep of the house belonging to Mr Flemming, a prominent non-conformist minister in the district. Mrs Flemming sustained her with bread and butter and sympathy; the muddle was sorted out, and mother and child were admitted to the workhouse. But the baby afterwards died of bronchitis said to have been contracted that cold day. The report of the inquest continued: 'The Coroner said the worst of it was that a sturdy beggar, who knew how to go about it, could get anything he wanted, but a poor girl was turned aside.'

How had the antique machinery of local government – the vestry – coped with the enormous change and growth in the borough during the first half of the nineteenth century? The answer, not surprisingly, is 'very badly'. The subject of local government in St Pancras, and its major task, the administration of the Poor Law, would require a book on its own to do it justice, and it constitutes in any case part of the history of St Pancras parish as a whole rather than of Kentish Town. Very briefly, the traditional method of local government in each parish had been by open vestry, a sort of parish council presided over by the vicar and church-wardens but which every parishioner had the right to attend. By the eighteenth century, with the slow but steady influx of people into areas like St Pancras and the adjacent parish of St Marylebone, and in particular the appearance of a substantial number of middle-class people who liked to run matters their own way, this form of homespun democracy was beginning to seem too cumbersome and disorganised. In Marylebone in 1768 a handful of local landowners managed to persuade Parliament to pass a Local Act converting the Open Vestry to a Select Vestry consisting mainly of themselves. St Pancras then attempted to follow suit, but met with greater difficulty. At the turn of the century a twenty-year fight ensued, led by Thomas Rhodes, the farmer of the southern end of the parish whose lands extended into Marylebone also, and who served at various times as a churchwarden and as an Overseer of the Poor. As the duties and responsibilities of the vestry, particularly towards the poor, increased in proportion with the population, he became a powerful local figure. When the Select Vestry was finally introduced in 1819 he naturally became one of its first members, along with the Duke of Bedford, the Lords Camden, Somers, Mansfield, Dartmouth, Southampton and prominent local citizens. He did not finally die till 1856, when he was ninety-three, and the parish had been transformed out of all recognition from the area he had known as a boy and young man.

Of the change to Select Vestry, Walter E. Brown, who was cemetery clerk to the vestry right at the end of the nineteenth century, just before it became the Borough Council, has written:

> . . . the people were somehow blindly feeling their way towards representative government in local affairs. The Select Vestry was supposed to be a step in that direction, but it was soon discovered to be a retrograde one. Inefficient as it was for the performance of the many duties that accumulated, the old system, at least, was self-government; but the Vestry created under the new Act rendered great landlords and property owners absolute masters of the situation . . . It is not to be supposed that the rate-payers, who were increasing daily in power and numbers, were content to allow the representatives of an oligarchy to usurp those rights which should be exercised by themselves, and to consent to be, so to speak, wiped out in thus summary manner. The result was that, for ten years, constant quarrels took place . . .

These quarrels, then and later, centred mainly on provisions for the poor and the poor rate levied to pay for these. By the Act of 1819 the

Directors of the Poor became subservient to, and were elected by, the vestry: in practice, they were often the very same clique. The 1820s saw a number of petitions to Parliament from irate ratepayers, who resented the fact that they were asked to do nothing but indeed pay the rates, and in 1832 with the New Vestries Act the system was modified: in future the ratepayers were to choose and elect the vestry rather than the vestry being self-selecting and thus self-perpetuating. But there again in practice very much the same names cropped up. Two years later, the Directors of the Poor became the Poor Law Commissioners and there some new blood must have come in, for the late 1830s were marked by a series of expensive legal proceedings, the result of the Commissioners trying to have things their own way and the vestry 'protecting the interests of the rate-payers' (i.e. refusing to raise the poor rate). At one point two rival sets of Poor Law officials were in existence, both approved of by an unwise vicar trying vainly to keep the peace! Guerilla warfare continued, matters not helped by the fact that the workhouse built for 500 near the Old Church during the early years of the century was now accommodating over 1,000 and the whole poor relief system was cracking at the seams. Something of a climax was reached in 1852, when the vestry took the keys of the workhouse away and wanted to dismiss the Master. The Poor Law Commissioners claimed they had no right to do this, and the vestry fought back with handbills and posters proclaiming 'Invasion by the Poor Law Commissioners of the Rights and Privileges of the Vestry and Ratepayers'. The Commissioners finally backed down, but the rows went on.

In 1855 the Local Management of the Metropolis Act changed matters considerably, even if it did not put an end to endemic wrangles between those responsible for levying money and those responsible for spending it, or to running complaints about the state of the workhouse, whose surroundings (Agar Town and St Pancras Cemetery) had become very insalubrious. By the time of the Act the internal affairs of St Pancras parish were so disorganised that special mention of it as a notorious case was made in Parliament by Sir Benjamin Hall, who drafted the Act, which paved the way – to use the metaphor that seems apt – for a lot of physical tidying up in Kentish Town. The sixteen inefficient local paving boards were superseded. Regular strings of gas lamps began to replace the old, intermittent naphtha flares along the main streets; a lot more sewers got laid – so much so that when, some ten years later, it was revealed at a vestry meeting that the parish had not actually got the power to prevent a builder building houses without drainage, at least one vestryman was surprised to hear it. (The road in question was Chester Road, off York Rise, part of the northern end of the district then rapidly developing and filling up with railway porters, drivers, ticket collectors and their families.) But old-style corruption did not disappear just like that. Instructive is a newspaper report of a Ratepayers' Association Meeting which took place in September 1867:

> In reference to the erection of district relieving offices, the proposal with regard to paying 17s. 6d. per foot frontage for building ground in Mansfield Place, Kentish Town [now Holmes Road], was very warmly discussed; the price was considered exorbitant, and fault was found with Mr Joseph Salter for pushing the matter so strenuously in the Vestry, he being the agent for the estate. It had been said that the landlord demanded a higher price on account of the depreciation of the adjoining property by the proposed erections; but this was a very poor reason for asking so high a sum: there was already on the site a public house, a railway and a manufacturey, and the neighbourhood was about the lowest in all Kentish Town.

This Joseph Salter was a significant figure in the area for many years – one of those Thomas Rhodes-like characters with a finger in every local pie. Only, as Rhodes typified his own generation by being a farmer-turned-builder, Salter typified his by being an insurance office agent, auctioneer, rent-collector and ultimately estate agent with a special line in valuations for railway compensation. He set up shop in New Chapel Place in 1854, just as the building explosion in Kentish Town was really getting under way: a few years later, as his family rapidly expanded, he moved his business premises up the street to Holmes Place, which later became 311 Kentish Town Road. The business remained there, as 'Salter Rex', till 1975, when new offices were built nearby. It is still the chief estate agent in Kentish Town.

Joseph Salter was at various times auditor to the vestry, Chairman of the Board of Works (he opposed the Metropolitan Improvement

Rate in 1866) and a Poor Law Commissioner who was re-elected as a Guardian when the Gaythorne-Hardy Act of 1867 finally severed the long and acrimonious partnership of the Poor Law administrators and the vestry. Another Salter, Jonathan, whom I believe to have been Joseph's brother and owner of a prosperous drapers in Camden Town, was similarly a vestryman and a Poor Law Guardian and was eventually presented with a gold watch in return for fifty years service. (A fact which gives pause for thought, when you consider the vicissitudes both vestry and Poor Law had gone through in that period.) Jonathan Salter's attitude to his duties can best be summed up by the fact that, when the matter of distributing new clothing to children in the workhouse came up, he 'wished the new style of clothing to be given to the best conducted children'. Joseph, however, as a father of twelve, seems to have been of a rather more charitable turn of mind, provided his own interests were not at stake: it was his suggestion that, at Christmas 1867, 'some small toys should be supplied to the [workhouse] children . . . the Master was authorised to expend £2 in their purchase.' At all events he had inspired sufficient respect and gratitude by the time he died in 1876 to have a granite fountain and drinking trough erected in his memory at the corner of College Gardens – a scrap of green space at the junction of Royal College Street and St Pancras Way, which the vestry had earlier managed to preserve from being turned into roadway.

The horses for whom the drinking trough was a kindly thought have long vanished, except for the occasional scrap-iron dealer's cart, and the trough is dry, but the fountain still works on one side and is an amenity for the drunks, tramps and other isolated misfits sometimes to be seen in the gardens, sheltering under the reverberating railway bridge that spans it.

10

With Gas and Attendance

I have in my possession a little book, dated 1864 and sold then for one shilling, entitled *How I Managed My House on £200 a Year*. At an early point in this minutely detailed account we have the archetypal Victorian clerk, and paterfamilias in prospect, telling his wife that he has found a house for them in an expanding suburb 'near Islington':

> The house at thirty pounds, which stands in the open space of garden ground, close to the field of forty acres, will be just the thing for us. I should think it would be some years before the now pretty view can be built out. It is only three miles from London, perhaps a little more to the office, but that does not signify. The house is just the one for us; I mean the finished one of the four houses near to the church which is in progress. We shall have no neighbours yet, and I have observed very common people do not live in semi-detached houses; they like to congregate near a market, and so ought we, as a matter of economy, but I think fresh air better than very cheap food. So, little wife, it is settled . . .

It is instructive to compare this, and the description that follows of their removal to this new, exciting, remote spot, with the description in George Grossmith's *Diary of a Nobody* of the Pooters moving into what might be precisely the same house, thirty years later:

> My dear wife Carrie and I have just been a week in our new house, 'The Laurels', Brickfield Terrace, Holloway – a nice, six-roomed residence, not counting basement, with a front breakfast-parlour. We have a little front garden; and there is a flight of ten steps up to the front door, which, by the by, we keep locked with the chain up . . . We have a nice little back garden which runs down to the railway. We

were rather afraid of the noise of the trains at first, but the landlord said we should not notice them after a bit and took £2 off the bill. He was certainly right, and beyond the cracking of the garden wall at the bottom, we have suffered no inconvenience.

It is interesting that, despite the impeccable respectability of the Pooters (Mr Pooter is a senior clerk in the firm where he had been for the last twenty years) there is a slight implication of social decline where the house is concerned. It was not, obviously, intended by the builder that the inhabitants should leave the front door locked all the time and come and go 'to the little side entrance, which saves the servant the trouble of going up to the front door, thereby taking from her work'. Moreover the possession of only *one* servant (two was then the upper-middle-class norm) is an indication intended to place the Pooters irrevocably in a certain category. The nature of life in the inner suburbs was by then recognised by everyone; it was fossilising into a joke, and George Grossmith, Pooter's creator, was one of those who helped to crystallise it. He was born and grew up in the Camden – Kentish Town area: he knew all about that sort of life. There is even a subtle innuendo in the address 'Brickfield Terrace, Holloway'. Most of Holloway proper, like Tufnell Park, was not laid out till the late Victorian era, but Weedon Grossmith's illustration clearly shows a house of the late 1850s or 1860s. The point is that, by the end of the century, the practice was in vogue of euphemising an address in barely-respectable Kentish Town as 'Holloway', 'North St Pancras' or 'Highgate Rise'. For Kentish Town had lost, by the last quarter of the nineteenth century, the battle to remain a desirable area. Palmer, writing in 1870, remarked 'the green fields . . . have passed away, and lines of streets connect it with the Holloway Road'. Less than twenty years later, the *London Argus* was uncompromisingly damning about the place: 'The district today has not much to recommend it. It is one of those shabby, prosaic, monotonous residential quarters that could well be spared from the Metropolis.'

People were to go on saying that, in various ways, for the next sixty years. The era of 'slum clearance' was as yet only on the horizon but was in sight – that middle-class and bureaucratic obsession with destroying the habitat of people who have no say in the matter, in the name of progress, morality and a Brave New World. A curious idea seems to have got about, which is still to be found today, that the evils of what was coming to be called 'suburban sprawl' can be considered in isolation from the needs of the population which have created the sprawl in the first place. William Morris spoke of the growth of London as a 'spreading sore . . . swallowing up in its loathsomeness field and wood and heath without mercy and without hope'. In fact, of course, Kentish Town like most of the other old suburbs couldn't possibly be 'spared from the Metropolis' because, apart from anything else, very large numbers of people lived in these areas. In 1881 the population of St Pancras reached its highest level ever – 236,258 (it has been decreasing slightly but steadily ever since). The number of houses, however, was more or less the same – under 26,000 – as it had been ten years earlier, when the population was 15,000 fewer. So evidently the overcrowding had become slightly worse. Most of the worse-crowded areas were not in Kentish Town itself, except for a few pockets in west Kentish Town, but it is clear that a lot of houses by then even in the relatively 'nicer' streets, were already in multi-occupation, and most remained so from then on.

Lodgers were very much a feature of Victorian and Edwardian life in both the working classes and the lower-middle class, though sometimes in the latter a polite pretence was maintained, for the landlord and the neighbours, that the outsider was a friend visiting. Indeed couples just setting up together commonly rented a house bigger than they needed, intending to balance their budget by installing some docile sub-tenant in the 'first floor front' or the 'third floor back'. The song of the period, *Our Lodger's Such a Nice Young Man*, presents the archetypal one, a young man come to London to work, of slightly higher social class than his landlord and landlady and on occasions a source of violent marital upheaval. It will be noted that Gowing, Mr Pooter's rather more knowing friend, is a lodger in someone else's house. But frequently couples or even whole families took what were called 'apartments' in someone else's house; local newspapers of the late nineteenth century are full of advertisements for these at 20 words for 6d. – 'Apartments, furnished – Drawing and Bedroom or Bedroom with use of Parlour, with or without Board', 'To Let, a Drawing Room floor of Three or Four Rooms. Gas if required. Use of kitchen.' A frequent phrase is 'With gas and attendance'; presumably these had by then become the recognised signs of a civilised existence. Occasionally when advertising for 'a General Servant' a prospective employer would stress the fact that lodgers were *not* kept, which gives one a certain insight into the life led by a general servant in houses where lodgers were a feature. Other landladies seem simply to want a tenant who would be as little trouble as possible: 'Unfurnished room – first floor – suitable for a widow, or single person without occupation.'

That advertisement strikes a chill to the heart. Why the person offering the room should prefer an occupationless lone person to one who had at least a job to go to to dilute the absolute solitude and monotony of his or her life, it is hard to see. Presumably the advertisement is saying in code that a lodger of some modest means and therefore gentility is wanted rather than a 'shop girl'. One recalls General William Booth's passionate remarks on the subject:

> In London at the present moment how many hundreds, nay thousands, of young men and young women, who are living in lodgings, are practically without any opportunity of making the acquaintance of each other, or of anyone of the other sex! The street is no doubt the city substitute for the village green, and what a substitute it is!
>
> It has been bitterly said by one who knew well what he was talking about 'There are thousands of young men today who have no right to call any woman by her Christian name, except the girls they meet plying their dreadful trade in our public thoroughfares.' As long as that is the case, vice has an enormous advantage over virtue; such an abnormal social arrangement interdicts morality and places a vast premium upon prostitution. We must get back to nature if we have to cope with this ghastly evil. (*In Darkest London*, 1890)

General Booth approaches the subject from a different angle to that usually adopted by twentieth-century commentators, but in essence the diagnosis of the 'lonely bed-sitter syndrome' is the same. This remained a significant element in the life of the inner suburbs throughout the first half of the twentieth century, and is only dying out now under pressure of cumulative social change, greatly increased council ownership of property, and the unfortunate effects of several well-intentioned Rent

Acts, which have turned the renting of rooms into a complex legal situation which erstwhile landlords and landladies are afraid to enter.

It is to be hoped that as the nineteenth century drew towards its close, and a mild emancipation of women began to create for the first time a host of female office workers living in something like independence and travelling about on the new Metropolitan Railway and the 'Twopenny Tube',* it was possible for people in places like Kentish Town to find company elsewhere than on the street. Bicycling clubs flourished in the 1890s; with the chances they offered for informal, unchaperoned but essentially respectable and healthy trips to the neighbouring countryside, they were a considerable force for social liberation. Pooter's friends Gowing and Cummings are both eager subscribers to the *Bicycle News*. Lupin, Pooter's unsatisfactory son, does not go in for anything quite so energetic, but prefers the opportunities for making new acquaintances offered by amateur theatricals: he is a leading light of the 'Holloway Comedians', and it was there that he met Daisy Mutlar who, without being (of course) a Bad Girl, is the prototype of the 'fast young lady' of the period.

Even Lupin, for all his tiresome behaviour, his slang and his over-high collars, subscribes basically to exactly the same set of social rules as his quintessentially respectable father. Lupin associates with City types who give him dubious tips about shares, but *never* with members of the working class, not even servant girls. The Pooters' one servant, Sarah, seems to be young, and inevitably lives, in such a small house, at close quarters with her master and mistress: Pooter actually comes upstairs and paints her wash-stand and towel horse bright red for her, for which she is unaccountably ungrateful, but it never seems to enter anyone's

---

* The Northern Line itself was planned in the 1890s and finally opened in 1907. It was originally envisaged that the line would stop in Kentish Town, but it was later decided to extend it to Archway. (Further extension to Finchley and Barnet came a generation later.) South Kentish Town, between Camden Town and Kentish Town, was closed between the wars. It was considered too close to the stations on either side for it to earn its keep. It had been originally intended to name it 'Castle Road'. Had this name persisted, the whole of southern Kentish Town would now, no doubt, be known as 'the Castle Road area'. Such is the power of transport.

mind that she might be seen as a conceivable object for Lupin's free-floating desires. By the same token Sarah, no doubt, kept herself to herself and would not have dreamed of paying attention to the grocer's boy, who only appears as a dishevelled figure picking the paint blisters off the back door. He would have come (say) from Harmood Street or Inkerman Street, while the Pooters lived in (say) Leighton Road or Islip Street, near but on the opposite side of the district. From Harmood Street and its purlieus too would have come the little step girls who, in respectable streets, came and scrubbed the front doorsteps for house-wives like the unfortunate Mrs Pike, who were too poor to employ a servant but too conscious of their precariously maintained status to want to be seen cleaning the step themselves. Frederick Willis, who in old age wrote *A Book of London Yesterdays* about his own youth, delineates the social hierarchy in such districts with precision:

> The step girl was a child of about ten or eleven, progeny of the poorest section of local society, and free from the terrifying restraints of class consciousness . . . This child, member of a class similar to the Untouchables of India, provided her own apron (an old sack torn in half) and for a few coppers removed the fear of social ostracism from the housewife . . . The young servant girls were, of course, members of a higher grade of society, and they had to maintain their dignity when dealing with the untouchables, but when they went out with the Lady of the House on a shopping expedition, which frequently happened, they always walked at a respectful distance in the rear, carrying a large shopping bag. Meanwhile, no doubt, their mistress's husband was grovelling at the feet of a wholesale draper in St Paul's Churchyard. Thus society was kept in its proper station all along the line.

A constant preoccupation with 'the terrifying restraints of class consciousness' is indeed breathed out by the musty, long-unread pages of the local press of the period. Disproportionate numbers of the people of both sexes inserting small ads seemed to wish to give private music lessons or occasionally drawing and painting lessons – the traditional resorts of the impecunious gentry too poorly educated to do anything but pass on their minor skills to pupils who would end up as ill-equipped for life as themselves. No doubt between taking in lodgers and teaching scales to the daughters of local shopkeepers, you could maintain something that would pass for a middle-class existence. To many of the struggling 'music masters' and the like, 'taking a job as a clerk', even had one been available, would have seemed a form of social defeat almost worse than loss of respectability. If a gentleman could not have a proper profession (which in strict terms meant the law, medicine, or the Church), then at least he could claim status by clinging to artistic pretensions.

Yet for the large working class of areas like Kentish Town 'a job in an office' was the pinnacle of ambition. To this end, 'Mutual Improvement' societies, private schools and evening schools flourished, both before and after the establishment of the Board Schools in 1870, for Board Schools only offered the 3 Rs. Typical was the 'Camden Hall Evening School for Young Men . . . Book keeping, arithmetic, reading and writing etc'. A day school that flourished in the area was frankly called 'The Camden and Kentish Towns Middle Class School . . . Terms a Guinea and One-and-a-half guineas. No extras except Greek and German.' Others had more imposing names, such as the 'English and Foreign Collegiate School, Bellevue House' – which impresses till you realise that it is in the Kentish Town Road. 'Collegiate' was a favourite, somewhat empty term to designate a private school at the period; even the redoubtable Miss Buss used the word for the name of the school she first founded in Camden Town in 1851, where George Grossmith is alleged to have been an usher. When she founded her second school, the Camden School for Girls, in 1871, she was aiming at a slightly lower social class than the 'gentlemen of limited means' who fathered the clientele of the North London Collegiate School, and charged lower fees in consequence. Her new pupils – forty at the start – were the daughters of clerks, tailors, 'civil servants', builders, grocers, curates, a cattle salesman, a boarding house keeper, a boot maker, a police inspector, a piano tuner and a jeweller. Miss Buss found their ignorance of the most normal items of general knowledge 'beyond belief'.

Very large numbers of people in the course of the nineteenth century managed to hoist themselves from humble, usually rural beginnings into the urban middle class, but it appears that still more were constantly hoping to make this grade by one means or another. The Kentish Town inhabitant who inserted the following advertisement possibly got a better response to her offer than the legion trying to sell the less fundamental drawing or music lessons: 'Ladies of Neglected Education: Instructive Reading and Writing Lessons by an easy method, privately given by A Lady. Terms moderate.' 'You too can be a lady', in fact. Just as much of Kentish Town was built on the over-optimistic assumption that there were large numbers of people of professional status and means just waiting to come and live there, so many of the lower-middle and working-class people who did in fact come to occupy the houses possibly had aspirations beyond their station which were similarly destined to be unfulfilled. The Board Schools may not have provided a clerical education, but they did provide near-universal literacy and implanted in the minds of both pupils and parents the idea of social betterment. Twenty years after their establishment, General Booth was writing: ' . . . Another great evil is the extent to which our Education tends to overstock the labour market with material for quill-drivers and shopmen, and gives our youth a distaste for sturdy labour.' Somewhat earlier, a correspondent to the *Camden and Kentish Towns Gazette* voiced the same opinion:

> In some parts of London it is impossible to find a sufficient number of skilled workmen in various departments both of useful and ornamental art; such as joiners and decorators, and even carpenters and metal-workers. The young men who ought to supply demand prefer starving on the 'beggarly respectability' of office work. There is a growing dislike to manual labour amongst the lower section of middle class which is painfully apparent to those who see much of commercial life. Parents are eager to get their sons into houses of business where they may maintain the appearance, if not the standing, of gentlemen. The City is crowded with well-educated lads who are doing men's work for boys' wages.

This is the paradox of the late nineteenth century – that whereas there was a superficial (and much advertised) increase in 'refinement', as cheap public transport replaced the walk to work, education replaced child-labour, gas-light replaced oil lamps, paving replaced mud, sewers replaced cess-pits and middens, bathrooms began to be a common feature even at lower middle-class level and the streets were beautified with drinking fountains and urinals – while all these embellishments were coming to the inner suburbs, their social status was steadily sinking to the low point at which it remained for the next half-century. Well might the St Pancras vestry – finally reformed from its bad old practices – pride itself on its street cleaning, its road widening, its public baths, its early introduction of electricity, its new progressive image. Such things had become the only possible saving graces in a district which, from about 1850, had gradually transformed itself from a place of beauty and charm into the physical embodiment of Matthew Arnold's 'dismal, illiberal life'. Today, we are already seeing the London of the turn-of-the-century through the distorting glass of nostalgia: when we look, for instance, at the photographs taken by London Transport in 1903 and 1904 of the entire route under which they were preparing to build the Northern Line, we are attracted by the vital appearance of the streets, the elaborate lettering of the shop-signs, in particular by the absence of motorised traffic. Now that the motor car and the grandiose follies of town planners have between them wiped out much of this old urban habitat, we mourn it and feel that it must have been a good one. But at the time it had its own horror, and struck a fear into the minds of sensitive or historically-minded people which, though rational up to a point, was nevertheless not entirely explicable in rational terms. Cobbett's 'Wen', Morris's 'spreading sore' – significantly both are metaphors of disease within a body: evidently there were felt to be dark forces at work within the huge body of the metropolis which were effectively beyond control. Nor was it just a question of spreading houses infecting the country, but also of chronic decay within the already-built quarters. Making use of the same metaphor, a modern commentator has written:

> By the 1860s . . . slums were oozing out not just over east and south London but north as well. They pursued the middle classes along the main roads and up alongside the railway tracks, seeping in wherever an estate had relaxed its guard, wherever industry had lowered the desirability of a district or wherever the housing market hit a bad patch . . . It became a sort of plague, infecting one area after another. (Simon) Jenkins, *Landlords to London*, 1975)

The middle classes responded to this threat by flight, building new homes further and further out (future areas for the plague to strike) and by developing an obsession with the likelihood of this or that district 'going down' which lasted all through the first half of the twentieth century and was frequently a self-fulfilling prophecy. Sensing whether or not a place was 'going down' was like picking up a bad smell: some people were better at it than others, but everyone sat round sniffing, alert for the first signs. The word 'slum' itself began to be used more and more casually and subjectively, so that a 'slum' came to be almost any street where lived people of a perceptibly lower class than oneself. Thus in the perception of the upper middle classes who had disappeared into the blue hills of Hampstead and Highgate and beyond – to Welwyn and Radlett and all that part of ex-rural England later publicised as 'Metroland' – virtually the whole of the old inner ring suburbs became indiscriminately 'the slums': a country as undiscovered as Darkest Africa, where coughing men in mufflers sold matches on 'greasy' street corners, and 'slum children' in torn pinafores 'never saw a blade of grass'. Meanwhile there was, in reality, plenty of grass, and trees, in many parts of Kentish Town, Camden Town, Islington, Hackney, Clapham, Brixton, Lambeth and even in Bermondsey and Deptford. There were also large numbers of entirely self-respecting and comfortable people, who might well have declared, as Mr Pooter did in the end, that they loved their homes and their neighbourhood and did not want to move. But in their own eyes these people were living not of course *in* slums but rather uncomfortably near them. 'Slums' in people's reminiscences are always two or three streets away, never quite on their own doorstep.

Thus Alfred Grosch, who was born in 1888 in west Kentish Town, wrote towards the end of his life:

People were brutal and pugnacious. Kentish Town in those days possessed an unenviable number of slum streets down which police-men went as seldom as possible, never if they could avoid them. I could name a dozen such streets within a stone's throw of our house . . . The houses were more like dens than human dwellings. They had been houses, but landlords, concerned only with what could be obtained from them by way of rent, had long ceased to spend money on them, and in consequence brickwork and woodwork rotted for want of paint, while vermin had rendered internal decoration a sheer waste of

money . . . Barefoot, hungry children, clad in rags, were a common
sight as they raked over the refuse heaps of Queen's Crescent, a market
place, in search of half-rotten fruit to eat. Drunken women were
frequently to be met with at any hour of the day, sometimes with
children in their arms . . . (*St Pancras Pavements*, 1947).

Obviously there was some basis for this lurid picture: murders did
occur, typically arising from fights in public houses; a gang called (by
the local paper) the 'Malden Road Roughs' made a nuisance of themselves; there were some pockets of genuine slum property, mainly on
the Holmes Estate adjoining both Malden Road and Queen's Crescent,
where were some of the oldest buildings in the district. But one also
senses in Grosch's account the almost paranoid fear of the respectable
tradesman for the class beneath him, and the wish to regard this class as
another form of life. His father owned a corn-and-seed business at 10,
Malden Road, where 'Trade was good, the premises in a fine position':
clearly he must have had other customers besides the brutal, the
pugnacious and the hungry: 'My father's shop . . . stood at the bottom
end of Malden Road, being fifth from the beginning in a row of shops
that went to 18, even numbers. The corner shop, a tea-grocer's, was kept
by a bearded and most gentlemanly tradesman . . . He affected a black
apron – my father always wore a white one – and an alpaca jacket. On
Sundays, should it chance that we met him out, there would take place a
very grave and dignified hat-raising ceremonial.' Hardly a slum shop-
keeper. The next shop was a coffee shop and dining rooms, then a bacon
shop. Then came a watch-maker and jeweller's 'kept by very nice and
neighbourly people with several sons, and able to afford a maid'. Then
came the corn-and-seed-business, then an umbrella makers, then a toy-
shop, then an oil-and-colour shop 'whose chief assets were two pretty
and vivacious daughters'. Round the corner in a mews was a blacksmith.
Opposite, across the tramlines, was the Mother Shipton.
    By chance, although a large part of Malden Road and its backstreets
was redeveloped in the late 1960s and early 1970s, pub, mews and run of
shops are all still in existence. It may be instructive to add here what the
shops are at the time of writing. The corn-and-seed merchants now sells
second-hand office equipment, as does its neighbour (same firm). The

corner shop where the gentlemanly grocer lived is a Neighbourhood Aid Centre, its window decorated with cartoon posters about tenants' rights. The coffee and dining rooms used to be a junk furniture dealer's but has in recent years gradually elevated itself into a true antique shop. The bacon shop is the headquarters of Task Force, another of those bene-volent enterprises which now cluster as thickly in west Kentish Town as the old 'slum missions' and soup kitchens ever did. Then come two shuttered shops – also a feature of Kentish Town today – and then a 'Centre for Re-cycling' which opened in the optimistic belief that patrons would bring to it and take from it objects of roughly equivalent value, but which soon degenerated into a dumping ground for rusting, broken pushchairs, dismantled water-heaters of an obsolete pattern and sodden sofas with the stuffing sprouting like fungus. The oil-and-colour shop where lived the 'two pretty and vivacious daughters' is now a cheap clothes-boutique called 'Route 24' – the number of the bus that has replaced the Malden Road trams.

What, one wonders, would Alfred Grosch make of this heterogeneous collection? How would he diagnose the relative social rise or fall of the area from it? His own admission of the subjective element in these matters is significant. When he returned to Malden Road as a young man after a few years away, 'There was no disguising the fact that Number 10 and its surroundings were dirty and dreary. Indeed I am convinced that they were never otherwise, but had only seemed so when lit up by the early enthusiasm of my parents . . . ' Those who have moved away from an area long ago are more likely, even if their childhood was a happy one, to see it as a bad area from which they have 'escaped', and to exaggerate the slums of their childhood as a form of self-dramatisation. In contrast those who have remained in the same area, though they may admit on questioning that in their youth there were streets where they were not allowed to go, are more apt to harp on vanished elegances. Another survivor of Grosch's era, today's oldest inhabitant in trading terms, who has been selling stationery and books in the High Street since 1917 in the shop where his father sold cut-price three-volume novels before him, became eloquent as he recalled for me the lost world of small shopkeeping:

It was all so different then, I really can't convey it . . . Kentish Town
High Street was a lovely place then. It was all shops like ourselves –
grocers and clothing shops, private businesses. There was a corn-
chandler's opposite and next door a greengrocer's. The greengrocer
kept horses out at the back because he used to trade in them. He
always wore old-fashioned farmer's corduroys with a two-button
flap in front and he used to stand there with his hand in one pocket
and a wad of money there, just over his stomach. One morning he
said to my father, slapping his stomach, 'I've just paid for the freehold
of this place.' So my father made enquiries and managed to buy the
freehold of ours too. It was a lucky thing he did, with the way rents
go up today . . . I remember Mr Dunn, the owner of the hatter's next
door to us. He used to come and upset his poor manager by just
arriving in the morning and staring at the window display and then
he used to come in here for an hour or more and talk to my father,
smoking a lovely big cigar. You could smell it after he had gone. And
when he died he left in his will that Dunn's were to go on doing as
much business with us as possible – and they did for a while, but of
course that's all forgotten now, Dunn's isn't even there any more . . .

   I remember the houses in Caversham Road and round there were
really beautiful; everyone had servants and some people kept carriages.
I used to go and deliver *Punch* and things to them, the evening when it
came . . . And when they ordered books we'd send a letter down to the
City warehouses that evening, and the very next morning I'd go down
there on the twopenny tram and by the time I got there the books
would be all ready for me. You can't do that now – people won't do
those sort of things. It takes weeks to get an order now. We were open
from eight in the morning till seven at night, nine on Saturdays – and
on Christmas Eve we'd open till midnight. It was all so different.

A similarly fond account of the High Street in the past was given to me
by an old gentleman long resident in Suffolk, who had lived in Kentish
Town as a small boy around the turn of the century. One can only
mourn with him the disappearance of the specialised tobacconist, with a
window full of lacquered and gilded jars, where the proprietor blended
individual mixtures for 'his' customers; and also the Vicarage Farm

Dairy, where glazed china milk pails covered with butter muslin stood on bare wood scrubbed 'gleaming white' and where 'the only break-away from the pure austerity of white was in a fair-sized coloured figure of a negro boy holding a heap of real eggs in a china basket, and looking very proud of them'. It is interesting, how often the words 'scrubbed' and 'spotless' and 'snowy white' occur in reminiscences such as these, when you consider that the one characteristic of London of the period on which everyone agrees is its formidable and all-pervasive griminess. Is this pristine brightness, like the 'fields' alleged to have been still existing in areas like Kentish Town at the same era, a figment of the elderly imagination, part of the mythic quality a long-gone childhood assumes in memory? Or was it genuine, the result of heaven-knows-what un-ceasing efforts on the part of individual housewives and shopkeepers, whose work was their life and who knew no other?

This correspondent, incidentally, also put forward the *other* classic view of the childhood habitat – not the lost world of enchantment where the white-gowned dairy keeper appears as an elderly fairy godmother but the frightening and squalid world from which, by social betterment, one has managed to escape. He wrote that his family's house in Holmes Road was situated near (but *not* in) an area of complete poverty and sordidness, centring on Litcham Street,

> a terraced street of three-storied houses on both sides, mid-Victorian I should say, that had come down by 1900 to social degradation; a filthy street, the pavements defiled with rheum, the houses crowded with teeming families of uncouth and unlettered people, several families in one house – a hundred people living in accommodation intended for tens. Two houses were run as common doss houses at which vagrants could sleep for 2*d.* or 3*d.* a night; the sweep lived there, the rag and bone man lived there and from the windows not a few ravaged faces gloomed down upon you from between frowsty cobwebs of curtains; if no curtains a piece of newspaper would do.

He was emphatic, in making the point that this 'forbidden territory' was only a slum pocket:

Litcham street was the nadir of a small ganglion of streets consisting roughly of Weedington Road, Warden Road, Carleton Street (*not* Carleton *Road*) and a few others. This ganglion was surrounded by moderately healthy and clean streets . . . Although adjacent to it, almost contiguous in fact, Holmes Road was a model of cleanliness and quietitude perfectly untroubled by its unsavoury neighbour – a strange and constantly occurring phenomenon in London.

This 'ganglion' has virtually all gone now. Most of Weedington and Warden Roads disappeared under some bland flats apparently made of breeze blocks *c.* 1960, and what was left of them went in the Grafton Ward town-planning holocaust of ten years later. Litcham Street went *c.* 1930, as part of the earliest* clearance scheme in the district: even its name was changed – to Athlone Street – and its rotting houses were replaced by solid tenement blocks which, in the manner of such housing, long served to perpetrate the street's low-class character, but which are now finally acquiring a patina of age and respectability. Even the name of the large board school there was changed, in a determined effort to eradicate its reputation as the roughest in the district, but it never really thrived and is now an Evening Institute only. If you went looking for 'slums' there now you would not find them, merely the drabness of small industries; still less would you find slums in the adjacent Crimea area, where the small houses, once the resort of the shabby-genteel and the down-right poor, are now eagerly bought and renovated by those who can afford today's property prices. The traditional social geography of the old inner suburbs has been turned back-to-front, with the back streets now the favoured oasis of peace, jealously protected by environmental traffic schemes, while social decay and disintegration have moved to the main streets. It is Kentish Town High Street, like many others, that is now a battered and fragmented travesty of its former self, a place of litter, noise, dust, 'To Let' boards and a solid mass of barely moving cars at each rush-hour tide. Many of the upper floors of the houses are accessible only through the shop and therefore, with the

* A huddle of 'poor cottages' at the fork by the *Castle* had been removed in the 1890s, but this was part of a road-widening scheme. They were replaced by blocks of the 'model dwellings' variety.

passing of the family-owned business, moulder – dead places of mice, old packing-cases and windows that will no longer open.

Fossilised concepts of value in the minds of rating authorities and ground landlords have brought huge increases in rent and rates for High Street properties in recent years, and ironically this has itself been a big factor in the transformation of such streets from thriving business communities into semi-wildernesses. But in any case the problems of combining, in one and the same street, the role of major traffic artery and shopping place have, in the mid-twentieth century, become almost insuperable. Through the congested high road of Kentish Town, hemmed in by railway land and inflexible residential developments, was filtered, by the end of the nineteenth century, much of the combined London-bound traffic of Holloway, Highgate, Hornsey and Muswell Hill. A generation or so later had been added to this the traffic generated by a vast ring of new suburbs – the Finchley, Barnet, Totteridge belt. Commuting had become a way of life for millions. The obsession with living 'further out' than London's heart, which had done much to shape Kentish Town in the eighteenth century, by the twentieth century was doing much to ruin it. The hamlet strung out along a travel route of mediaeval times had become by degrees a place whose whole nature was deformed by the needs of the masses travelling daily through it by road and rail.

My Suffolk correspondent dated this modern transformation from about 1910, when 'the village-like style came to an unnatural end under the wheel of the motor car and the electric tram. . . . After that there was inevitably a decline in general conditions. I remember it as getting progressively dustier, more noisy and untidy.' Grosch too was un-favourably struck by the new trams when he returned after an absence. The horse trams whose advent had been hotly debated by the vestry *c.* 1870 were merely a logical variant on the horse omnibus, itself a direct descendant of the stage coach, but by the early 1900s 'The horse trams had disappeared from Malden Road, and in place of them had come huge, noisy, clanking, electrically driven vehicles that roared up and down the road like monsters from the works of Jules Verne or H. G. Wells.' Not for nothing was the tram, during the relatively brief period of its prime, the novelist's and poet's favourite symbol for all that was prosaic and crushing in urban lower-class life. (Only now that it has become extinct does this monster, seen in memory, acquire romance and charm). The existence of tram routes was, in its day, a remarkably accurate pointer to the social status of an area, though whether a tram-line actually led to an area declining or merely confirmed a pre-existing decline is debatable. Thus Kentish Town High Street acquired a double set of tram-lines, even though it was so narrow at one point that the double line had to merge for a few yards into a single one, and these continued up Fortess and Junction Road to Archway. Up the Highgate Road, however, they only continued as far as Parliament Hill, at which point gentility took over in the shape of the St Alban's-Brookfield Estate. The lines did not penetrate east Kentish Town at all, even in spacious Caversham Road, but in west Kentish Town they ran along Prince of Wales Road and Malden Road to narrow, depressing Fleet Road on the fringes of Hampstead, which had been acquired as a speculation by Joseph Salter (the surveyor mentioned in the last chapter) and was eventually covered with uncompromisingly low-grade houses, because there was a fever hospital nearby and the choosier residents of Hampstead proper shunned the place.

It is no accident that Sir John Betjeman's poem* on the Kentish Town he knew in his childhood describes a tram-ride – or yet that a tram figures prominently in the memories of an elderly Kentish Town bootmaker whose family history is so typical that it may perhaps stand for the history of the many. Fred Dorsey (as I will call him) was born in 1891, the second of the eighteen children of an engine driver. His grandfather had been a foreman platelayer, a countryman who was sent to London in 1866 to oversee the building of line-junctions on the Midland Railway land at Kentish Town: many of the next generation went into the railway. But Fred Dorsey has a leg deformity which made him unfit for manual work: his family planned that he should be a tailor, but 'I always liked boots, I really wanted to make them.' It wasn't an exclusive trade – there are literally dozens listed for the district in the directories of the period – but young Dorsey had his way and was apprenticed. After working for a while for one master he lost his job but

---

* Printed at the end of this book on page 237.

had £40 saved. A man who was not a bootmaker himself but was proprietor of such a business in Torriano Avenue, offered to sell him the lease cheap – workmen had left and set up nearby in competition to him and 'trade had gone right down'. Fred Dorsey agreed to buy and together they went to the agent, but he maintained that the ground landlord would never agree to a single man having the lease. (Perhaps it was too easy for single men to disappear in the night without paying what they owed?) But Fred Dorsey was not to be deterred – 'I thought a bit, and then I went to see my young lady, see, and I said "What say we get married? You can stop with your sister and I'll stay where I am too." Because I had no other money at all beyond that forty pound.' It turned out that the girl's sister disapproved of the idea of the marriage and it would have been awkward for her to stay there, but they got married anyway. It was 23 November 1914, when young men without lame legs were marching off to war.

Coltman, the greengrocer that used to be on the corner of Fortess Walk [an eighteenth-century house with a mansard roof, a last surviving fragment of Willow Walk] had promised to lend me a pound to get married on, but when I came for it on the wedding morning – that was the day before I got possession of the shop – Mrs Coltman said 'I'm ever so sorry, Fred, but my husband says to tell you he's had such a bad week he can't lend it to you.' . . . Well, I was walking up and down there, outside the Bull and Gate, wondering how to get the money – for I hadn't a penny in the world – the time was getting on and I knew my missus-to-be would be waiting for me down at the Vestry Hall for the wedding at twelve o'clock. Well this tram come by, with the driver ringing his bell. It stopped at the stop. 'Hallo Fred!' the driver says to me. Well I hardly knew him and didn't like to ask him for the money, but I was desperate, see. So I asked him, and explained, and he said 'We're on our way to the depot now. You go and stand over the other side of the road and wait till we come down again.' So I did that, walking up and down again, and it was getting later and later. And after twenty minutes or so the tram came down, ringing its bell again, and he had the money for me. A bag of sixpences and shillings, ten bob's worth, and another bag, all coppers, pennies and ha'pennies, because that was what they mostly took on the trams! And I got on the same tram down to the Town Hall – 'Jump on,' says Harry, 'don't worry about the ha'penny fare!' So down I went, with the bags of money, and there was my missus-to-be already there and getting worried, with the witnesses. 'Oh Fred,' says she, 'I was wondering where you were.' 'Ah, I went to the bank, love,' I says, and she believed me, because of that bag of coppers. . . . ' Course, I told her the truth afterwards.

By the end of the day he had just 2½ *d*. left. The young couple spent the first night of their married life on newspaper on the floor of the shop, with a penny rasher of bacon, a ha'penny worth of potatoes, a borrowed frying pan and a penny packet of Woodbines. In 1975 when I talked to him, Mr Dorsey was still smoking Woodbines, still wearing his own hand-made leather boots, and still living behind the same shop, now a hardware business run by one of his sons. His wife had been dead some years, but nine of his twelve children were still alive. He was just screwing up his courage – successfully, as it turned out – to go on an old people's holiday to the Costa Brava organised by Camden Council.

It might have been the same tram that bore Fred Dorsey down to St Pancras and fifty years of wedlock that, in the opposite direction, bore the young John Betjeman in the same year to the more rarified end of the borough 'where stucco houses in Virginia creeper drown' after an afternoon's shopping in Kentish Town:

When the Bon Marché was shuttered, when the feet were hot and
    tired,
Outside Charrington's we waited, by the 'STOP HERE IF REQUIRED',
Launched aboard the shopping basket, sat precipitately down,
Rocked past Zwanziger the baker, and the terrace blackish brown,
And the curious Anglo-Norman parish church of Kentish Town.

In reply to a letter from a member of Camden History Society in 1971, Sir John wrote:

The tram was a number 7 and it was brown when it was LCC . . . Hampstead Heath then had buttercups and dandelions and daisies in the grass at the Parliament Hill Fields end. Daniels* was a kind of

Selfridges and it was on the corner of Prince of Wales Road, or very near that corner. There was a cinema higher up on the same side and there I saw my first film, very early animated pictures; it was called the 'Electric Palace' . . . The Bon Marché was an old fashioned draper's shop . . . Opposite Kentish Town station was a Penny Bazaar and next to that was Zwanziger which always smelt of baking bread. Then there was an antique dealer and a picture framer and a public house . . . Then there was some late Georgian brick houses with steps up to their front doors, then the always-locked parish church of Kentish Town (that was the one I referred to in the poem. It was rebuilt in Norman style in 1843 by J. H. Hakewill and seems to have no dedication). It was very low. Then there was Maple's warehouse, always rather grim, then some squalid shops and a grocer's shop called Wailes which was very old-fashioned. Then came Highgate Road station with a smell of steam and very rare trains which ran, I think, to Southend from a terminus at Gospel Oak. Then there were some rather grander shops with a definite feeling of suburbia . . . I remember thinking how beautiful the new bits of Metroland Villas were in the newly built Glenhurst Avenue, and my father telling me they were awful. Then there was the red brick gloom of Lissenden Gardens and Parliament Hill Mansions . . .

These later blocks were built in the Edwardian period, evidence of a passing conviction on the part of the British that the future for the middle classes lay in large family flats like those to be found in Continental capitals. The belief did not survive the First World War and the vast expansion of 'Metroland' into London's countryside in the 1920s, but the blocks themselves remain, desirable homes because of their proximity to Parliament Hill, but contriving to turn a few acres of land there into a simulacrum of one of the duller districts of Paris, Vienna or Warsaw.

From the blackened, train-shaken heart of Kentish Town to the airy pseudo-rural heights only a short tram-ride away – that theme of contrast and social juxtaposition crops up again and again in the

---

* It has other literary associations. The writer V.S. Pritchett's parents met while working there. [G.T.]

reminiscences of men and women old enough now to remember the time when 'the poor were different from us'. To the young John Betjeman, taken by his mother to visit a poor family in Falkland Place ('I then thought it was a slum, but I now realise it was charming Middlesex cottages'), 'the courts of Kentish Town' must have seemed as mysterious as the circles of an unplumbed underworld. Indeed the Dante's Inferno metaphor for such areas was extensively used by an adult writing at exactly the same time – Compton Mackenzie, whose *Sinister Street* was published in 1913.

If Betjeman was essentially an outsider riding through on a tram to Highgate, Michael Fane, the hero of *Sinister Street*, is far more so. His view of our area is worth quoting at length because it is so entirely typical of the view the moneyed, leisured classes held of all inner city districts at that period and for the next forty years. In the upper-middle-class imagination they had become No Go areas, 'impossible' places where gruesome domestic slaughters occurred (see Crippen) and whose very names would bring a smile to sophisticated lips – 'My dear, Kentish Town! You *can't* go there . . . Where is it, anyway?' Ten years later John Buchan, in *The Three Hostages*, was to settle on a fanciful version of Gospel Oak ('shabby gentility on the very brink of squalor') as a suitable locale for the heart of his mystery, in the person of a blind spinner speaking in verse, but it is *Sinister Street* which provided the archetype for all such writing:

> . . . Ever since Mrs Pearcey's* blood-soaked perambulator Kentish Town had held for [Michael] a macabre significance: of the hellish portals mystery and gruesomeness were essential attributes. The drive was for a long time tediously pleasant in the June sunshine; but when the cab had crossed the junction of the Euston Road with the Tottenham Court Road, unknown London with all its sly and labyrinthine romance lured his fancy onwards . . .

* A celebrated double-murder of 1890. Mrs Pearcey's (actually Piercey) effigy, with accessories, including a stick of toffee allegedly sucked by the murdered baby, may still be seen at Madame Tussaud's. The main protagonists of this drama all lived in the Kentish Town area.

Presently upon an iron railway bridge Michael read in giant letters the direction Kentish Town behind a huge leprous hand pointing to the left. The hansom clattered through the murk beneath, past the dim people huddled upon the pavement, past a wheel-barrow and the obscene skeletons and outlines of humanity chalked upon the arches of sweating brick. Here then was Kentish Town. It lay to the left of this bridge that was the colour of stale blood. Michael told the driver to stop for one moment, and he leaned forward over the apron of the cab to survey the cross-street of swarming feculent humanity that was presumably the entering highway. A train roared over the bridge; a piano organ gargled its tune; a wagon-load of iron girders drew near in a clanging tintamar of slow progress. Michael's brief pause was enough to make such an impression of pandemoniac din as almost to drive out his original conception of Kentish Town as a menacing and gruesome suburb. But just as the cab reached the beginning of the Camden Road, he caught sight of a slop-shop where old clothes smothered the entrance with their mucid heaps and, just beyond, of three houses from whose surface the stucco was peeling in great scabs and the damp was oozing in livid arabesques and scrawls of verdigris. This group restored to Kentish Town a putative disquiet, and the impression of mere dirt and the noise and the exhalations of fried fish were merged in the more definite character allotted by his prefiguration.

Thus fortified in his fantasy by the smell of frying fish, Michael manages to find even the relatively banal and airy Camden Road sinister; the exhortations posted in front of a chapel he passes seem to him 'spiritually malevolent', and the oblongs of garden behind the houses 'circumscribed secretive pleasure grounds in the amount of life they could conceal'. As a monument to the ferocious and unrealistic class-separations of the era, in which the everyday habitat of one class, by no means the poorest, is made to seem as exotic as Outer Mongolia, *Sinister Street* would be hard to equal. But its author was one jump ahead of his characters after all, for presently we realise Michael is being gently mocked. As his cab makes the return journey from the disappointingly ordinary Seven Sisters Road, when he began to examine the Camden Road as a prospective place of residence, it became suddenly dull and respectable. The locked-up chapels and the quiet houses declined from ominousness into respectability, and he wondered how he had managed only a quarter of an hour ago to speculate upon the inner life they adumbrated. Nothing could be less surreptitious than those chatting nursemaids, and in one of the parallelograms of garden a child was throwing a scarlet ball high into the air.

Thus, to some a 'lovely place' or a 'much-loved district', to others at exactly the same period 'a slum . . . where only a blackened elm, an ill-grown privet hedge and some stunted lilacs told of the more cheerful past', to neo-romantics a world of gas-lit mystery, to others 'one of those shabby prosaic monotonous residential quarters that could well be spared from the Metropolis', Kentish Town continued its own life into the twentieth century as a small part of the largest city in the world. No one recorded it, few people took an interest in it: the people who would once have done so had almost all moved away. At long last, after hundreds of years, its upper-class connections seemed to be over. Was this the end, was its final destiny to be simply swept away in some future large-scale urban clearance project, its very identity as a sub-merged village lost, even perhaps to its name? Many people, in the first half of the twentieth century thought so – if they thought about such an area at all. But, as it turned out, they were wrong.

11

As far as we have got

(1977)

There seems to be an unspoken agreement among local historians that the time after, say, 1900, or 1914 at the very latest, does not count as history and therefore cannot be worth serious interest. This, allied to the other widespread antiquarian fallacy – that once a district becomes part of an urban conurbation it ceases to have an identity of its own – has resulted in a gulf in the middle distance of the historical vista, roughly corresponding to that period when the old inner London suburbs became invisible to the educated middle classes except as Lowryesque landscapes seen from behind the windows of a moving vehicle.

It is true that, except for some suburban-style residential development in the northern end of the district (much of Brookfield Estate, the Holly Lodge Estate) Kentish Town probably changed less between 1920 and 1940 than it had done at any time in the previous hundred years. It had assumed – for the time being – its definitive urban form. What changed was the countryside further north, as fields receded from Archway to Highgate, from Highgate to Finchley, from Finchley to Southgate and Barnet, and this new ocean of neo-London, though unseen from Kentish Town, had the effect of making Kentish Town itself greyer and shabbier, more congested with commuter trains, buses and cars passing through, less and less favoured by those who could afford to live anywhere else. This is one reason – though only one – why the geographical un-discovered country of that era is now an undiscovered country in chronological terms. The middle classes, who had once cared about the district enough to document its existence on paper and to collect the ephemera of its day-to-day events, were simply no longer there to do so.

But the upheavals of the post-1945 era have in any case played strange tricks with people's perceptions of the years between the wars, that time which is not quite yet the past, picturesquely framed, but is certainly not the present either, and which confusingly has the characteristics of both then and now. Some of those middle-aged to elderly people to whom I have talked in Kentish Town solve the problem of putting their own memories into some sort of perspective by treating the past of forty or fifty years ago 'as if it was yesterday', and criticising the present accordingly, ignoring the massive social changes that the 1940s and 1950s brought. These are the people who are convinced that 'the area has gone down dreadfully'; they miss the signs of a homogeneous working- and lower-middle-class culture (scrubbed doorsteps, net curtains, polished knockers, hatted, all-white people in the street) which characterised their childhood and youth. They cannot interpret the much more fragmented and socially diverse appearance of the district today. Other people of similar age adopt the opposition approach, treating their youth as if it had taken place not *c.* 1930 but about 1870 or even earlier: a long-vanished Dickensian world of contrasting plenty and want, typified by the opulent displays of geese and hams outside the shops and the children they knew who 'couldn't come to school because they had no boots to come in'. It is true that a pre-1914 way of life (boot-clubs, open shop-fronts, gaslights, cobbles, horse-drawn carts) *did* persist for longer in London's invisible regions than it did in, say, Kensington or the Home Counties, but one senses that the antique features of the inter-war period are exaggerated by some informants as a way of distancing the whole period and thus rendering it powerless to provoke either regret or fear in the present. While their more pessimistic and past-bound neighbours are muttering about immigrants moving in and the district going down, they themselves incline to the belief that the place is going up – 'look at the prices houses are fetching now' they say wonderingly, with reason. 'And we've got a television writer living in our street now. It isn't like the old days, you see.'

It isn't indeed like the old days, but the flat discrepancies in people's perception of the social movement of the district relate not just to their subjective standpoints but to a genuine social dislocation in the area over the last fifteen years or so. The place is now more socially mixed than it has been, probably, for the last hundred years, and not only in overall terms, taking one street with another, but perceptibly, street by street and house by house. Near-poverty lives side by side with near-affluence. Ironically, the one social element which, today, is under-represented in Kentish Town is the very one which dominated it in the days of clerks and pianoforte makers: the Registrar General's Class 3 – the lower-middle-class white-collar worker or skilled artisan, with a wife and young family.

It would be interesting to chart in detail the social development of Kentish Town in the twentieth century, through the grey years, through the Second World War and the artificial depression of property values that followed it when the thousands of terraced streets that ringed central London were supposedly hardly worth the bricks of which they were built – and on to the unforeseen, gradually swelling property boom of the late 1950s and 1960s, which took everyone by surprise, most of all town planners, and whose reverberations are still continuing. But, apart from the fact that such a description, using an inner London district as a microcosm for an era of profound social change, would be a book in itself, we are still too near to the period to perceive it clearly. We can see what happened, sometimes in superabundant detail, but not always what those happenings meant. Moreover the major issues of the century – the traffic problem, the housing problem, the perpetual tussle between the forces of private enterprise and the forces of municipalisation, all of which are very much in evidence in Kentish Town – are still continuing. There are no firm conclusions yet to be drawn, and any progress report to date can be only that: ephemeral stuff, full of partisan attitudes that are themselves material for the local historian of the future. Those who, halfway through this period, notably in 1944, made sweeping assumptions about the district and about the future nature of urban society in general turned out to be not just wrong, but profoundly and even disastrously wrong. If we have learnt little else from those mistakes, we can at least learn the folly of making premature judgements on the nature of our own times.

What I am offering in this chapter, then, is not local history so much as the stuff of future local history. If, by the year 2000 (where the arbitrary frontier of the future seems to be fixed at the moment) Kentish and Camden Towns, Islington, Kilburn and Kennington, Hackney and Lewisham, have declined (as some people think they will) into urban 'jungles' on the American model, dangerous to cross after dark and full of racial tensions, then I shall have been wrong in my particular set of assumptions and deductions. But no more wrong than the band-waggoners of the late 1960s property boom, who painted a radiant if daunting picture of the streets of these inner suburbs soon to be as uniform as Chelsea or Belgravia with white stucco, Thames Green front doors, flower boxes, reproduction Georgian railings, and Minis, Volvos and Mercedes lining the pavements.

The 'menacing jungle' theory of urban areas has had a long run. In 1924, John Buchan was writing 'London is like the tropical bush – if you don't exercise constant care the jungle, in the shape of slums, will break in.' The general implication here is of social mobility and flux – families moving out, others moving in, moonlighting – an erratic, febrile existence. Yet a very different writer, Montagu Slater, wrote of exactly the same sub-district (Gospel Oak) at the same period in very different terms: he was born and brought up there and to him it was as stable as a country village: 'There are about twenty streets on the side of the hill ending in a little circus with trees. Nobody left the place much except to go to work, and there were plenty of the women who knew less about London than people do in Manchester. The local pubs and the flea-pits, the pubs, the billiards-hall, the open-air market gave them all they wanted' (*Once a Jolly Swagman*).

This subjective impression is borne out by facts. Still today in Kentish Town there are substantial numbers of people who were born in the area and have lived there all their lives, though usually at a number of different addresses. Frequently their parents and sometimes their grand-parents lived there also, like the boot-maker quoted in the last chapter, or like the elderly proprietor of a chemist's shop who, in 1975, fought an unsuccessful rearguard action to try to stop his late-eighteenth-century house – 109 Highgate Road – from being demolished. (He stood on the pavement opposite for several days watching it come down.) The ancestors of most arrived with the houses and the railways in the middle of the last century, but I came across one family who claimed descent from much further back: a Kentish Town builder called Morgan who died at ninety-five in 1973 used to trace his family back to the Morgans of eighteenth-century days. Again and again I found exemplified the importance people attach to their roots and to their physical habitat actual or remembered – an aspect of the human psyche which, in the past thirty years, has been treated with the most cavalier disregard by those who believed themselves in possession of a moral brief for altering the urban landscape. I do not say that these authorities have been worse in this respect than the power-holders of the previous century, but they have not been better.

Three different overlapping but conflicting images of urban landscape have been jostling one another for public acceptance for much of this century – the city district as a shapeless near-slum, as a tightly-knit village community, and as the raw-material for the creation of a new, purpose-built habitat to replace the worn-out one. Each has a certain validity, but each is capable of being over-emphasised regardless of the others. The concept of 'slum clearance' began in the nineteenth century, and the original motive was not even altruism or a passion for social equality so much as concern for public health: the 'dens and courts' of places like Somers Town were felt to be breeding grounds for disease which might then spread to more salubrious areas. The Metropolitan Association for Improving the Dwellings of the Industrious Classes, which was founded in 1842 and erected its first 'Model Buildings' in St Pancras had, it is true, something of the spirit of all subsequent re-housing enterprises, but its critics were quick to point out that in fact it was not catering for the neediest classes. As John Hollinshead wrote in *Ragged London* (1861),

> At St Pancras they have done nothing for the worst class in Somers Town and Agars Town, and they have wasted their means on a class who are well able to help themselves . . . The costermongers, the street hawkers – the industrous poor – are still rotting up their filthy, ill-drained, ill-ventilated courts, while well-paid mechanics, clerks and porters, willing to sacrifice a certain portion of their self-respect, are the constant tenants of all these model dwellings.

That, in essence, has been one of the standard complaints about subsidised housing ever since, and it is one that modern councils seem to be as far from solving as ever. The only fundamental difference today is that, whereas in previous generations 'filthy, ill-drained, ill-ventilated courts' at least did exist to house those not eligible for model housing, council ambitions since the Second World War have become so sweeping that many of the traditional alternative forms of accommodation have simply disappeared. With hindsight, it is hard now to understand why municipal authorities all over England failed to realise that if they pulled down 'slum property' – which, almost by definition, means crowded, unregulated property – and replaced it with dwellings built to more rigorous specifications and designed for a higher standard of living, *inevitably* the result would be a net loss in the amount of accommodation actually available, and a rise in rents. Moreover there is always a gap, sometimes a long one, between the time when old houses are emptied of their inhabitants and the time when these inhabitants can be moved back into new accommodation in the same district – always provided that they have not, in the meantime, been irretrievably dispersed elsewhere. The statement, endlessly reiterated in the post-war years, that such-and-such a borough council had produced X hundred new homes in the previous year, has been all too frequently a pious fraud, though a fraud usually believed in implicitly by council officers. The aura of moral rectitude which surrounded the concept of slum-clearance was so pervasive and so attractive to people of almost every political shade of opinion but particularly to those with doctrinaire concepts of the Brave New World they should be helping to build, that it took decades before the moral imperative began to be seriously questioned.

Of course some genuine slum-clearance was needed. Photographs of Somers Town taken in 1924, the year the St Pancras House Improvement Society was formed largely to get rid of it, show fetid courts which would indeed have been difficult to improve. The same applies to the Litcham Street area (see previous chapter), demolished *c.* 1930. Four years later new blocks were announced for part of Harmood and Ferdinand Streets, and Leighton Road on the other side of Kentish Town was getting its first block – Kennistoun House, on the old courtyard-and-gallery pattern which has proved a good deal more serviceable than many subsequent designs. (The rents at Kennistoun House were at first 13s. 4d. per week for two rooms, 16s. 1d. for three and 18s. 2d. for four: this was still the era of the culture of poverty when a penny more or less counted. Twenty-six years later the same block was to achieve a brief fame when it was the scene of some noisy rent riots, including a siege with the main protagonists barricaded in their rooms.)

Kennistoun House at least was not true slum-clearance, and nor was the block further up the same road on the opposite side, which opened in 1939 replacing much of Peckwater Street. They were simply a general confirmation of the area's social levelling-down.* Other pre-war blocks that went up in those years represented a genuine housing gain, in that they were built on land not previously used for housing: e.g. Montague Tibbles (now, with 1960s refinement, renamed 'Penshurst') on the site of the old Tailors Almshouses, and the York Rise Estate on land adjacent to, and previously owned by, the railway.

It was not till the Second World War was on the way to being won that the Brave New World machine really got into gear, and, in doing so, gradually altered and expanded the concept of 'slum clearance' far beyond anything that early improvers could have foreseen or intended. By then, highly permissive legislation existed to enable councils to acquire properties by compulsory purchase in order to carry out 'improvements'. What the legislators did not realise, what indeed no one realised, was the extent to which this power would presently be abused by councils to carry out grandiose schemes that owed more indeed to the visions of le Corbusier than to the real needs and wants of the population of urban areas.

Among the generation of town planners who entered the profession after the War, 'comprehensive redevelopment' was considered, for ideological reasons, the only proper approach. Many of these planners are still with us, disillusioned and nervous men in middle age who are yet – as one of them said to me – 'too old dogs to learn new tricks'. A moral prejudice is the hardest thing to replace, and highly moral was what the planners of the 1950s and 1960s did indeed believe they were being when they destroyed the very street patterns in the name of progress, unnecessarily jettisoning the architecture of the past wholesale as if only by that method could they jettison the social evils of the past as

---

* Mr Pike's house was by now a doctor's surgery, and one of the few in the road not in multi-occupation.

well. It was a classic example of throwing the baby out with the bath-water, or of a ritualised gesture disguised in a gloss of rationalisation.

What no one admitted till well into the 1960s, when whole com-munities had already been destroyed in London and elsewhere and large tracts of once-living urban landscape had been turned into deserts of windy concrete towers set on useless doylies of ownerless grass, was that 'slum' is almost entirely a relative concept, and that much so-called 'slum clearance' has been no more than a form of conspicuous con-sumption and political self-advertisement. Most of the true, irredeemable slums of London had already gone by the mid-1950s, but by then the machinery of slum clearance was so well established as a part of the local authority apparat that, like a blind monster, it went nosing round for more. And of course it found them, for there is nothing like announcing that a certain street or district *will* be demolished under some future slum-clearance scheme to ensure that its fabric and social status have indeed deteriorated by the time the bulldozers arrive, perhaps years later. Private tenants will have sold up and left, landlords will have ceased to do repairs, no grants will have been forthcoming for improvements. A once self-respecting and thriving community will have become an area of sheet iron screens, vandalised windows, squatters, refuse and scrawled slogans. Lo, a slum has been created, a prophecy has fulfilled itself. Planning-blight has been to the mid-twentieth century what bad speculative building was to the nineteenth, but at least the Councillor Agars of that time did not make sanctimonious remarks about the virtue of their activities.

How did Kentish Town fare in this situation? The answer is, much better than some places, but that is not saying much. Fortunately in the 1930s, when slum clearance began to be adopted as a Labour Party crusade, Kentish Town was not quite poor enough to attract great attention, in view of the limited funds available in that unprosperous time. But at the end of the Second World War all the signs were that the Borough of St Pancras was about to enjoy the attentions of Brave New Worlders in no uncertain way. The County of London Plan (1944) specifically labelled Kentish Town 'an area in need of removal'. It was, according to the planners, 'an inchoate community . . . peppered with small industries.' What the prevailing opinion of the time did not allow is that the presence of industry was a sign not of sickness but of a viable community. In any case most of the small industries of the area were not (and are not) of a type that create excessive noise or smell. The remnants of the piano trade lingered on, the many mews, empty of horses, were being taken over by branches of the motor repairing business. The ugly building fronting Highgate Road (site of the entrance to Weston's Retreat) was a lino factory, and the nooks and corners of the old streets contained many small workshops that made envelopes, boxes, wire gadgets, toys, patent medicines. Since then, with the coming of the Greek Cypriot community in the 1950s, minor branches of the rag-trade have moved in, often into parts of the large factories from which the tide of piano-making had steadily retreated. Small industries in which local people can find work near their homes have been an essential part of inner London districts, ever since they assumed their metropolitan identity. To apply to them the same criteria that one applies to suburbs built purely as residential quarters, is inappropriate. Yet 'zoning' – industry here, living space there – without flexibility or regard for pre-existing situations was one of the basic concepts of the County of London plan, and one that still lingers, destroying jobs and bedevilling planning applications. Ironically it led, by the 1960s, to a certain amount of destruction in Kentish Town of existing homes, particularly in the Holmes Road area, on the grounds that they were in an area 'zoned as industrial'.

The Plan of 1944 was on a grand scale and, like all such spectacular exercises it contained ideas which would have been good ones – if other considerations could have been discounted. The best idea was a far-sighted scheme for co-ordinating the main-line, suburban and tube railways in a more rational manner, something of which London is still, today, in considerable need. Had this project been carried through, Kentish Town railway station and Kentish Town tube station would no longer be sitting absurdly side by side opposite the Assembly House with no connection between them. The North London railway line would have been put underground for most of its length, and would in effect have become a branch of the Underground corresponding physically to the District Line and appearing on the Underground map. (Instead it is today the 'Secret Railway', a line of few trains, semi-derelict, and only kept open at all through constant agitation by the parents of children who use it as a cross-route to various schools within the borough.) The other great obsession of the 1944 Plan was the need for new ringway roads through London, a subject that has been furiously debated ever since. GLC road planners of recent years, locked in perpetual battle with militant residents' associations, must have thought with wistful nostalgia of the days when their predecessors could airily announce that the Euston Road 'would' become part of the A Ring Road while the B Ring 'would' cut across Camden Town. Also proposed was a 'Parkway' connecting Primrose Hill with Parliament Hill, and a new 'green lung' between Camden Road and Agar Grove. Such ideas are of the kind which sound attractive on first hearing, but which, on analysis, prove to be based on the belief that the ideal human habitat is Welwyn Garden City and that urban habitats of a totally different order should be altered to conform as far as possible to this ideal, and that the urban areas through which these parkways, lung etc. would be carved were somehow non-areas that did not count. Both these misconceptions dominated town planning for the next twenty-five years and are not extinct today. Even in the early 1970s Camden Council (which superseded St Pancras Borough Council with the GLC reorganisation in 1966) were still demolishing streets of houses to create 'green spaces' (sacred phrase!) often in places where they were not particularly useful or where the surrounding traffic management schemes had rendered the roads too dangerous for children or elderly people (the chief users of gardens) to cross. A classic example of this type of planning misjudgement will be found adjacent to Hawley Road.

Confronted with this Plan, St Pancras Borough seems to have felt a vague unease, a conflict between the idea that anything so splendidly forward-looking must be applauded and the lurking suspicion that they did not actually want a higher authority to try to turn them into Welwyn Garden City – a project which even the most sanguine of them must have suspected was doomed to failure. The good qualities of an urban environment as a place to live, work and play are quite other than the good qualities of a garden suburb, and if you attempt to change the town habitat too drastically you risk losing its essential qualities without gaining those of another type of place. But it was not till 1962 that an

American, Jane Jacobs, wrote *The Death and Life of American Cities*, suggesting what large numbers of humbler people like Montagu Slater and the local shop-keepers had known all along: that an environment of streets and alleys can be a friendly one, catering adequately for most of the needs of the inhabitants. The Plan contained a sop-sentence or two about 'retaining and encouraging the life of the communities', but there was no suggestion how, in the presence of the new bisecting road schemes, this was to be achieved. The response of the Borough Council was to shuffle their feet and suggest 'various modifications' – including the abolition of the 'green lung' and the shifting of the B Ring Road out of the heart of Camden Town to the southern part of Kentish Town, an area where it long lurked in spirit. (Indeed this phantom road, resurrected by the GLC in the 1960s as the Motorway Box, effectively blighted for years the prospects of the streets in its neighbourhood – Jeffries Street, Ivor Street, the tops of Camden Street, Royal College Street and St Pancras Way, one of the oldest and most architecturally homogeneous corners of the district. At least the question mark over their future in the 1950s and 1960s saved these streets from being demolished for a new estate.) In the catalogue to an exhibition of its own in 1947, entitled 'St Pancras of the Future', the Council stated: 'It will be seen that, if it is possible to carry out the provisions of the County of London Plan, St Pancras tomorrow will differ widely in appearance from St Pancras today and offer better amenities to its inhabitants. It is for us, as citizens of London and residents and workers in St Pancras, to help to turn the proposals into realities.'

The same booklet contained the information that in 1939 (the last years for which figures were available) almost half the houses in the borough had been occupied by more than one family. What such statistical pronouncements hid was the fact that these houses, many of them three storeys high plus basement, had never been intended to house one small nuclear family apiece even when new. Typically they had sheltered in addition servants (sometimes four or five of these in a large house such as those on the Camden Road), extra relatives, or lodgers. But to speak of house-sharing as if it were an unmitigated evil was the standard prelude to the Council's inevitable next remark about its plans for building self-contained flats: 'In order to gain open ground space, each block of flats will be built as high as each site will reasonably allow.'

It is painful now to reflect on the docility with which people accepted this and other arbitrary dictates about their future way of life. 'They', the Council, were felt to know best, and anyway the building of new homes was a sign that peace was here, wasn't it? Not much building had taken place after the First World War, despite promises, and this had been a source of resentment. An interesting example of the patriotism of the period combined with a sense of regret at destruction is to be found in the preamble to Grosch's reminiscences, quoted in the preceding chapter: 'Personally, I should like to see some effort made to preserve one or two rows of these streets and houses in which lived a people who did a very great deal to make, and hold, that Empire of which we are so proud today.'

That was written in 1947, the very year that the first large chunk of the Empire (India) detached itself. But what is interesting about Grosch's remark is not so much its backward-looking flag-waving but its calm concept of a future in which *everything* in his native district would be swept away in the interests of progress. If public opinion had reached such a point that people accepted this awesome prospect as a matter of course, no wonder local councils believed they could do absolutely anything they liked, with arbitrary powers greater than those of any private landlord. They could, and did – in London's East End, in Birmingham and parts of Manchester. They did not go quite so far in Kentish Town. But it was a close thing. The exhibition of 1947 blandly laid out plans for property that was to be demolished in ten years, in twenty years and in thirty years, with no apparent perception of the social shifts and changes that might take place in that period and the consequent impossibility of predicting decay with any accuracy. The future, it was felt, was on the point of arriving, and once it had arrived it would be there for good, unchanging and unchangeable.

Even when the actual future became the present and took (as it was bound to) a different form from that predicted, the static, mythic future with cloud capp'd glass towers, filled with contented socialist workers and set on billowing greensward, was not displaced from the imaginations of architects, planners and politicians. In 1962 when, after a spell in eclipse, Labour regained power in St Pancras, the cherished visions of the immediate post-war period were at once put into execution as if nothing had happened in the 1950s to render them obsolete.

What had in fact happened was an unprecedented shift in the public estimation of the value of inner London housing property. The visions of the post-war planning generation (concepts which themselves dated back to the early Fabian movement) were all constructed on the basic assumption that urban properties started life as desirable, became steadily less desirable over the course of several generations and finally declined to a state of near worthlessness. To purchase them compulsorily at the 'end of their life' would not therefore pose any great financial problem for the local authority or be met (of course) with any opposition, since the inhabitants would be only too grateful to be moved out. House property was a wasting asset, as the descendants of Victorian speculative builders would tell one another, sadly creeping round unmodernised properties for which they could ask only minimal rents. What neither they nor the local authority foresaw was that, from the middle 1950s onwards, house prices in hitherto despised inner suburbs began mysteriously to climb.

The trend started in Islington, where a complex of Georgian squares had indeed been overlooked for too long, but as it spread to Primrose Hill, Fulham and Camden Town around 1960 and to Kennington and Kentish Town a year or two later, a bemused public and a number of delighted estate agents began to realise that though the architecture was an important factor in this reassessment of worth, the crucial factor was a house's position. The very nearness of these areas to central London, which for all the earlier part of the century had been a disadvantage in most buyers' minds, had become *the* selling point. While it would be untrue to say that no one, any longer, cherished dreams of a country cottage in Mill Hill, it became apparent that a substantial section of the upper and middle classes were now prepared – even eager – to live in the very areas from which their parents and grandparents had departed for greener fields.

The reasons for this radical shift have not to date been adequately explained, but a number of factors can be suggested. It would be simplistic to suppose that previous generations had just failed to notice the convenience of living near to town and near to buses, tubes and shopping centres, and that it only needed a few pioneers to point the way for light to dawn. The truth must surely be that, between the later nineteenth century and the 1950s, the disadvantages of the old inner areas were marked enough to outweigh the advantages. An important consideration during this period was, simply, the dirt of life near the centre. We tend now to forget – and many people approaching adulthood have never known – the sheer filth of London in the days when every household was warmed by one or more coal fires and all trains were steam. In Camden and Kentish Towns the train smoke alone from all the shunting yards must have ensured that the districts remained unattractive to middle-class families. It is surely no coincidence that these districts began to appeal again to the middle classes around 1960, precisely at the time when the steam trains were being withdrawn for good and when the clean air legislation that followed the 'smog' scare of the late 1950s was beginning to have a real impact on people's heating arrangements.

Socially, too, the situation had changed somewhat, even before the moneyed 'outsiders' began to arrive. To be working class in the late 1950s was to be enjoying a new prosperity and new health and welfare amenities of which previous generations had never dreamed. In a nutshell, the working classes no longer seemed 'different from us' to the young middle-class generation who were themselves enjoying a *less* sheltered and privileged life than many of their parents. Servants, in the traditional sense, had disappeared. The gulf between the young working-class wife pushing her small (planned) family in a pram, and the young upper-middle-class wife pushing *her* family in a similar but often rather smaller pram, was genuinely less than it had been at any earlier times. The schools, playgrounds and doctors' surgeries of traditionally working-class areas no longer filled the emancipated middle-class parent with forebodings about germs and swear words.

Other factors are harder to pin down. It is said that the revival of a taste first for Georgian and then for Victorian architecture has had much to do with the way the inner suburbs have become visible again: the 'leprous, peeling facades' and 'Victorian monstrosities' of the 1920s and 1930s observer had by 1960 become 'delightful period properties'. But did this shift of view help to provoke the rediscovery of the Victorian districts, or did the fashion for all things Victorian which reached its chic peak about 1970 actually stem, in part, from the fact that people had already sought out Victorian town architecture for other reasons? A taste for urban stucco rather than suburban mock-timbering is the superficial expression of something much deeper – a rejection of the rural idyll in favour of a more sophisticated and cosmopolitan one, fashionably egalitarian. Over large parts of southern England the country village, in its traditional form, had died, killed off by various things including the influx into it of moneyed refugees from places like Kentish Town. It was the children and grandchildren of those refugees who returned, with a new if disguised romanticism, to seek another village – a village in the city.

Obviously the country's prosperity in those never-had-it-so-good years, however misguided and illusory it now seems in retrospect, meant that there was far more money available for house purchase than there had been in the depressed inter-war period, and this in itself tended to have an inflationary effect on concepts of value. Prices for small terraced houses will only rise from £500 to £1000 to £2500 to £7000 to £15,000 and upwards in the space of a decade or so if the money is in fact there. It was this same prosperity that produced the municipal redevelopment bonanza. Ironically, the beginning of the 1960s, when prices really began to rise steeply, was just the time when councils like St Pancras began to set the machinery in motion for long-cherished schemes, regardless of the fact that some at least of the supposed 'slums' due to come down were now valuable, well-modernised properties. Private interests and municipal attitudes were thus set on an inevitable collision course.

In 1964 a Town Planning Consultant's Report was issued for west Kentish Town, the old Southampton Estate. Today, it makes curious reading. A certain sophistication had crept in since the days when domestic heaven was supposed to lie at the top of a tower block with acres of space around it. High rise blocks had already come in for a lot of criticism, though it took the collapse of Ronan Point block in East London in 1968 to provide pig-headed local planning officers with a face-saving excuse for changing their policy. The authors of the 1964 plan appear to have been aware of the dangers of having 'ground that belonged to everybody and nobody . . . an anonymous expanse of

building blocks having neither front nor back, beginning nor end . . .
the recognised urban values thrown out with the bathwater.' And yet
the comprehensive redevelopment plan they produced was, in many
respects, a recipe for just that. Virtually the whole of west Kentish Town
was to be demolished and replaced with blocks of varying heights, most
of them not set along road systems. Many of the minor streets were to
disappear altogether. In the Crimea area tower blocks were to be constructed. The basically ruthless and high-handed attitude to the
landscape of people's lives is betrayed by the remark 'Of the old streets
only Kelly street is worth preserving . . . ' In other words the criteria for
'slum clearance' had stealthily shifted over the years from 'Is this in
such bad condition it needs knocking down?' to 'Is this of sufficient
architectural interest to be worth making out a special case for keeping
it?' Somewhere along the line the declared purpose of local authority
redevelopment had been lost.

Once again, the planners had some good ideas. They made much use
of the term 'penetration' and the text accompanying the plan explained
it in terms of vistas and through-walks, with the North London Railway
viaduct retained and exploited as a landscape feature. There was the
preoccupation with communal leisure activities which seems to have
been a permanent feature of all town planning pipe-dreams from
Hampstead Garden Suburb on, and there was also provision for a
'quarter . . . of studios, workshops, clubs and secondhand shops' –
without any awareness that such things never flourish in new, custom
built property which is by definition too expensive for them. The
artificially created open spaces of the County of London Plan were also
revived.

Bits of this plan eventually came to pass, to the accompaniment of
furious protests, arguments, counter-arguments and public meetings.
But really 1964 was too late – by just a year or two – to introduce
anything quite so high-handed. Two years earlier, similarly sweeping
plans for the area north of Queen's Crescent (Grafton Ward and Gospel
Oak) were set in motion, and were to take – except in Oak Village itself,
which had become an enclave of battling, wealthy owner-occupiers –
their relentless course. Over the next fourteen years much of the area
that had been 'home' to Grosch before 1914 and to Montagu Slater

between the wars was reduced to a wasteland of one kind or another – emptied, boarded houses, churned earth, blocks that the local people christened 'Colditz'. It was partly *because* of this that, by the mid-sixties, public opinion, in the form of Civic Societies and local residents' associations, was at last becoming mobilised to fight municipal domination. Much to their own surprise, the Council, the fairy-godfather giver of new homes, found that they had a fight on their hands.

It was unfortunate, but inevitable, that the people who first took up the battle were the articulate middle-class newcomers to the district rather than the long-term working-class residents. For a while, the whole issue threatened to degenerate into a political battle across class divisions – a view of the matter fostered by some councillors, who found it convenient to cast the people who opposed redevelopment in the role of capitalist baddies which enabled the goodies to be the traditional deserving poor whom the Council was only trying to help. The baddies, it was suggested, were decadent in their obsession with conserving the old, and were thereby depriving the working classes of their right to have bathrooms. Yet in fact the working classes had, if anything, more to lose than the middle classes if their streets were destroyed. They would have less chance of moving elsewhere and would have to accept what they were given in the way of a council flat. But for so long the idea had been promulgated that only by knocking everything down and starting all over again could you achieve water-tight roofs and indoor lavatories, that many ordinary people began to believe this was indeed the only way and to look askance on 'Save Our Street' campaigns. Once again, as centuries before, a middle-class presence in Kentish Town was having its effect, and no one, at first, knew quite how to take this.

A woman I visited in 1975 in her new flat south of Queen's Crescent (a fragment of the 1964 plan that did finally get itself built) had been the founder and leader of a tenants' association which had set itself to oppose the local Civic Society over *their* opposition to the Council's plans:

We were sick of sharing the toilets, that was the main thing really. We never stopped to think that the Council could have put us in new baths and toilets like they're doing in some of these streets now instead of pulling the whole lot down . . . People didn't think much about these things then – they've changed a lot since. Personally I could never see why they pulled Maitland Park down [a piece of 1950s redevelopment]. It was beautiful there . . . and Prince of Wales Crescent used to be a really nice place too. It was all small shops and a little post office. I lived in two rooms there when I was first married. Now everyone's been moved out and its all horrible, full of squatters . . . It shouldn't have happened really.

The social problem was in fact much more complex than it was made to seem, either by the Council or by the new middle-class owner-occupiers. The latter claimed, with truth, that they were saving a large part of Kentish Town from turning into the sort of desert which great tracts of south and east London had become, and thereby benefitting their working-class neighbours as much as themselves. However it was also indisputable that many of them, however innocent and well-intentioned in themselves, were only there occupying those particular houses at all because working-class tenants had been displaced from them. 'Gentrification' began to be used as a ready-made sneer on the lips of those who were, inevitably, articulate and middle class themselves but did not want to see themselves that way. They pointed out – again, with some truth – that the fabric of nineteenth-century housing was being preserved and restored at the expense of the teeming life it had previously sheltered. Notoriously, houses in multi-occupation were emptied of their numerous tenants, by house agents not always over-scrupulous in their methods, in order that each might be sold to just one middle-class family.

What these critics did not admit, however, was that this evil in the private sector was paralleled by their own shortcomings in the public sector. For the old houses had provided a pool of cheap, rented accommodation, sub-standard perhaps but flexible – and this was just what council housing did not provide. If you were a short-term tenant without security of tenure, between being displaced by a comparatively wealthy family and being displaced by a redevelopment scheme there was not much to choose. Worse, even if those occupying parts of terrace houses when the moment came for redevelopment did get allotted council flats, it still meant that the stock of easily rentable accommodation was steadily being eroded.

One group affected were the hard-up newcomers to London who had traditionally always found their first shelter in little-regarded places like Kentish Town. Paradoxically, this student and sub-student world was, by the late 1960s, bigger than it had ever been before. All over west Kentish Town houses that would once have provided the accommodation wanted were being emptied by the council in preparation for redevelopment, but many of them remained empty for years before the bulldozers arrived. The solution was obvious, and people took the law into their own hands, all the more so since this coincided with the radical chic of the period. The early squatters in Kentish Town, around 1970, were mostly organised through relatively respectable bodies such as Student Community Housing. They came to some agreement with the council, who were themselves inclined to take a tolerant, fashionably liberal attitude towards them, and paid a minimal rent and rates. For a brief period the condemned houses lived again, as 'community shops' were opened with varying degrees of success, people made and sold yogurt (that accepted sign of pure ideals), handbags, African drums. But these authorised squatters were followed by others, less benign. At first even these tended to be people with some kind of ideological axe to grind, real or bogus, but they were soon followed by people without even such moral pretensions, who squatted merely for convenience – semi-criminals, drug addicts, alcoholics, runaway teenagers, the human flotsam which *has* always floated to the slums, in every century, and now readily invaded the slums which the council, in its unwisdom, had created with planning blight. Council attitudes to squatting were forced to harden. Meanwhile other local residents, infuriated by the litter left around, by the way the milk was stolen from their doorsteps every morning, by the shouts and loud music in the night, and by (I quote) 'the naked copulation in the gardens', decided to take the law into their own hands in their turn. One night the police in Holmes Road were telephoned and told that if they didn't 'do something' about the squatters in Marsden Street (off Malden Road) someone else would. Someone else did, and a battle followed in which a nest of squatters were routed, it is said, with pitchforks, and several of them ended up in hospital.

I do not believe the pitchforks. I think they are an imaginative touch put in to indicate the (literally) grass roots nature of local feeling over the issue. But they are none the less significant for all that.

The disappearance of cheap flats and rooms to let brought other evils in its train besides squatting by outsiders. Young local people, sometimes from families that had been in Kentish Town for generations, could no longer find 'two rooms in Prince of Wales Crescent' when they got married. This particularly affected the sort of couple with ambitions and a certain standard of living, who had no intention of instantly starting a large family to qualify for priority on Camden's long housing lists, or yet of bringing up a couple of children for years in Mother's front room. These were the Class 3, the lower middle class, actual or potential, who moved out to remote suburbs, a loss to the district. Blandly, in self-congratulation, Camden's Director of Housing remarked in a pamphlet published in 1971 that 'steadily the proportion of privately rented flats must be expected to fall and, with a vigorous housing programme the number of Council dwellings must be expected to increase'. Yet well before this point it had become obvious that the community was becoming socially polarized in an undesirable way between council tenancy and owner occupation. It was glumly predicted that by the year 1984 (or whatever arbitrary date was chosen) the whole of the Kentish and Camden Town areas and indeed the ring of comparable districts right round London would be parcelled out into expensively gentrified streets and, in utter physical and social contrast to them, one-class ghetto estates of council flats.

For the supreme irony of council estate construction is that it has ultimately proved socially divisive and anti-egalitarian. Partly this is due to the physical nature of most estate architecture – the way it turns its back on prevailing street patterns and, in discouraging through-traffic, inevitably discourages outsiders from entering on foot also. Many estates, indeed, are as much unknown territory to people living in the adjacent streets as if they were in another neighbourhood altogether. But another important divisive factor is the constraints placed upon council tenants, the petty regulations about door-painting and petkeeping, the general lack of real privacy despite the much vaunted 'self-containment'. Few people would be council tenants, at least not in a flat, if they had any financially feasible alternative, and it is significant that vandalism is far worse on estates than it is in the more mixed social communities of the streets. If you live in a house in a street then you are of the community of that street and, by extension, the whole area, whether you occupy a whole house or a self-contained basement flat or two rooms and a shared bath on the landing. If you live on a Council estate, however, you live 'in Lenham' or 'in Baxton' and you are instantly labelled.

Some of these drawbacks in the council housing system are, of course, the product of several factors beyond the control of individual councils. It is hard to see how, today, under any system, a good supply of cheap rented accommodation could be maintained in London, given that people will no longer tolerate the overcrowding they put up with in the past. It is a moot point whether, had public authorities *not* attempted to control the situation so heavily since 1945, but had allowed the traditional *laissez faire* system of private landlordism to continue, the result today would on balance be better or worse. It would certainly be different.

One change of council policy in the last few years in Camden is, however, doing much to bridge the widening gulf between council tenant and owner-occupier. Many of the houses originally acquired in the early 1960s with a view to demolition are now being done up and re-let to council tenants, which pleases both the prospective tenants and the middle-class conservationists. It may be that time will expose certain follies in this policy too, and certainly it has its critics ('Throwing good money after old bricks'). But for the time being it seems a good idea – and, what is more important, a modest, piecemeal, flexible idea which does not involve taking long-term expensive decisions that cannot easily be revoked. Indeed it is a measure of the success of this policy that its results do not jump to the eye. The numbers of nineteenth-century houses now in council ownership in Kentish Town, including the whole of the Christ Church Estate and much of the Bartholomew Estate which were acquired at an auction in the 1950s, is far greater than a casual observer would suppose walking round the streets. Such an observer, seeing a pleasant house, restored in appropriate style without the alarming picture windows and glass and iron front-doors that characterise some private conversions, is more apt to assume that its owners are 'another middle-class family that has moved in'. Hence the idea that Kentish Town is steadily going up and can only continue to rise, gains further currency.

The fact is, however, that after the social and physical upheavals of the 1960s, the district has probably reached another period of near stability. Including modern estates, the Council now owns more than half the housing in the area, and this has effectively put a stop to any lingering property developer's dream of it even becoming another Chelsea or Hampstead. At the same time, its dangers seem to be, for the moment, past. No Motorway Box will mutilate its southern area. No more vainglorious schemes will attempt to transform it out of all recognition: for the moment local authorities have run out of both steam and money. The slums of the future – and the near future at that – will not be found in 'inchoate communities . . . peppered with small industries' like Kentish Town, but in the bleakly coherent wastelands of places like the Pepys Estate in south London or the Ben Johnson estate in Stepney, or Woodberry Down in north London.

Paradoxically, the various threats to Kentish Town's very existence that have been posed since 1945 may have played an important part in sharpening people's ideas about what life in an urban area is or ought to be. Between the wars, when districts like this stagnated, no one took much interest in them except those who wished to change them. Not until they seemed to be trembling on the brink of extinction, their rows of terraces apparently doomed to pass into history like the open fields and the timbered farmhouses before them, did people of all classes stop and ask themselves what, in fact, was still good about these places, or whether they really wanted them knocked down. The prolonged wrangles over demolition which at first had threatened to divide the articulate newcomers from the resigned long-term inhabitants, in the end united them, albeit temporarily. The final saving of Harmood Street by public outcry, and the final defeat and loss of the elegant curve of Prince of Wales Crescent, which received coverage in the national press, were topics of interest shared by everyone. Here, as in other comparable areas all over London but perhaps particularly here, local enterprises began to flourish in the late 1960s: local news-sheets were published, street festivals were held, organisations for helping people with commodities ranging from legal advice to psychodrama, appeared in every street. A Neighbourhood Advice Centre, financed by the Camden Council for Social Services was set up. Some eighteen residents' and tenants' associations came into being within a square mile of streets – significantly, the level of all this communal activity was far higher in west Kentish Town, where there had been so much trouble and strife, than in the relatively calmer district to the east of the high road which no one had tried to pull down. A free-floating and at first slightly mysterious organisation called Inter Action settled in Kentish Town, in the misguided belief that here was a forgotten district no one was doing anything about. Having discovered their mistake they nevertheless stayed, occupying a derelict medicine factory where the director's office was still panelled in mock-Jacobean, and busied themselves with a variety of causes such as open spaces (that King Charles's Head of reformers) and street games for children, always referred to in an approved radical style as 'the kids'. Some people thought they were Maoists and others that, on the contrary, they were not all that different in their basic attitudes from the Mission Hall clergymen of a hundred years ago. But nearly everyone was pleased when, in 1974, they succeeded in opening a riding stable, allotments and a miniature 'farm' (goats, chickens, a donkey, a calf) on a segment of railway land with old stabling and stock sheds.

It was an inspired idea. As a symbol of the new urban peasantry, as a focus for the idea of the village that lurks disguised in city streets and as a means of creating a sense of the revival of the lost past, it could not be bettered. Look, it seemed to be saying, the fields are not only sleeping underneath: they are *here*, exposed once again, with people working in them, tending animals, learning about real things, doing things instead of gazing into shop windows and television sets. The 'farm' soon became, and is still, the focus for all sorts of myths: people were eager to believe that it was an actual fragment of farmland overlooked for a hundred years and miraculously rediscovered like the Sleeping Beauty's domain, that the 'farm buildings' (in reality Midland Railway stabling) were the remains of the eighteenth-century Mortimer's Farm.

The earth itself is indestructible – the tough, sticky London clay studded like a currant cake with the fragments of other lives. But what stands on the earth seems more like a geological formation. A hundred years ago this image was already used by a foreign observer (Karl Capek) to describe the amazing agglomeration of terraced housing that met his eye, but today, when the terraces are broken and interspersed with so many more recent deposits, the metaphor seems still more appropriate. The buildings of different periods, themselves converted or modified in different ways, are mixed together like stratified rocks that have been churned up not once but several times by changes in the social climate. Temperate, sunny eras have deposited elaborate fanlights, stucco mouldings, cornices and parapets; colder eras have peeled stucco and rotted trimmings, making facings porous. Successive ice ages have left piles of masonry like great rocks standing out above the more delicate roofscape of slates – piano factories, engine sheds, model dwellings, greyly serviceable blocks with stone dressings, post-War follies in rough-cast concrete. In the 'urban sprawl' the petrified tide-marks of earlier building waves are still clearly visible: here the airy stuccoed facades give way to heavier, mid-Victorian ones with porticoes, here these in turn lie alongside late-Victorian debased Scottish baronial style. Here is an untouched segment of Edwardian red-brick and hung tile, here a slice is missing and in its place (brought hither by a glacier from a distant suburb?) is a piece of 1930s by-pass architecture. Here traffic sweeps noisily round a new traffic island, there children play in a pot-holed, ancient unmade lane under flowering trees.

The surface vegetation the houses currently wear is equally varied. In one run of near-identical houses, the blistered chocolate and margarine paint of pre-war days, endlessly proving how 'serviceable' it is, may be flanked on one side by fresh white rendering and a stripped pine front door and on the other by a neighbour done up like a doll's house, each individual brick picked out in mauvish-pink by its Greek Cypriot owners. The house at the end of the run, slightly bigger than its neighbours, its path squared in black and white tiles of long-ago elegance, presents a sorrier sight than any of the others. Its area railings, taken during the war supposedly to make armaments but actually to rust in a field in Lincolnshire, have been replaced by a sagging cat's cradle of stakes and wire, the steps where maids once lingered are covered with green slime and blown chip papers; ragged Robin grows at the bottom. In tribute to a respectable past, all its windows are occluded with dirty net curtains, but in one of them a pane of glass has been blocked for years by a cornflakes packet. In another stands a little Sacred Heart, facing the street: perhaps He enjoys watching the goings-on in the new adventure playground opposite. From His vantage point He cannot see that the house next door has been sanded all over and now presents the pristine, bright yellow appearance it must have presented around 1840, before a hundred years of London grime had come to darken it. Actually this startling new façade is a façade in every sense, for, in currently approved fashion, the occupants have restored the outside to a perfect simulacrum of what it must once have been, new eight-paned windows and all, but have transformed the small-roomed interior into a barn-like Paradise of rolled steel joists, spotlights and a spiral staircase leading to a studio in the roof-space. Their bleak good taste is not much admired by the neighbours who have seen inside, particularly not by the ones further up the street whose own identical house is completely smothered in Virginia creeper and whose front patch is a riot of sunflowers, roses, geraniums and garden gnomes.

The Indians arrive in their shining car, full of wives and large-eyed children. They run the small grocers in the next street (open till nine at night seven days a week) which they bought three years ago from the Greeks.

An alsatian pads past, very busy. A woman with a pram and eyeshadow eyes it suspiciously.

In the pub at the corner someone is washing the cut-glass windows. Posters advertise 'Disco' and 'Topless Go-go dancers', but most of the time the place wears an air of intense respectability.

An old man dodders past with woollen gloves and a shopping bag. His wife has sent him to Sainsburys to get him out from under her feet.

A rather angry-looking young woman in a long, crumpled cotton skirt goes by, pushing a double push-chair vigorously in front of her containing two small children of disparate colours. Relic of a high-minded commune of squatters, she has now, as an unsupported mother, been rehoused by the council.

A colony of Irish workmen arrive and prepare to dig up the pavement.

The accents of the young ones are just as strong as those of the older men. Ireland itself must be half empty these days, but the Catholic churches in North West London are well filled.

A man in a dark suit with a briefcase passes on his way to the tube and County Hall. His wife is just getting the car out to take the children to school (a state primary school, but not the nearest one).

Two blowsy women, mother and daughter, with cigarettes in their mouths at the same angle, are taking huge bundles in the direction of the launderette. A brisk young husband in jeans, bound on the same errand, overtakes them.

In an upstairs room of a house opposite someone is typing.

Parliament Hill Fields

SIR JOHN BETJEMAN

Rumbling under blackened girders, Midland, bound for Cricklewood,
Puffed its sulphur to the sunset where that Land of Laundries stood.
Rumble under, thunder over, train and tram alternate go,
Shake the floor and smudge the ledger, Charrington, Sells, Dale and Co.,
Nuts and nuggets in the window, trucks along the lines below.

When the Bon Marché was shuttered, when the feet were hot and tired,
Outside Charrington's we waited, by the "STOP HERE IF REQUIRED",
Launched aboard the shopping basket, sat precipitately down,
Rocked past Zwanziger the baker's, and the terrace blackish brown,
And the curious Anglo-Norman parish church of Kentish Town.

Till the tram went over thirty, sighting terminus again,
Past municipal lawn tennis and the bobble-hanging plane;
Soft the light suburban evening caught our ashlar-speckled spire,
Eighteen-sixty Early English, as the mighty elms retire
Either side of Brookfields Mansions flashing fine French-window fire.
Oh the after-tram-ride quiet, when we heard a mile beyond,
Silver music from the bandstand, barking dogs by Highgate Pond;
Up the hill where stucco houses in Virginia creeper drown –
And my childish wave of pity, seeing children carrying down
Sheaves of drooping dandelions to the courts of Kentish Town.

A Note on Sources

originally compiled 1977, revised 2010.

Apart from the published works listed in the Bibliography and the files of defunct local newspapers in the Camden Archives and Local History Centre, I have drawn on a variety of unpublished sources of material. The most important of these is the Heal Collection, a large and valuable accumulation of documents, transcriptions of manuscripts, newspaper cuttings, prints, water-colours, maps, site-plans, posters and other historical ephemera, amassed over two successive generations by members of the Heal family – the owners of the furniture shop in Tottenham Court Road. All the material relates, broadly, to St Pancras parish and its environs. This Collection was presented to the local borough council in 1913, and forms an important core to the Camden Archives, which are in any case extensive and excellent. The Heal contribution is a goldmine for the researcher; in the 1970s it had been little exploited, and its existence was one of the reasons for my decision to write this book.

Camden Archives also possesses several manuscripts relating to the parish of St Pancras at various dates. When I was writing this book, and for many years afterwards, the manuscript regarded by all concerned as the most important and interesting was the one I refer to in the text as 'Woodehouse's book'. I wrote then 'It has occasionally been called a "journal", but in fact it is more in the nature of an historical and contemporary account of the district. It was compiled shortly after 1700 by one William Woodehouse (Wodehouse, Woodhouse etc. – his own spelling varies), who was almost certainly the occupant of the house that nearly three centuries earlier had been occupied by William Bruges the Garter King at Arms. His book also includes transcripts of Court hearings over which he presided as a JP, and a printed pamphlet on witches of an earlier date.' Readers of this book will see that I refer to Woodehouse and the information he supplies a number of times.

No doubt was ever cast on Woodehouse's authenticity when I was writing: there was merely a slight surprise expressed by the then chief archivist of Camden that he had not actually found Woodehouse's name in any register of Justices of the Peace. I was not till 2002 that an article by Patrick Nother, a journalist and researcher, appeared in Camden History Society Review No. 26 (see Bibliography). In the course of work for a book of his own on Kings Cross, Nother had found incontrovertible evidence that 'Woodehouse' had patched together for his observations on St Pancras a number of reports, belonging roughly to the same period, lifted from other districts and contained in various other fairly recondite works. Moreover, upon analysis, all the various authentic-looking bits of paper which made up 'Woodehouse's Book' turned out to be of nineteenth century origin. In other words, the work is a forgery.

Interested readers may study Nother's trenchant and closely argued article for themselves. But the fact remains that, though Woodehouse himself probably never existed, the concoction that bears his name is a skilful and well-informed one, generally appropriate to a district such as St Pancras in the early eighteenth century. It contains no anachronisms, no improbabilities; it has cut and pasted real-life evidence from else-where. Most likely (Nother has concluded) it was not originally intended to deceive, but was more in the nature of parlour-game between two or more skilled antiquarians. So, although if I were writing my book today I would not of course quote Woodehouse, I do not think any new reader will have their overall picture of old St Pancras hopelessly perverted by the Woodehouse references I have had to leave in the text.

Another fragmentary manuscript of some sixty years later (genuine, this time) is also in the Camden Archives. This is the memorandum book on his house in Kentish Town compiled by the Rev. Dr Stukeley, the one-time rector of St George's, Bloomsbury. Another is the account of Kentish Town dating from the middle of the nineteenth century, but taking a retrospective look, compiled by one William Elliott and subsequently (according to the inscription) copied and enlarged by Samuel Wiswould (the author of *Charities of St Pancras*, 1963). At least one commentator (C. H. Denyer, a Mayor of St Pancras in the 1930s and editor of a useful short history of the borough) has confused Mr Elliott's book with that written and published by J Bennett earlier in the century

(*Some Account of Kentish Town*, 1821), but this is an error. A third, but less informative manuscript compiled in the nineteenth century was the work of one Edwin Roffe; he (like Bennett, but a generation later) was the owner of a printing business in the area.

A fourth manuscript, anonymous this time, will be found not with Camden but in the Museum of London archive. This is a journal, the work of a school-teacher in a British (ie. Congregationalist) School in some unspecified district, who visited London and London schools in the summer of 1853 by way of a busman's holiday.

The originals of the Cantelowes Manor Court Rolls and the St Pancras Parish registers are deposited in the London Metropolitan Archive. This Archive also holds some pictorial material, once in the Library of the Greater London Council, and a file of the work of A. Crosby, the water-colourist who made detailed drawings of the Fleet River and Morgan's Farm. This was, till recently, in the Print Room of the Guildhall Library.

A large series of photographs of Camden and Kentish Town High Streets, taken by the promoters of what became the Northern Line underground circa 1900 when the line was being planned, and once the property of London Transport, is now in the possession of the Camden Archives. They also have the original of J. F. King's 'Rolls' or 'Panorama' of Kentish Town, as described in the text, a valuable and beautiful document and an important source both pictorially and factually. It has been reproduced by the London Topographical Society, with notes by John Richardson, in association with the London Borough of Camden.

In the Camden Archives, too, will be found the archives of St Pancras Almshouses to the year 2000. Also the Archives of St Pancras Housing Association, including their estates at York Rise and at Athlone Street, and a report of housing conditions in the latter area made in 1933.

The original Census forms are lodged in the National Archives, erst-while Public Record Office, now at Kew. They make microfilm copies available for consultation – as do Camden Archives for their own district. The researcher of today will find many more documents transcribed or microfilmed and indexed than was the case a generation ago, but he or she is correspondingly less likely to enjoy the privilege and pleasure of browsing original documents in the way that I once did.

I am most grateful to Malcolm Holmes, long-time archivist of Camden, now retired, for his help in bringing the Sources and Bibliography up to date. Also to Paul Barker, journalist, writer, expert on things urban and, like myself, an inhabitant of Kentish Town for many decades, for his interest and acumen.

Revised Bibliography

Altick, Richard, *Victorian People and Ideas*, 1974.

Arnold, Matthew, *Friendship's Garland*, 1866.

Ashton, J., *The Fleet*, 1888.

Baker, Alan R. H., and Harley, J. B. (editors) *Man Made the Land: Essays in English Historical Geography*, 1973.

Barnes, E. G., *The Rise of the Midland Railway*, 1966.

Barnes, William, *A Century of Camden Housing*, 1971 (pamphlet published by Camden Borough Council).

Barker, T. C. and Robbins, M., *A History of London Transport*, 2007.

Barton, Nicholas, *The Lost Rivers of London*, 1992.

Bebbington, Gillian, *London Street Names*, 1972.

Bennett, J., *Some Account of Kentish Town*, 1821.

Bernstein, Henry T., 'The Mysterious Disappearance of Edwardian London Fog', in *The London Journal* Vol. I, No. 2, 1975.

Birch, J. B., *Brown's Dairy*, 1910 (privately printed pamphlet).

Booth, General William, *In Darkest London*, 1890.

Briggs, Asa, *Victorian Cities*, 1963.

Brown, Walter E., *St Pancras Book of Dates*, 1904, *St Pancras: Open Spaces and Disused Burial Grounds*, 1902, *The St Pancras Poor: a brief record of their treatment etc from 1718 to 1904*, 1905, *From Open Vestry to Borough Council 1718–1900*, 1900 (all privately printed for St Pancras Borough Council).

Buchan, John, *The Three Hostages*, 1924.

Burchell, Doris, *Miss Buss's Other School*, 1971 (Published by the Frances Mary Buss Foundation).

Cansick, Frederick Teague, *Cansick's Epitaphs of Middlesex*, 1872.

Cooke, M. E., *A Geographical Study of St Pancras*, 1932.

Coppock, J. T. and Prince, H.C. (editors) *Greater London*, 1964.

Denyer, C. H. (editor) *St Pancras Through the Ages*, 1935 (Borough Council publication).

Dickens, Charles, *The Old Curiosity Shop*, 1841.

Dickens, Charles, *Dombey and Son*, 1848.

Dyos, H. J., *The Study of Urban History*, 1976.

Dyos, H. J., *Victorian Suburb: a study in the growth of Camberwell*, 1973.

Dyos, H. J. and Wolff, Michael (editors) *Victorian City: Images and Realities*, 1999.

Girouard, Mark, *Victorian Pubs*, 1984.

Godfrey, Walter H. and Marcham, W. McB, *Survey of London*, Vol. XVII, 1936, XIX, 1938 and XXIV, 1952 (published by the LCC).

Goldsmith, Oliver, *A Citizen of the World*, 1760.

Gomme, Sir George Laurence, *London in the Reign of Queen Victoria (1837–1897)*, 1898.

Gordon, W. J., *The Horse World of London*, 1893.

Grosch, Alfred, *St Pancras Pavements*, 1947.

Grossmith, George and Weedon, *Diary of a Nobody*, 1892.

Guizot, Francois P. G., *An Embassy at the Court of St James*, 1840.

Harrison, *A History of London*, 1775.

Hole, James, *The Homes of the Working Classes, with Suggestions for their Improvement*, 1866.

Hollinshead, John, *Ragged London*, 1861.

Hoskins, W. G., *English Landscapes*, 1977.

Howitt, William, *The Northern Heights of London*, 1869.

Hughson, David, *London*, 1809.

Ilive, *Survey of London*, 1742.

Jacobs, Jane, *The Death and Life of Great American Cities*, 2002.

Jenkins, Simon, *Landlords to London; the story of a capital and its growth*, 1975.

Jeffcot, Eric, 'Old Roads' (article in *St Pancras Journal* Vol. 8, No. 1).

Kellet, John R., *Railways and Victorian Cities,* 1979.

Laslett, Peter, *The World We Have Lost,* 1968.

Lee, Charles E., *St Pancras Church and Parish,* 1955 (published by the Parochial Church Council).

Lee, Charles E., *The Northern Line,* 1973 (published by London Transport).

London, Hugh Stanford, *The Life of William Bruges,* 1960 (published by the Harleyian Society).

Lysons, Daniel, *The Environs of London,* 1796.

Mackenzie, Compton, *Sinister Street,* 1913.

Mayhew, Henry, *London Labour and the London Poor,* 1861.

Miller, Frederick, *St Pancras Past and Present,* 1874.

Mitchell, R. J. and Leys, M. D. R., *A History of London Life,* 1958.

Morell, R.C., *The Story of Agar Town,* 1935 (privately printed).

Morris, William, *The Earthly Paradise,* 1870.

Morris, William, *Hopes and Fears for Art: Five lectures,* 1882.

Murray, J. F., *The World of London,* 1843.

Norden, John, *Speculum Britanniae,* 1549.

Olsen, Donald J., *Town Planning in London,* 1982.

Palmer, Samuel, *St Pancras,* 1870.

Parker, Rowland, *The Common Stream,* 1975.

Pepys, Samuel, *Diaries,* 1659–69 (first published 1841).

Pevsner, Nikolaus, *The Buildings of England: London,* 1952; revised edition by Cherry, Bridget, 1998.

Pike, E. Royston, *Human Documents of the Victorian Golden Age,* 1974.

Platt, Colin, *The English Medieval Town,* 1976.

Priestley, Harold, *London, the Years of Change,* 1966.

Rasmussen, Steen Eller, *London, the Unique City,* 1934.

Richardson, John, *The Local Historian's Encyclopedia,* 1993 (published by Historical Publications).

Robbins, Michael, *A History of the North London Railway*, 1974.

Rodgers, Betsy, *A Georgian Chronicle: Mrs Barbauld and her Family*, 1958.

Rudé, George, *Hanoverian London: 1714–1808*, 1971.

Saunders, Ann, *Regent's Park*, 1969.

Schlesinger, Max, *Saunterings in and About London*, 1853.

Sheppard, Francis, *London 1808–1870: the Infernal Wen*, 1971.

Simmons, Jack, *St Pancras Station*, 2005.

Simond, Louis, *Voyage en Angleterre*, 1812 (Paris).

Slater, Montagu, *Once a Jolly Swagman*, 1944.

Stowe, John, *A Survey of the Cities of London and Westminster*, 1598.

Summerson, Sir John, *Georgian London*, 1991.

Taylor, Nicholas, *The Village in the City*, 1973.

Thompson, F. M. L., *Hampstead: Building a Borough, 1650–1964*, 1974.

Warren, Mrs., *How I Managed my House on £200 a Year*, 1864.

Willis, Frederick, *A Book of London Yesterdays*, 1960.

Wiswould, S., *The Charities of St Pancras*, 1863 (privately printed).

Zwert, Peter, *Islington*, 1973.

ANONYMOUS PUBLICATIONS:

Gleanings in St Pancras, 1906 (privately printed).

St Pancras of the Future (a catalogue of exhibition held in 1945); *St Pancras Today* (a catalogue of exhibition held in 1947); *The End of One Story: a souvenir of the Borough of St Pancras*, 1964; *West Kentish Town: Town Planning Consultants' Report*, 1964. All Borough Council Publications.

Camden Scene: Planning survey, 1975.

Old Euston, 1938 (Published by *Country Life*).

The story of the Governesses' Benevolent Institution, 1961.

St Pancras Notes and Queries, 1903 (Extracts from *The St Pancras Guardian*, 1897–1903).

CAMDEN HISTORY SOCIETY PUBLICATIONS:

Le Faye, Deirdre, *Mediaeval Camden,* 1974 (pamphlet).

Howells, Coral Ann, 'Small Boy on a Kentish Town Tram', in *Camden History Review I,* 1973.

Read, Elizabeth J., 'the Remarkable Baroness Burdett-Coutts' in *CHR I.*

Newman, Leslie T., 'It All Began with J.C. Bach' in *CHR I.*

Richardson, John, 'The St Pancras Affair', in *Camden History Review II,* 1974.

Lee, Charles E., 'Transport and the Social Scene', in *CHR II.*

Franklin, Richard, 'All Hallows-Gospel Oak', in *CHR II.*

Lee, Charles E., 'Plentyfull Sprynges at Hampstede Hethe', in *Camden History Review III,* 1975.

Conquest, Richard, 'The Black Hole of St Pancras', in *CHR III.*

Franklin, Richard, 'How Different from Us!', in *CHR III.*

Other relevant material will be found in the quarterly *Newsletters* of the Camden History Society, Nos. 1–37, 1970–1976.

See also the *St Pancras Journal,* published monthly by St Pancras Borough Council between 1947 and 1965.

The privately printed books and pamphlets relating to St Pancras will be found in Camden Libraries' local history collection.

Since *The Fields Beneath* first appeared there have been a number of other publications which, while they have not contributed to the book, may be of interest to its readers. I would cite particularly Lesley Marshall's *Kentish Town: its past in pictures,* published by the London Borough of Camden in 1993, and two more books by John Richardson, *Kentish Town Past,* 1997 and *A History of Camden,* 2000. There has also been much activity by the Camden History Society, which has published a series of street-by-street historical surveys that includes *Streets of Kentish Town,* edited by Steven Denford and David Hayes, 2005, and *Streets of Gospel Oak and West Kentish Town* by the same editors in 2006. Steven Denford has also published with Camden History Society *Agar Town: the Life and Death of a Victorian Slum,* 1995.

The Camden History Society has also continued to publish its regular Reviews containing specialised articles. In addition to the list cited above, I add the following articles as being of general relevance to Kentish Town:

Tindall, Gillian 'Where was the House that Bruges Built', CHS Review 4, 1976.

Ellis, John, 'The Spiritual Strength of Kentish Town, a Survey of Methodist Chapels', CHS Review 5, 1978.

Lewis, Ella M, 'A Kentish Town Grocer's in the Great War', CHS Review 8, 1980,

Baker, Ena, 'Shopping in Kentish Town', CHS Review 11, 1984.

Ridge, Althea, 'W. Flint, Ironmongers of Kentish Town', CHS Review 12, 1984.

Whyman, Desmond, 'Butchers' shops in Kentish Town', CHS Review 20, 1996.

Cox, Jane, 'Spreading the Gospel in Gospel Oak: All Hallows, the "cathedral of North London" ', CHS Review 20, 1996.

Renton, Peter, 'The North West London synagogue in Kentish Town', CHS Review 23, 1999.

Tindall, Gillian, 'The Destiny of Bower Cottage, a study of St Margaret's Nursery, Kentish Town', CHS Review 23, 1999.

Damp, Christopher, 'Kentish Town Congregational Church and the Congregational Churches of Camden', CHS Review 24, 2000.

Barnes, William, 'A Short History of Oak Village', CHS Review 25, 2001.

Nother, Patrick, 'The mystery of the "Woodhouse Journal": forgery, criminal deception or Victorian parlour-game?' CHS Review 26, 2002.

Gretany, Marion, 'Eleanor Palmer's Gift Charity in Barnet and St Pancras', CHS Review 28, 2004.

Harrison, Gerry, 'A Watershed in NW5: Kentish Town Baths 1901–2006', CHS Review 30, 2006.

A Note on Nomenclature

'Town' in a proper name in Old and Middle English does not indicate a town in the modern sense, but simply any form of inhabited place. When the 'town' has indeed been in existence since then, it is commonly found shortened to 'ton': until the nineteenth century one often finds 'Kentishtown' run together in one word or, earlier, even truncated to 'Kentisston'. Perhaps its reversion to two separate words (with the modern emphasis on the latter one) was assisted by the establishment, *c.* 1800, of Camden Town, a planned suburban development with its name invented by analogy with its older neighbour up the road. Within a few years of Camden Town's establishment, Somers Town, and later Agar or Agar's Town, similarly named after their ground landlords, made their appearance in the south of the old parish of St Pancras; and in Pentonville we have a Frenchified version of the same thing.

Various theories have been put forward to explain the Kentish part of the name. The most memorable, as well as the least probable, is the one repeated by Gillian Bebbington in her otherwise admirable book *London Street Names*. She states 'Probably the first owner came from Kent', and goes on 'It is significant that the medieval manor of Kentish Town followed the ancient Kentish custom of gavelkind, whereby a dead man's land was divided equally between all his sons and daughters and lots were drawn to decide the ownership of each.' But the evidence for this in Kentish Town is sparse, and moreover had been rejected many times by other commentators. The truer, if duller derivation is probably from the common place-name particle 'ken' or 'cain', variously interpreted as a Celtic word for a green wood or a river. (I would also put up the suggestion of the Celtic *canto*, meaning border.) Following on this, a convincing theory is that Kentish is a corruption of 'Ken-ditch' – i.e. the ditch or watercourse of the Fleet. Some authorities have derived Ken from Caen in Normandy, and indeed that spelling of the particle was current for centuries in Ken Wood, the estate a couple of miles up the hill. Others, noting the similarity between 'Kentish' and 'Ken Wood' have concluded that the names are linked, and both possibly traceable to the same landlord. Ralph de Kantewood, who was Dean of St Paul's after the Norman Conquest, seems to have owned both, and granted lands near St Pancras church to St Paul's, from which time dates a long line of ecclesiastical ground landlords. But did Ralph de Kantewood give his name to the district, or did he in fact take his name from it? Lysons (*Environs of London*, 1796) managed to slide out of the issue by suggesting both possibilities at the same time, which does not make sense.

Lysons also seems to have been the person responsible for starting a rogue theory, which has gained wide currency, that 'Kentish Town' is a corruption of 'Cantelupe Town', after a Roger de Cantelupe who was prebendary of Kentish Town under St Paul's in 1249. Certainly the manor whose lands covered much of the area came to be known as Cantelowes or Cantlers. But, as I have said, Ralph de Kantewood was on the scene almost two hundred years before the prosperous and powerful Cantelupe family, and the forms 'Kentisshton' and 'Kentissetone' crop up in documents that pre-date the Cantelupe ownership. No doubt it was mainly the coincidence of two rather similar-sounding names applied to the same district that gave rise to the belief that both were versions of the same common origin, but Lysons fuelled the confusion by interpolating the name 'Cantelowes' in parentheses into his translation of the entry for St Pancras in the Domesday Book. Subsequently later historians such as Samuel Palmer copied his translation but omitted the parentheses, thus making it seem as if 'Cantelowes' appeared in the original source. In this way are errors handed down from one writer to another, developing a persistent life of their own.

A Word on Manor Houses

Nineteenth-century amateur historians seem to have had manor houses on the brain; they readily identified any and every large old house as 'the old Manor House' and frequently, for good measure, Bruges's house as well, and these errors have been perpetuated. As I have stated in the text, Morgan's Farm, the house built for Sir Thomas Hewett in the early seventeenth century on what later became the Christ Church Estate, was not a manor house, though nearly all the pictures in various collections that are labelled 'Kentish Town Manor House' or words to that effect depict this building. When they don't, they depict another building with still less claim to the title: a stuccoed, single-gabled, apparently eighteenth-century gentleman's residence situated in Willow Walk just behind what is now Fortess Road. (Under the bogus name of 'Cantslow Manor', it was demolished by the Metropolitan Board of Works for road-widening in the 1890s.)

It is virtually certain that both the St Pancras manor house and the Cantelowes manor house – mediaeval buildings which, by the time of the Commonwealth Survey in the mid-seventeenth century had declined into mere farms – stood much nearer to St Pancras Old Church than either of these spurious ones. I believe, in fact, that they were originally sited fairly near one another on opposite sides of the King's Road (the present-day St Pancras Way). Those sufficiently addicted to historical detective work to wish to know *why* I believe this, are invited to read my article on the subject in the *Camden History Review IV* (Camden History Society publication, 1976). As an indication of the difficulty of interpreting disparate, fragmentary sources correctly, and the unwisdom of believing implicitly in any map of manorial holdings including the one in this book, I will confine myself here to pointing out that the usually scholarly and authoritative LCC *Survey of London* volumes contradict themselves on this point. Volume XIX confidently (and, I believe, correctly) plots Cantelowes Manor House on the west of the

King's Road, while Volume XVII states with equal confidence that it stood at roughly the same level on the eastern side of the road. Neither volume plots St Pancras Manor House at all.

Acknowledgements

(1977)

Standards of historical research have risen so much in the last twenty years or so that we seem to be living in a golden era of urban studies. The anatomy of the town is receiving an unprecedented amount of attention, and anyone working in this field today must acknowledge, as I do, a substantial general debt to forerunners like Sir John Summerson and Steen Eller Rasmussen. I also owe a great deal to more recent leaders in this field such as H. C. Dyos, Donald J. Olsen, J. T. Coppick, H. C. Prince, Peter Hall, and to the editors and writers of the recent Secker and Warburg *History of London* series.

I have other, more specific thanks to offer: first and foremost to John Richardson, Chairman of the Camden History Society, who has been more than generous with advice and help and with the loan of his own transcriptions from local manorial records and parish registers; also to other members of the History Society council, and particularly to Mrs Coral Howells for permission to use a letter written to her by Sir John Betjeman. Much gratitude also to the staff of the local history section of Camden Libraries, particularly to Malcolm Holmes, who has given me a great deal of incidental help. Also to Miss Joan Walton of Athlone Street Branch Library for her suggestions and interest. My thanks also to the staffs of the London Library, the London Museum Library, the Greater London Council Members' and Picture Libraries, the Guildhall Library, and most especially to John Walford of the Public Record Office, who very kindly made original Census forms available to me when I protested to him on the difficulty of working from microfilm when comparing one decade with another. Also to P. C. Beddington, the Librarian of Gray's Inn Library, for supplying me with information concerning the inglorious career of H. H. Pike.

So many people in the Kentish Town area have given me help of one kind or another that it would be invidious to mention names. My only regret is that I have not been able to use much more of what each of them has told me: inevitably, when working on a book of this type, one amasses a wealth of usable material which has to be reluctantly excluded for reasons of space. Particular thanks, however, to F. J. Napthine for allowing me to consult hitherto unpublished work of his own, and to Mrs Rose Deakin for supplying me with some figures relating to Census material.

I am grateful to Phillip French for several recondite suggestions concerning the appearance of my chosen area in literature; to Sir John Betjeman and his publishers, Messrs. John Murray, for permission to reprint his poem 'Parliament Hill Fields'; to the publishers of the late T. S. Eliot, Messrs Faber, for permission to reprint seven lines from *East Coker*, and to Messrs. Macdonald and Jane for permission to reprint a passage from Compton MacKenzie's *Sinister Street*.

Finally, very many thanks to Simon Jenkins, editor of the *Evening Standard* and author of *Landlords to London*, who read the manuscript for me and made a number of helpful comments, all of which I have tried to follow.

Gillian Tindall

Photographic Acknowledgements
(1980)

1   From a print by Storer in the author's collection.

2 and 3
   Original watercolours in the Crosby Collection, Guildhall Library.

4   From a print in the author's collection.

5   From the original in the Museum of London.

6, 7, 8 and 9
   Extracted from maps in the possession of Camden Libraries'
   Local History Collection.

10a   Courtesy of Camden Libraries' Local History Collection.

10b   From an original in the Heal Collection, courtesy of Camden
   Libraries.

11a   From the London Transport Collection, Camden Libraries.

11b   Photograph by R. G .Lansdown.

12   From the London Transport Collection, Camden Libraries.

13a and b
   Photograph by R. G. Lansdown.

14   From the London Transport Collection, Camden Libraries.

15   Courtesy of the GLC Picture Library.

16   Photograph by R. G. Lansdown.

About the Author

In her long career, Gillian Tindall has written novels (one of which won the Somerset Maugham Award), two biographies, and a large number of short stories for print and radio, but she is now best known for her books of 'micro-history'. Each of these takes a specific place, house or obscure group of people at a past date, and uses this to tell a story of much wider historical meaning. Her *Celestine, Voices from a French Village* has been paricularly aclaimed (and won her an honour from the French government) as has her *The House by the Thames*, but her first book of this kind was *The Fields Beneath*, first published in 1977 and in many subsequent editions. The area of London that it covers has been her home now for more than forty years, though she has a similar stake in a village in central France and also a long-term relationship with Bombay/Mumbai. She is married, with a son and grandsons.

Index